T0252117

PRINCIPAL COMPONENT NEURAL NETWORKS

Adaptive and Learning Systems for Signal Processing, Communications, and Control

Editor: Simon Haykin

PRINCIPAL COMPONENT NEURAL NETWORKS

THEORY AND APPLICATIONS

K. I. Diamantaras

Aristotle University
Thessaloniki, Greece

S. Y. Kung

Princeton University

A Wiley-Interscience Publication

JOHN WILEY & SONS, INC.

New York / Chichester / Brisbane / Toronto / Singapore

Library of Congress Cataloging in Publication Data:

Diamantaras, Konstantinos I.
    Principal component neural networks : theory and applications /
K. I. Diamantaras, S.Y. Kung.
      p.   cm. — (Adaptive and learning systems for signal
processing, communications, and control)
    "A Wiley-Interscience publication."
    Includes bibliographical references and index.
    ISBN 0-471-05436-4 (cloth : acid-free paper)
    1. Neural networks (Computer science)   I. Kung, S. Y. (Sun Yuan)
II. Title. III. Series.
QA76.87.D53   1996
006.3—dc20   95-242

10 9 8 7 6 5 4 3 2

To Anthoula
and
Se-Wei

CONTENTS

PREFACE

The area of neural networks has witnessed considerable growth in the last decade owing mainly to the advancement of new techniques motivated from biological information processing as well as the progress made in modern microelectronic technology. Artificial neural networks have derived their power from a combination of novel network structures and powerful new learning techniques (such as the Hebbian and back-propagation rules). They have demonstrated convincing success in many applications, including pattern recognition, data modeling, image processing, signal processing, etc.

Principal Component Analysis (PCA), on the other hand, represents a classical statistical technique for analyzing the covariance structure of multivariate statistical observations. The principal components are the most important linear features of the random observation vector. Through PCA many variables can be represented by few components, so PCA can be considered either as a feature extraction or as a data compression technique. PCA is also closely related to least-squares techniques in estimation theory, the Karhunen-Loève (KL) transformation in time series and image processing, and the singular value decomposition (SVD) in numerical analysis. PCA and these related methods are indisputably very important in applications of signal/image coding, processing, and analysis.

This book systematically explores the relationship between PCA and neural networks. It studies issues pertaining to both neural network models (i.e., network structures and algorithms) and theoretical extensions/generalizations of PCA. The ultimate objectives is to provide a synergistic exploration on the *mathematical*, *algorithmic*, *application*, and *architectural* aspects of principal component neural networks.

In the literature there is a plethora of neural models performing PCA. They basically fall into two categories: those originating from the Hebbian learning rule and those that use least squares learning rules such as back-propagation. This book attempts to present them, as much as possible, under a unified formulation. Various extensions and generalizations of PCA are also provided, which relate to many methods in signal processing, pattern recognition, control theory, etc.

The mathematical background assumed for the reader is that of college calculus and probability theory. It is expected that the readership will be from a variety of disciplines such as mathematics, statistics, neuropsychology, artificial intelligence, and engineering. Therefore, we attempt to present the subjects in their entirety.

Basic background in mathematics or neurobiology is provided either in review chapters or in the appendices. Consequently, more confident readers might prefer to skip introductory parts such as, for example, Chapter 2, which contains basic material in linear algebra.

Application, in addition to theory, represents an important part of the book. Principal component techniques have been successfully applied in many data processing problems, such as high-resolution spectral estimation, system identification, image compression, pattern recognition, etc. Each chapter contains a selected list of application examples from various areas. Our intention is not to fully cover the application spectrum of neural PCA models but to provide ideas and motivations for adopting such models.

Research on hardware issues relating to the implementation of PCA neural processing remains largely virgin territory. Nevertheless, it holds a very promising future. High-speed, real-time, and massively parallel implementation is an important and fast developing frontier for artificial neural networks (ANNs) in general, and principal component neural models should be no exception. The key lies in integrating two information processing technologies: *adaptive processing* and *parallel processing*. Various plausible digital and analog parallel implementations are described in Chapter 8.

This book is an outgrowth of the Ph.D. thesis of the first author at Princeton University. However, considerable changes have been made to the original manuscript, putting emphasis on mathematical background and putting effort into presenting as many contributions by other workers in the field as possible. Since this is a fast-growing area, it is almost impossible to make sure that all methods published to date are included. For our part, we have made special efforts to filter through major contributions and to provide an extensive bibliography for further reference. Nevertheless, we realize that there may be oversights on critical contributions on the subject. For these, we would like offer our apology. More importantly, our sincere thanks go to the many researchers whose contributions have established a solid foundation for the topics treated in the book.

We have benefited greatly from enthusiastic and enlightening discussions with our friends and colleagues. Our sincere appreciation goes to the series editor, Professor Simon Haykin, for his timely encouragement and valuable suggestions. Our special thanks to Professor Kurt Hornik whose collaboration essentially produced Chapter 5, and Ms. Yunting Lin for her contribution in Chapter 8. We are very grateful for the valuable and constructive suggestions from Professors V. Poor and S. Kulkarni at Princeton University. We have been very fortunate to work with Mr. George Telecki of John Wiley & Sons, Inc., who has provided sound professional assistance on this project. Finally, we wish to thank the Department of Electrical Engineering at Princeton University for offering a scholarly environment and convenient infrastructure for research.

K. I. Diamantaras
S. Y. Kung

Thessaloniki, Greece
Princeton, New Jersey

1

INTRODUCTION

Pattern recognition and data compression are two applications that rely critically on efficient data representation. The task of pattern recognition is to decide to which class of objects an observed pattern belongs. The patterns within a class may vary considerably so that matching the observation with some characteristic template may be an inefficient classification procedure. Take for example the recognition of handwritten characters: the same letter varies considerably when written by different people, or even by the same person but under different circumstances, e.g., slow writing versus quick writing. Another example is speech recognition: a phoneme has considerably disparate waveforms when uttered by different speakers.

It is therefore desirable to extract measurements that are invariant or insensitive to the variations within each class. The process of extracting such measurements is called *feature extraction*. The *features* constant within a class but different between classes help the classifier, which typically follows the feature extractor, improve its performance (see Fig. 1.1a).

The compression of data, on the other hand, is motivated by the need to save the number of *bits* to represent the data while incurring the smallest possible distortion. The bit rate is a valuable resource in data storage or transmission applications. For example, in High-Definition Television (HDTV) the bit rate required for 1500 × 1000 color images (24 bits per pixel) without compression at 30 frames per second is 1 Gbit/sec! The cost of a channel with such transmission capacity, or the cost of magnetic storage or memory of appropriate size to hold even short uncompressed movies, is prohibitive. This makes compression a necessity rather than an option. Typically a compression system comprises a coder and a decoder. The coder maps the high-dimensional data into a small number of parameters while the decoder maps these parameters back into data space (see Figure 1.1b). The coding process is in a sense a special type of feature extraction. In this sense, both applications

1

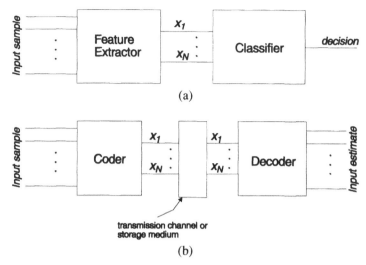

Figure 1.1. Feature extraction applications: (a) a typical pattern recognition system involves a feature extractor followed by a classifier; (b) a data compression system includes a coder and a decoder subsystem: the coder may include a feature extractor for representing the high-dimensional input data with few parameters.

of pattern recognition and data compression share a very similar mathematical framework, especially in the preprocessing phase.

1.1 STATISTICAL ANALYSIS OF DATA

In many applications, such as those described above, we encounter large sets of data. Statistical analysis is an effective mathematical manipulation that provides models for the data and finds hidden relationship among them.

Let us suppose that we are given a set of observations corresponding to some measurable quantities. These quantities could describe some physical system, e.g., a car, a nuclear reactor, etc. Or they could represent some human activity/behavior, e.g., the stock market, students' performance in exams, etc. Suppose that each observation is represented by a set of n numbers, each corresponding to a unique variable of the system, such as the temperature in the engine of a car, the price of a certain stock in the stock market, or a student's grade in a particular course. This set of numbers forms an n-dimensional *vector* $x = [x_1 \quad x_2 \quad \cdots \quad x_n]^T$ (the superscript T denotes transposition).

A particular system at a particular point in time is characterized by a specific observation vector. For example, the closing prices of the stocks in the New York Stock Exchange on June 1, 1995, were specific numbers forming a multidimensional vector. However, these specific numbers could not be precisely known prior to June 1, 1995. Since observed variables with uncertainty are commonly modeled by random numbers, we are really addressing a *statistical observation* rather than just an observation.

We would like to quantify the amount of unpredictability in a statistical observation. If the data are not completely unpredictable we would like to best predict them. Finally, we would like to know how accurate a prediction may be achieved.

The variables in a statistical observation follow some probability distribution. If the variable x_i takes on discrete values its probability distribution is simply

$$p_{x_i}(x) = \text{Prob}(x_i = x).$$

If x_i takes on continuous values, for example in the set of the real numbers $\mathbb{R}$, then we define

$$p_{x_i}(x) = \frac{\text{Prob}(x \leq x_i \leq x + dx)}{dx}.$$

The estimation of the probability distribution gives us some critical information about the data. However, it also has drawbacks: (a) it is not always easy to compute, and (b) it ignores the relationship between different variables in the observation.

Another popular way of describing the data is through the use of the *second order statistics*, namely the *mean*

$$\bar{x} = E\{x\} = \begin{bmatrix} E\{x_1\} & \cdots & E\{x_n\} \end{bmatrix}^T$$

and *covariance* between each pair of variables:

$$r_{ij} = E\{(x_i - \bar{x}_i)(x_j - \bar{x}_j)\},$$

where E is the expectation operator. The parameters r_{ij} can be arranged to form the $n \times n$ covariance matrix

$$R_x = E\{(x - \bar{x})(x - \bar{x})^T\}.$$

The expectation $\bar{x}$ is typically a poor predictor of x unless the variances $r_{11}, \ldots, r_{nn}$ are very small. This happens only when the data have small deviations from the constant vector $\bar{x}$, whence the data come close to a constant observation. Clearly, this is not a very interesting case.

The significance of the parameters r_{ij} however should not be ignored. They bring about the statistical relationship between two variables via the ratios $\rho_{ij} = r_{ij}/\sqrt{r_{ii}r_{jj}}$. If $|\rho_{ij}| \approx 1$ then x_i is strongly *correlated* with x_j, whereas if $\rho_{ij} = 0$, then x_i, x_j are *uncorrelated*. The more correlated the variables the easier it is to predict one from the other. Unfortunately in most situations $|\rho_{ij}|$ is not close to 1 for many pairs i, j.

In order to formally treat the issue of predictability or unpredictability, we need to first define what we mean by "prediction." In general, a given variable x_i may not be predictable from a single variable x_j but from a combination of some or all other variables in the multivariate observation. Suppose that we could identify m

deterministic functions $f_1, \ldots, f_m$, for some $m < n$, such that

$$f_1(x_1, x_2, \ldots, x_n) = 0$$

$$\vdots$$

$$f_m(x_1, x_2, \ldots, x_n) = 0.$$

Given the values of $p = n - m$ variables, the remaining m variables can be determined from the above m constraints. The solutions may not be unique, but they generally form a finite set.

Unfortunately, such functions are almost impossible to determine a priori, unless f_i's are constrained to belong to a specific class of functions S. The simplest and most tractable family of functions are the linear functions which are described by the following general formula:

$$f(x) = f(x_1, \ldots, x_n) = w_1 x_1 + w_2 x_2 + \cdots + w_n x_n,$$

where $w_1, \ldots, w_n$ are constant parameters. In two dimensions the equation $f(x) = 0$ corresponds to a line, in three dimensions the same equation corresponds to a plane, and in n dimensions it corresponds to an $(n - 1)$-dimensional *hyperplane*. A set of m equations

$$f_1(x) = w_{11} x_1 + \cdots + w_{1n} x_n = 0$$

$$\vdots$$

$$f_m(x) = w_{m1} x_1 + \cdots + w_{mn} x_n = 0$$

corresponds to the intersection of m hyperplanes, which is in general a p-dimensional hyperplane, $p = n - m$.

Thus we have perfect linear predictability if the data lie on some common p-dimensional hyperplane. However, this is an unlikely situation in real applications. Instead, there is a certain error between any hyperplane and the given data

$$f_1(x) = \varepsilon_1$$

$$\vdots$$

$$f_m(x) = \varepsilon_m,$$

where $x = [x_1 \quad \cdots \quad x_n]^T$ is the data vector. The variables $\varepsilon_1, \ldots, \varepsilon_m$, are random variables. If we assume that $\bar{x} = 0$, then they have zero mean and finite variances.

For any given p, we would like to find the p-dimensional hyperplane that *fits* the data in an optimal fashion, in particular minimizing the mean square error

$$J = \sum_{i=1}^{m} E\{\varepsilon_i^2\}.$$

To that end we constrain the parameters to satisfy the normality condition $w_{i1}^2 + \cdots + w_{in}^2 = 1$ so as to obtain parameters corresponding to a true hyperplane instead of the trivial solution $w_{i1} = \cdots = w_{in} = 0$.

The optimal hyperplane defined by the equations $f_1(x) = 0, \ldots, f_m(x) = 0$ is called the p-dimensional **principal component subspace** of the data x.

For example, assume that $\bar{x} = 0$, and for $p = 1$ the minimal error $J_{\min}$ is zero. Then the optimal hyperplane is a one-dimensional line and every observation x falls on this line. It follows that there exists a fixed vector e_1 collinear with this line so that

$$x = ce_1$$

for some scalar c. The vector e_1 is called the **principal eigenvector** of x, and c is called the **principal component** of x. If e_1 is normalized (i.e., it has unit length) then c is equal to the *inner product* $e_1^T x$.

Clearly, in this particular example there is a large amount of redundancy among the n observation variables $x_1, \ldots, x_n$. The data can be perfectly described using just one variable c, provided that we know the (constant) principal eigenvector e_1. We say that the number of observed variables n is the *superficial dimensionality* of the data, whereas the *intrinsic dimensionality* is 1.

Staying with this example, the vector e_1 is a **linear feature** because it reveals the structure of the data with a simple linear relationship $x = ce_1$. If we had N observation vectors stored in a computer memory where each variable was represented by B bytes, then we would require a total memory space of $N \times n \times B$ bytes for storing the raw observation data. However, if we stored only the principal eigenvector and the principal components for each observation the required storage would have been $(n + N) \times B$ bytes. We have therefore practically a **data compression ratio** of $1 : n$ (for large N).

The above example is actually very simplistic. In reality the minimum error J is never zero. However, it is common that for some p quite smaller than n the error is very small; thus, the data can be reconstructed from p principal eigenvectors and p principal components with little distortion error. In this case the compression ratio is $p : n$.

Still, the example demonstrates the relationship between prediction, redundancy removal, feature extraction and data compression. The analysis into principal components or **Principal Component Analysis (PCA)** is a classical technique that does all those things in the linear domain and has, for these reasons, application in any problem where a linear model is appropriate. Such problems arise in signal processing, image processing, system and control theory, communications, etc.

1.2 ELEMENTS OF NEUROPHYSIOLOGY

The basic building blocks of the nervous system are called **neurons**. They are excitable cells numbering approximately 10 billion (10^{10}) in the human brain. They are composed of the cell body or **soma**, where the cell nucleus is located, and

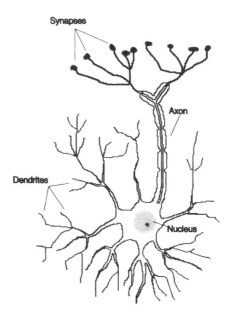

Figure 1.2. Schematic diagram of a neuron.

processes (projections) that come out of the soma and are classified into **dendrites** and **axons** (Fig. 1.2). Dendrites are input devices through which the neuron receives signals from other neurons. There is usually only a single axon per neuron and it serves as its primary output device, which may either connect to other neurons or may terminate into muscle tissue, serving as a control signal for the muscle activity. The axon is a long fiber which *arborizes* (branches) extensively into many threads. A typical axon may branch out to 1000 different points, thus creating a dense network of neural connections when added with the other 10 billion or so axons and their arborizations. The points of contact between an axon branch and a receiving neuron are called **synapses**. There are estimated to be approximately 10^{13} to 10^{14} synapses in the human brain.

Neurons are classified into three classes according to their location and functionality: *afferent* (incoming), *efferent* (outgoing), and *interneurons*. Afferent neurons are sensory cells specialized into receiving signals from the environment, e.g., light (in the retina), sound vibrations (in the cochlea), etc. Efferent neurons (also called motor neurons) are the units carrying out the brain output which controls the muscular contractions and glandular secretions of the body. All other neurons in between are called interneurons and are assumed to be involved in the processes of perception, thought, memory, etc.

The transmission of signals between neurons is performed through a complex electrochemical process. Generally, when the electrical potential on the cell membrane gets above a certain threshold the axon fires an electrical pulse, called the **action potential**, of fixed amplitude and duration which travels through the axon body to the receiving neurons connected with it. After the axon fires it gets into a

refractory period of duration τ_f, during which it is not ready to fire again. Thus, the frequency with which the axon may fire cannot exceed $1/\tau_f$.

Although the firing of the neuron is to some degree a random phenomenon [1, 2] it depends mainly on the combined potentials received as inputs at the neuron's synapses. The strength of the synaptic potential at a certain synapse depends on many factors, including the strength of the stimulus signal, the geometrical characteristics of the synapse, the electrical characteristics of the cell membrane, the relative position with respect to the other synapses, the width of the fiber, etc. Synaptic potentials are summed up and compared with the threshold potential leading to the axon's firing or resting state.

There are two kinds of potentials as well as two kinds of synapses: (i) *inhibitory synapses* produce hyperpolarizing potentials that tend to prevent the neuron from firing, whereas (ii) *excitatory synapses* produce depolarizing potentials that tend to bring the membrane potential closer to the firing threshold. Some combinations of input signals can produce both depolarizing and hyperpolarizing potentials that cancel exactly each other and leave the neuron in an electrically neutral state. It is also possible that either the total depolarizing potential is stronger than the total hyperpolarizing one—in which case the neuron may fire if the potential exceeds the threshold—or the hyperpolarizing potentials prevail, leaving the neuron in a resting state.

A simplified neuron model was proposed by McCulloch and Pitts [3] in 1943 (Fig. 1.3). The neuron is considered to be a binary threshold device with n inputs $x_1, \ldots, x_n$, one output y, a threshold level θ, and n synaptic weights $w_1, \ldots, w_n$ that account for the different efficiencies with which the synapses affect the neural potential. The model is summarized as

$$y = f\left(\sum_{i=1}^{n} w_i x_i - \theta\right), \tag{1.1}$$

where $f(\cdot)$ is the unit step function:

$$f(x) = \begin{cases} 1 & \text{if } x \geq 0, \\ 0 & \text{otherwise.} \end{cases}$$

Model (1.1) is quite imprecise: for example, it ignores the stochastic nature of neural firing, it simplifies the combined input as a weighted sum of the stimuli,

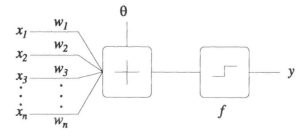

Figure 1.3. The simplified diagram of a neuron according to McCulloch and Pitts.

although it is known that some nonlinear effects take place, etc. In addition, neurons fire pulse trains rather than a single pulse. However, this can be captured by a simple generalization of the model in which the signals x_i and y correspond to firing frequences rather than action potentials. In this generalization the nonlinear function f is not just a step function but rather a *sigmoid function*, such as

$$f(x) = \frac{1}{1 + e^{-x}}, \tag{1.2}$$

so the frequency can go from 0 to some maximum value which is equal to the inverse of the duration of the refractory period (here normalized to 1). Generalizing in this way, we ignore the phase of the pulse sequences, assuming that it is not important, at least in some applications. This is a simplifying hypothesis which is, however, used by a major part of the theory of neural computation. It will be also used throughout this book.

1.3 THE VISUAL CORTEX AND FEATURE DETECTION

The mammalian visual system is one of the best-studied large-scale biological neural structures. Research in this area has been very fruitful and the results very enlightening and often surprising. The early findings of this effort and the description of the classical model for mammalian vision is presented by Hubel and Wiesel [4, 5].

The processing path of optical information in mammals consists of many stages briefly described as follows:

(a) First, the light is received in the *retina*. This is a layer of photoreceptors that lies in the inside back wall of the eye and contains two kinds of sensors: *cones* and *rods*. Cones help us see details and color but do not respond in dim light. Rods work in dim light conditions.

(b) The retinal photoreceptors feed the *ganglion cells* (also in the retina), whose axons form a bundle called the *optic nerve* that leaves the eyeball from a small pit in the back of the eye. This pit does not contain any photoreceptors, and thus it is a "blind spot." The part of the retina with the highest concentration of photoreceptors is called the *fovea*. It is a rod-free area and is the center of our gaze.

(c) The left and right *lateral geniculate nuclei* receive inputs from both left- and right-eye ganglion cells.

(d) The *primary visual cortex* in the back side of the brain receives input from the lateral geniculate nuclei.

Of course, the neurons at the visual cortex send and receive information to and from other parts of the brain so that the optical information fuses with other sources of information, memory, etc., in order for the animal to form its response to the

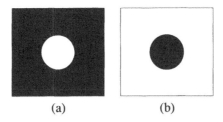

(a) (b)

Figure 1.4. (a) On-center stimulus; (b) off-center stimulus.

external stimuli. Thus, the primary visual cortex is not the final destination for the optical information.

The first very interesting finding from the study of the visual path was that each ganglion cell responds only to stimuli exciting a certain part of the retina, called the *receptive field* of the cell. In addition, the stimulus that maximally excites the cell has a center-surround shape (see Fig. 1.4). Thus the ganglion cells operate as feature detectors. The "feature" is either a white dot with a black surround or a black dot in a white surround. Cells in the geniculate have similar center-surround properties.

In the visual cortex the neurons respond maximally to different and more complicated input patterns. They also have, in most cases, wider receptive fields than ganglion cells. The "simple cells" in the first visual area are responsive to bars or edges of a specific orientation and position in the visual field [5]. Other neurons respond maximally to edges moving in a certain direction within their receptive field [5], others are found to respond to a narrow range of spatial frequencies [6, 7], while others respond to specific colors [8]. Still another class of cells responds to horizontal disparities between the inputs from the two eyes [9].

In general, the neurons in the visual cortex behave like specialized *feature detectors*. Even as early as the retina the ganglion cells filter out the DC component and pass on the information concerning spatial discontinuities. It is those discontinuities that help us discern features in the objects we see, and it is with the help of these features that we "perceive" objects.

A still more interesting question than "what do the neurons in the visual path do?" is "how do they learn to do it?" In other words, how much of the wiring in the neural circuitry is determined prenatally by a genetic program and how much of it is learned postnatally?

Vision deprivation experiments in animals (e.g., by closing one eye for a certain period of time) show that the effect of deprivation at a very young age (soon after birth) is irreversible damage in the animal's vision. However, if the same experiment is performed in an adult animal the vision can be restored perfectly after months or even years of deprivation by simply opening the eye again [4, chapter 9]. For the cat the critical period in which deprivation produced severe damage is between the ages of 4 weeks and 4 months. For the monkey the corresponding period is between birth and 4 months.

This can only be explained if we accept that the neural circuitry responsible for vision is not completely mature at the time of birth and is subject to modifications (learning) at an early age. As the animal becomes an adult the circuitry becomes mature, and therefore subsequent deprivation does not affect the structure of the network significantly.

Scientists are divided into those who believe that most work is done by evolution—thus neural development is genetically dictated and feature detectors are only "tuned-up" by experience [10]—and those who advocate that neural plasticity is governed by a self-organizing principle which plays an essential role in the formation of feature detectors [11–14].

If the second scenario is true it seems unlikely that this principle would be a global one. It is rather expected that some local rule governs the self-organization of the brain, and any global plan would emerge as a result of local interactions among the neurons.

Theorists have actually developed simple local self-organizing laws, such as Hebb's law [15], for example, which in simulation produce results similar to the ones found in nature.

1.4 HEBBIAN AND HEBBIAN-TYPE LAWS

The Hebbian law was postulated by D. O. Hebb in the late 1940s [15] as a principle governing the self-organization of the neural assembly. Hebb's principle stated that if neuron A feeds neuron B, and A, B fire in a correlated fashion, then the strength of the synaptic connection between the two is increased. The increase of the synaptic strength is achieved through metabolic growth of the synaptic knob between the axon of A and the soma of B. Similarly, if neuron A does not participate in firing B for a long period of time, any synaptic knob from A to B decays and finally vanishes.

Hebb proposed this theory in order to explain the permanence of memory. The above associative law of metabolic change seemed the simplest idea and it turned out to be quite powerful. Apart from its simplicity the most attractive feature of this law was the fact that it did not require action at great distance. All the information determining the growth or decay of the synaptic strength is carried by local electrical potentials: that of the afferent axon and that of the efferent soma.

It must be noted that there has been no biological proof for the validity of the Hebbian law. Still, since its publication, the law has attracted a lot of attention, mainly for two reasons:

(a) It is a local rule; synaptic strengths are updated using the activation of the axon terminating at the synapse and the activation of the neuron that receives the axon.

(b) It demonstrates an intriguing relationship with PCA, the classical feature extraction technique described in Section 1.1.

In its simple form the Hebbian law translates into the following equation:

$$w(k + 1) = w(k) + \beta\, a(k)\, b(k),$$

where w is the weight of the synapse between A and B, and a, b are the activations of A and B respectively. The number β is a small step-size parameter, and k is the time index.

Assume now that B receives input from n neurons $A_1, \ldots, A_n$, and all the synaptic weights $w_1, \ldots, w_n$ are trained with the same Hebbian rule. Assume further that the activation of B is a linear function of its inputs:

$$b = \sum_{i=1}^{n} w_i a_i.$$

Then we find that (a) the weight vector $w = [w_1, \ldots, w_n]$ tends to become collinear with the principal eigenvector of the input data, but (b) the model is unstable.

Observation (a) is most interesting since it makes a connection between a classical feature extraction technique and neural network theory. Observation (b) is a problem, but, fortunately, it can be amended. If we can scale the weight vector or normalize it at each iteration so that we can keep its size within certain bounds, then we expect to extract some finite vector which is still collinear with the principal eigenvector.

Indeed, Oja [16] proposed an indirect normalization technique that he called *linearized normalization* and showed that his linear neuron "learns" the principal eigenvector of the input data as $k \to \infty$.

Oja's model inspired further work on the subject. Many different models have been proposed for the extraction of multiple principal eigenvectors. Some earlier models include Földiák's model [17], the Generalized Hebbian Algorithm (GHA) [14], the Adaptive Principal component EXtractor (APEX) [18], the model of Rubner and colleagues [13, 19], the subspace model [20], etc.

Simulations of simple Hebbian models present striking similarity with experimental observations. This does not imply that nature uses the Hebbian law, but rather shows that simple, local connectionist rules can be very powerful in a holistic sense, namely, when seen from the viewpoint of a large model composed of these rules, and encourages research along this direction. For example, Linsker [12] shows that a simple Hebbian-type network with multiple layers forms center-surround feature detectors in its third layer when trained with a smoothed Gaussian input noise. In the fourth layer orientation selective cells appear, and they are distributed in space in a topographical manner reminiscent of the one found in the cortex.

As another example, Rubner and Schulten [13] present two test cases: (a) opponent color processing and (b) orientation and spatial frequency selection. In the first case psychophysical evidence had showed that there exist an achromatic channel and two color-opponent channels: one red-green and the other blue-yellow. It has been found that principal component analysis of cone responses to a set of monochromatic stimuli produces exactly one achromatic and two color-opponent components. By using a Hebbian-type network the authors perform PCA on the input data and thus produce these color-related components.

In the second case they show that principal component analysis on a set of smoothed Gaussian input noise patterns (similar to Linsker's) using the same the network produces feature detectors which are orientation and spatial frequency selective. Similar results are observed by Sanger [14], using another Hebbian-type network which again performs PCA on the input data.

1.5 OUTLINE OF THE BOOK

Chapter 2 reviews some important concepts and theorems from linear algebra. We discuss concepts related to vector spaces, linear maps and matrices, with emphasis on orthogonal transforms and the eigenvalue decomposition. We also introduce Birkhoff's theorem, a very important tool which will be instrumental for our theoretical analysis in subsequent chapters.

In Chapter 3 we define the problem of principal component analysis purely from the statistical perspective. We present the basic PCA theorem, the theory of singular value decomposition (SVD), the Karhunen-Loève transform, and the relationships between the three. We also study the relationship between PCA and information maximization in the Gaussian setting. The chapter concludes with a brief exposition of the most common methods for eigenvalue decomposition from a numerical and algorithmic point of view. Examples and applications of PCA are also presented as aids to understanding and motivations for the theory.

Chapter 4 makes the connection between neural networks and PCA. The first half of the chapter studies the Hebbian law and its relatives, such as Oja's model, Földiák's model, the GHA model, the APEX model, Rubner's model, etc., in great detail, providing a theoretical analysis for each model. The typical network structure of these models is a linear network without hidden units, which either has or doesn't have a lateral connection subnetwork among the output units. A large number of other PCA models are also briefly introduced.

The second half of the chapter describes the relationship between the well-known back-propagation rule and PCA. Unlike the first half of the chapter the model of our study is a two-layer network with an equal number of input and output units but with a smaller number of hidden units.

Minor component networks and Linsker's model are also outlined. They are introduced as reference pointers to some related areas. Finally, we present applications of PCA models in speech processing, detection, and image compression problems.

Chapter 5 addresses the theoretical issue of the optimal linear compression transformation in a two-layer network with unreliable hidden units. This situation is similar to having a noisy channel that carries a linearly compressed signal. The optimal linear codec (coder-decoder) is defined only by using constraints either on the transformation parameters (i.e., the synaptic weights) or on the power of the transmitted signal.

We find that the problem is related to PCA, and that there is an interesting relationship between the noise power and the number of hidden units. We also discuss relationships between this result and classical results in information theory.

Chapter 6 presents three generalizations of classical PCA along three different paths: (a) the reduced-rank linear approximation problem, (b) the cross-correlation problem, and (c) the nonlinear PCA problem. The first two problems fall under the general heading of what we call *Asymmetric PCA (APCA)*. Each problem involves two signals: the first problem studies the least squares approximation of one signal from another through a reduced-rank mapping. The second problem studies the maximization of the cross-correlation between two signals. The first problem relates to the generalized SVD, while the second problem to SVD. Both problems collapse to ordinary PCA if the two signals are identical.

The third generalization path, that of nonlinear PCA, is studied through examples. The network structure corresponding to this problem is a two-layer network with reduced hidden layer with nonlinear hidden units.

The chapter concludes with application examples.

Chapter 7 extends ordinary PCA into the constrained PCA (CPCA) and oriented PCA (OPCA) problems. These extensions arise when components from certain subspaces are known to be undesirable. For example, certain subspaces could be known a priori to be contaminated by noise or interference. Such a priori knowledge will affect the selection of "best" representative components. In the formulation of constrained PCA, those unwanted subspaces are completely avoided. An application of CPCA in image noise removal is demonstrated.

Oriented PCA offers a more flexible formulation at a computational cost. It searches for an optimal solution oriented toward the directions where the unwanted direction has minimum energy while maximizing the projection energy of the signal. The OPCA can be shown to be closely related to the generalized eigenvalue problem of two random signals.

Chapter 8 looks into several very large scale integration (VLSI) implementational aspects of PCA neural networks. Many real-time applications require fast processing speeds, thus parallel (analog or digital) VLSI solutions are necessary and critical. The design of special-purpose architectures for neural PCA algorithms has been largely unexplored in the literature. For PCA algorithms, an attractive and cost-effective architectural choice is an array processor built on a locally interconnected network. This chapter demonstrates that all the PCA neural models are very parallelizable. To highlight this point, various plausible digital and analog parallel implementations are discussed. This paves the way for massively parallel processing, which represents a most viable future solution to real-time neural information processing.

2

A REVIEW OF
LINEAR ALGEBRA

In this review of basic concepts from linear algebra we define vector spaces, linear maps, matrices, and related concepts with emphasis on orthogonal transforms and the eigenvalue decomposition. We also introduce Birkhoff's theorem, a very important tool which will be instrumental for our theoretical analysis in subsequent chapters.

2.1 VECTOR SPACES

The fundamental concept of the vector space (or linear space) relates to almost all of the mathematical treatments in this book. Here we give a brief discussion that will provide the necessary basis for the analysis to follow in the succeeding chapters.

Underlying the concept of the vector space is the concept of the **scalar field**. A *scalar field* $\mathcal{K}$ is a set of numbers that is closed with respect to addition and multiplication; i.e., both the sum and the product of any two elements of $\mathcal{K}$ also belongs to $\mathcal{K}$. Both addition and multiplication are operators that take two arguments. They are commutative:

$$x + y = y + x \qquad x \cdot y = y \cdot x;$$

associative:

$$(x + y) + z = x + (y + z) \qquad (x \cdot y) \cdot z = x \cdot (y \cdot z);$$

they have a null element (called 0 for addition and 1 for multiplication):

$$x + 0 = x \qquad x \cdot 1 = x;$$

and multiplication is distributive over addition:

$$x \cdot (y + z) = (x \cdot y) + (y \cdot z).$$

Moreover, all elements of $\mathcal{K}$ must have an inverse in $\mathcal{K}$ with respect to addition, and all elements of $\mathcal{K}$, except for 0, must have an inverse in $\mathcal{K}$ with respect to multiplication.

The set $\mathbb{R}$ of the real numbers equipped with the standard addition and multiplication is a field, and this field will be mostly used throughout the book, although it will be rarely called a field explicitly. Other fields based on the standard addition and multiplication include the complex numbers $\mathbf{C}$, the rational numbers $\mathbf{Q}$, etc. It is possible of course to construct fields based on nonstandard definitions of addition and multiplication, but we shall not be concerned with such cases in this monograph.

A **vector space** can only be defined with respect to a field. More precisely, a set V is a *vector space* over a field $\mathcal{K}$ if

- V is closed under an operation called (vector) addition which operates on two elements of V and produces a unique sum in V.
- There is an operation called (left) multiplication which operates on two arguments: a scalar and an element of V and produces a unique result in V.
- Vector addition and left multiplication have the following properties:

  $\forall x, y \in V : \quad x + y = y + x.$

  $\forall x, y, z \in V : \quad (x + y) + z = x + (y + z).$

  There exists an element $0 \in V$ such that $\forall x \in V : \ x + 0 = x.$

  $\forall x \in V : \quad \exists y \in V : \quad x + y = 0.$

  Recall that 1 is the null element of the field multiplication. In left multiplication it has the property: $\forall x \in V, \ 1 \cdot x = x.$

  $\forall x \in V, \ a, b \in \mathcal{K} : \quad a(bx) = (ab)x.$

  $\forall x \in V, \ a, b \in \mathcal{K} : \quad (a + b)x = ax + bx.$

  $\forall x, y \in V, \ a \in \mathcal{K} : \quad a(x + y) = ax + ay.$

Vector spaces are also called **linear spaces**, while the elements of a vector space are called **vectors**. As an example, all ordered n-tuples made of elements from a field $\mathcal{K}$ form a vector space over $\mathcal{K}$ if the vector addition and left multiplication are defined as follows:

$$\forall x_1, x_2, \ldots, x_n, y_1, y_2, \ldots, y_n \in \mathcal{K} \qquad \begin{bmatrix} x_1 \\ x_2 \\ \vdots \\ x_n \end{bmatrix} + \begin{bmatrix} y_1 \\ y_2 \\ \vdots \\ y_n \end{bmatrix} = \begin{bmatrix} x_1 + y_1 \\ x_2 + y_2 \\ \vdots \\ x_n + y_n \end{bmatrix},$$

$$\forall x_1, x_2, \ldots, x_n, a \in \mathcal{K} \qquad a \begin{bmatrix} x_1 \\ x_2 \\ \vdots \\ x_n \end{bmatrix} = \begin{bmatrix} ax_1 \\ ax_2 \\ \vdots \\ ax_n \end{bmatrix}.$$

The zero element of the above vector addition is obviously

$$\begin{bmatrix} 0 \\ 0 \\ \vdots \\ 0 \end{bmatrix}.$$

A special case is the field $\mathcal{K} = \mathbb{R}$ equipped with the standard addition and multiplication. Hence, pairs of real numbers, i.e., the elements of $\mathbb{R}^2$, form a linear space. This space is often associated with points on the two-dimensional plane with reference to a specified coordinate system. Similarly, triplets of reals (the elements of $\mathbb{R}^3$) are often associated with points in three-dimensional space. In general, n-tuples of reals (the elements of $\mathbb{R}^n$) are said to form an n-dimensional space.

From now on we shall only deal with vectors that are n-tuples of reals for some n, unless otherwise stated. It can be shown that any abstract vector space V with finite dimension n is isomorphic with $\mathbb{R}^n$, so we are not really restricting ourselves too much except for considering only finite-dimensional spaces.

In terms of notation through the rest of this monograph vectors will be columns of numbers unless explicitly stated otherwise. Of course, there is no qualitative difference between column and row vectors except that column vectors are the most often adopted convention. We often write

$$[x_1 \ x_2 \ \dots \ x_n]^T \quad \text{to denote} \quad \begin{bmatrix} x_1 \\ x_2 \\ \vdots \\ x_n \end{bmatrix}$$

usually for the sake of conserving space on the page. The superscript T is called the **transpose**, and the transformation of a row vector to a column vector is called **transposition**.

Other examples of vector spaces include the set of polynomials with real or complex coefficients, and the sets of real and complex continuous functions on an interval $[a, b]$, when the operations of addition between polynomials (or between functions) and multiplication between scalars and polynomials (or between scalars and functions) are defined in the usual way. These particular examples of vector spaces are infinite dimensional.

2.1.1 Subspaces

A subset U of a vector space V, which is itself a vector space, over the same scalar field as V is called a **subspace** of V. For example, the set $U = \{[x, 0]^T, \ x \in \mathbb{R}\}$ is a subspace of $\mathbb{R}^2$ with the vector addition and left multiplication defined above (it is easy to check that U satisfies all the axioms of a vector space). On the other hand, the set $U_1 = \{[x, 1]^T, \ x \in \mathbb{R}\}$ is *not* a subspace of $\mathbb{R}^2$ because, among other things, it does not contain the null element of the vector addition $[0 \ 0]^T$. Of course, the same is true for every set $U_a = \{[x, a]^T, \ x \in \mathbb{R}\}$ with $a \neq 0$, $a \in \mathbb{R}$.

Only sets that contain the null element 0 of vector addition[1] may qualify for subspaces (or spaces for that matter). In fact, the set $U_0 = \{0\}$ containing only the null element of vector addition *is* a vector space and indeed the smallest one, in the sense that it is contained in any subspace but does not contain any subspace other than itself.

In geometrical terms a subspace of $\mathbb{R}^3$ is one of the following: (a) $\mathbb{R}^3$ itself (dim = 3), (b) a *plane* passing through the origin (dim = 2), (c) a *line* passing through the origin (dim = 1), (d) or the origin itself (dim = 0). The subspaces of $\mathbb{R}^n$ for any n are generally called **hyperplanes** except for $\mathbb{R}^n$ itself and the subspace containing just the origin.

Subspaces of the same space V have the following property:

The intersection of two subspaces is also a subspace. If the subspaces have finite dimension, their intersection has dimension less than or equal to the smallest of the two dimensions and it is equal only if one subspace is a subset of the other (or both are subsets of each other in which case they are identical).

Consider, for example, the intersection of two planes in $\mathbb{R}^3$ (Fig. 2.1). Only if the two planes coincide does their intersection have dimension 2.

2.1.2 Linear Dependence, Span, Basis, Dimension

The vectors $x_1, x_2, \ldots, x_k \in V$ are called **linearly dependent** if there exist scalars $a_1, a_2, \ldots, a_k \in \mathcal{K}$, not all zero, such that

$$a_1 x_1 + a_2 x_2 + \cdots + a_k x_k = 0. \tag{2.1}$$

The left-hand-side of (2.1) is called a **linear combination** of $x_1, x_2, \ldots, x_k$, and the scalars a_i are called the **coefficients** of the combination. The vectors are called **linearly independent** if (2.1) is true only when $a_1 = a_2 = \cdots = a_k = 0$, i.e., if there is no linear combination that results in 0 except for the trivial one which has all coefficients zero.

As an example the vectors $[1, 1]^T, [2, 2]^T \in \mathbb{R}^2$ are linearly dependent since $2\,[1, 1]^T - 1\,[2, 2]^T = [0, 0]^T$. Similarly the vectors $[1, 1, 0]^T, [0, 1, 1]^T, [0, 0, 0]^T \in \mathbb{R}^3$ are also linearly dependent since $0\,[1, 1, 0]^T + 0\,[0, 1, 1]^T + 3\,[0, 0, 0]^T = [0, 0, 0]^T$. On the other hand, the vectors $[1, 1, 0]^T, [0, 1, 1]^T$ are linearly independent since $a_1\,[1, 1, 0]^T + a_2\,[0, 1, 1]^T = [0, 0, 0]^T$ implies $a_1 = a_2 = 0$.

The **span** of a set $S = \{x_1, x_2, \ldots, x_k\}$ of vectors is the set of all linear combinations of those vectors and is denoted by span$(S) = \{y = a_1 x_1 + a_2 x_2 + \cdots +$

---

[1] In the rest of this monograph 0 denotes both the null element of vector addition and the null element of scalar addition. The meaning of 0 will be clarified only when it is not immediately clear from the context.

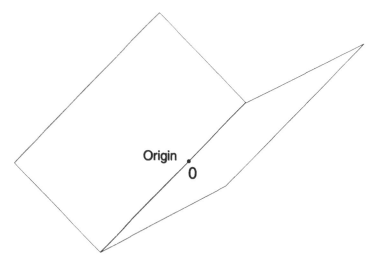

Figure 2.1. A line (subspace with dim = 1) is the intersection of two planes (subspaces with dim = 2). In general, the intersection of two subspaces has smaller dimension than the smallest of the two dimensions unless one subspace is a subset of the other.

$a_k x_k$, $a_1, a_2, \ldots, a_k \in \mathcal{K}\}$. For any set S, the set $U \equiv \text{span}(S)$ is a linear space. We sometimes also write $\text{span}(x_1, \ldots, x_k)$ to denote $\text{span}(S)$, and we say that the vectors $x_1, \ldots, x_k$ span U.

A set of linear independent vectors that span V is called a **basis** of V. In other words, every element of V can be represented as a linear combination of the basis vectors, and in fact this representation is unique due to the linear independence of the basis vectors. For example, the vectors $[1, 0, 0]^T$, $[0, 1, 0]^T$, $[0, 0, 1]^T$ are linearly independent, and every element $[x, y, z]^T$ of $\mathbb{R}^3$ can be written in a unique way as $[x, y, z]^T = x[1, 0, 0]^T + y[0, 1, 0]^T + z[0, 0, 1]^T$. Thus, the vectors $[1, 0, 0]^T$, $[0, 1, 0]^T$, $[0, 0, 1]^T$ form a basis of $\mathbb{R}^3$. Every vector space has a basis although not unique in general.

Notice that if we add one more vector z to a basis $x_1, x_2, \ldots, x_n$ of a space V then we destroy linear independence, for z is equal to some linear combination $a_1 x_1 + a_2 x_2 + \cdots + a_n x_n$, so $a_1 x_1 + a_2 x_2 + \cdots + a_n x_n - z = 0$. If we remove one vector from the basis then the remaining vectors lose the capacity to represent all the vectors in V. If, for example, we remove x_k from the basis, then x_k itself cannot be represented as a linear combination of the remaining vectors because otherwise $x_1, \ldots, x_k, \ldots, x_n$ would have been linearly dependent. Thus, the number of vectors in a basis is quite inflexible. In fact, if a space V has a basis with finitely many vectors then all bases of V have the same number of vectors. This characteristic number is called the **dimension** of V and is denoted by $\dim(V)$. If a space does not have a finite dimension, it has an infinite dimension, and the vectors of any basis can be brought into one-to-one correspondence with the vectors of any other basis.

2.1.3   Inner Product, Orthogonality

An *inner product* in a space V over the field $\mathbb{R}$ is a function $\cdot$ from $V \times V$ to $\mathbb{R}$ which obeys the following axioms

- $\forall x, y \in V : \quad x \cdot x \geq 0$ and $x \cdot x = 0 \Leftrightarrow x = 0$.
- $\forall x, y, z \in V : \quad (x + y) \cdot z = x \cdot z + y \cdot z$.
- $\forall x, y \in V, \; \alpha \in \mathbb{R} : \quad (\alpha x) \cdot y = \alpha (x \cdot y)$.
- $\forall x, y \in V : \quad x \cdot y = y \cdot x$.

In $\mathbb{R}^n$ the **Euclidean inner product**

$$x \cdot y \equiv x_1 y_1 + x_2 y_2 + \cdots + x_n y_n$$

satisfies all the above axioms. This is the most common inner product used in $\mathbb{R}^n$.

Theorem 2.1 (Cauchy-Schwarz). For any inner product $\cdot$ and for all $x, y \in V$

$$|x \cdot y|^2 \leq (x \cdot x)(y \cdot y).$$

It follows that

$$-1 \leq \frac{x \cdot y}{(x \cdot x)^{1/2}(y \cdot y)^{1/2}} \leq 1$$

for all $x, y \in V$. In particular, if $\cdot$ is the Euclidean inner product in $\mathbb{R}^2$ or $\mathbb{R}^3$, we define

$$\cos(\theta) \equiv \frac{x \cdot y}{(x \cdot x)^{1/2}(y \cdot y)^{1/2}}, \tag{2.2}$$

where θ is called the **angle** between the vectors x, y. In the geometric analogy θ is literally the angle (in rads) between the two vectors in two- and three-dimensional spaces (Fig. 2.2a). In higher dimensions the concept of the angle between vector is generalized by (2.2).

Two vectors x, y are called **orthogonal** if $x \cdot y = 0$, in which case we write $x \perp y$. If two vectors are orthogonal, (2.2) leads to $\cos(\theta) = 0$, or $\theta = \pi/2$. Thus in the conventional geometrical interpretation in two and three dimensions, two vectors are orthogonal (with respect to the Euclidean inner product) if they are geometrically perpendicular (Fig. 2.2b).

Some important properties and definitions related to orthogonality are stated here.

- If the nonzero vectors $x_1, x_2, \ldots, x_k$, are pairwise orthogonal then they are linearly independent.
- If the vector x is orthogonal to the vectors $y_1, y_2, \ldots, y_k$ then it is orthogonal to all the linear combinations of these vectors, namely x is orthogonal to all vectors in the subspace $S = \text{span}\{y_1, y_2, \ldots, y_k\}$. We say that x is **orthogonal to the subspace** S, and we write $x \perp S$.

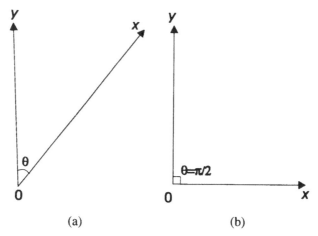

(a)   (b)

Figure 2.2. (a) In the geometrical interpretation the Euclidean inner product is related to the cosine of the angle between the two vectors. (b) The angle is $\pi/2$ iff $x \cdot y = 0$, in which case the vectors are called orthogonal.

- Let L be any subspace of a space V. The set of all vectors $x \in V$ such that $x \perp L$ is called the **orthogonal complement** of L. It is denoted by $L^{\perp}$, and it is itself a subspace of V.

2.1.4 Vector Norms

A **vector norm** is a measure of size for the elements of a vector space. It tries to capture and generalize the concept of the size of a line segment in the geometrical sense. Equivalently, it generalizes the concept of the distance between two points in the two-dimensional geometrical plane or the three-dimensional geometrical space. A *vector norm* in a space V over the field $\mathcal{K}$ (which is either the real or the complex field) is a function $\| \cdot \|$ from V to $\mathbb{R}$ which satisfies the following axioms:

- $\forall x \in V : \quad \|x\| \geq 0$ and $\|x\| = 0 \Leftrightarrow x = 0$.
- $\forall x \in V, \ a \in \mathcal{K} : \quad \|ax\| = |a| \, \|x\|$.
- $\forall x, y \in V : \quad \|x + y\| \leq \|x\| + \|y\|$.

Note that if $\cdot$ is any inner product in $\mathbb{R}^n$ then the function $f(x) = (x \cdot x)^{1/2}$ is a norm. It is straightforward to verify that $f(x)$ satisfies the first two axioms of the norm. For the third axiom we use the Cauchy-Schwarz inequality:

$$f^2(x + y) = (x + y) \cdot (x + y)$$
$$= x \cdot x + y \cdot y + 2x \cdot y$$
$$\leq x \cdot x + y \cdot y + 2(x \cdot x)^{1/2}(y \cdot y)^{1/2}$$
$$= (f(x) + f(y))^2.$$

Thus,

$$f(x + y) \leq f(x) + f(y).$$

Some properties of norms are

- $|\, \|x\| - \|y\| \,| \leq \|x - y\|$, for all $x, y \in V$.
- If the vector norm $\| \cdot \|$ is derived from an inner product $\cdot$, then

$$x \cdot y = \frac{1}{4} \left(\|x + y\|^2 - \|x - y\|^2 \right), \qquad \text{(polarization identity)},$$

$$x \cdot y = \frac{1}{2} \left(\|x + y\|^2 - \|x\|^2 - \|y\|^2 \right),$$

$$\|x\|^2 + \|y\|^2 = \frac{1}{2} \left(\|x + y\|^2 + \|x - y\|^2 \right), \qquad \text{(parallelogram identity)}.$$

We mention, however, that not all vector norms can be derived from an inner product.

Examples of vector norms for a vector $x = [x_1, x_2, \ldots, x_n] \in \mathbb{R}^n$ include

The Euclidean Norm

$$\|x\|_2 = \left(\sum_{i=1}^{n} x_i^2 \right)^{1/2}$$

(clearly, if $\cdot$ is the Euclidean inner product then $\|x\|_2 = (x \cdot x)^{1/2}$);

The Sum Norm

$$\|x\|_1 = \sum_{i=1}^{n} |x_i|;$$

The Max Norm

$$\|x\|_\infty = \max \{ |x_1|, |x_2|, \ldots, |x_n| \};$$

The l_p Norm

$$\|x\|_p = \left(\sum_{i=1}^{n} |x_i|^p \right)^{1/p}.$$

It is interesting to note that the Euclidean norm is a special case of the l_p norm for $p = 2$, the sum norm is a special case of l_p for $p = 1$, while the max norm is the limit of the l_p norm for $p \to \infty$.

In the rest of this monograph the notation $\| \cdot \|$ will denote the Euclidean norm $\| \cdot \|_2$ unless otherwise stated.

2.2 MATRICES

A mapping $\mathcal{A}$ from a vector space U with dimension n to a vector space V with dimension m (both spaces over the same field $\mathcal{K}$) is called a **linear transformation** if and only if it satisfies the following conditions:

1. $\forall x \in U, \, a \in \mathcal{K}, \qquad \mathcal{A}(ax) = a(\mathcal{A}x).$

2. $\forall x, y \in U, \qquad \mathcal{A}(x + y) = (\mathcal{A}x) + (\mathcal{A}y).$

Let $e_1, e_2, \ldots, e_n$ and $f_1, f_2, \ldots, f_m$ be fixed bases in U and V respectively. Then the transformation of the vectors e_i will be a set of vectors in V which can be represented as linear combinations of the basis vectors f_i:

$$
\begin{aligned}
\mathcal{A}e_1 &= a_1^{(1)} f_1 + a_2^{(1)} f_2 + \cdots + a_m^{(1)} f_m, \\
\mathcal{A}e_2 &= a_1^{(2)} f_1 + a_2^{(2)} f_2 + \cdots + a_m^{(2)} f_m, \\
&\vdots \\
\mathcal{A}e_n &= a_1^{(n)} f_1 + a_2^{(n)} f_2 + \cdots + a_m^{(n)} f_m.
\end{aligned} \tag{2.3}
$$

Any vector $x = \theta_1 e_1 + \theta_2 e_2 + \cdots + \theta_n e_n \in U$ maps to a vector $y = \xi_1 f_1 + \xi_2 f_2 + \cdots + \xi_m f_m \in V$, so

$$
\begin{aligned}
\xi_1 f_1 + \xi_2 f_2 + \cdots + \xi_m f_m = y &= \mathcal{A}x \\
&= \theta_1 \mathcal{A}e_1 + \theta_2 \mathcal{A}e_2 + \cdots + \theta_n \mathcal{A}e_n.
\end{aligned}
$$

Using (2.3) to expand the right-hand side of the above equation and from the fact that the expansion of a vector into a basis is unique, it follows that the coefficients of x and y satisfy the equations

$$
\begin{aligned}
\xi_1 &= a_1^{(1)} \theta_1 + a_1^{(2)} \theta_2 + \cdots + a_1^{(n)} \theta_n, \\
\xi_2 &= a_2^{(1)} \theta_1 + a_2^{(2)} \theta_2 + \cdots + a_2^{(n)} \theta_n, \\
&\vdots \\
\xi_m &= a_m^{(1)} \theta_1 + a_m^{(2)} \theta_2 + \cdots + a_m^{(n)} \theta_n.
\end{aligned} \tag{2.4}
$$

We say that the coefficients $a_1^{(1)}, \ldots, a_m^{(n)}$, form an $m \times n$ **matrix** if we arrange them in a rectangular array of m rows and n columns:

$$
A = \begin{bmatrix}
a_1^{(1)} & a_1^{(2)} & \cdots & a_1^{(n)} \\
a_2^{(1)} & a_2^{(2)} & \cdots & a_2^{(n)} \\
\vdots & & & \vdots \\
a_m^{(1)} & a_m^{(2)} & \cdots & a_m^{(n)}
\end{bmatrix},
$$

and we rewrite (2.4) as

$$
\begin{bmatrix} \xi_1 \\ \xi_2 \\ \vdots \\ \xi_m \end{bmatrix} = \begin{bmatrix} a_1^{(1)} & a_1^{(2)} & \cdots & a_1^{(n)} \\ a_2^{(1)} & a_2^{(2)} & \cdots & a_2^{(n)} \\ \vdots & \vdots & & \vdots \\ a_m^{(1)} & a_m^{(2)} & \cdots & a_m^{(n)} \end{bmatrix} \begin{bmatrix} \theta_1 \\ \theta_2 \\ \vdots \\ \theta_n \end{bmatrix} .
$$

Defining $\xi = [\xi_1, \ldots, \xi_m]^T \in \mathbb{R}^m$ and $\theta = [\theta_1, \ldots, \theta_n]^T \in \mathbb{R}^n$, we can write

$$
\xi = A\theta
$$

The operation between A and θ is called **matrix-vector multiplication**, and the product of this multiplication is another vector with the same or different dimension as θ, depending on the number of rows in the matrix A. In general, a $k \times l$ matrix operates on a vector of dimension l to produce a vector of dimension k.

A matrix is at first sight nothing but a rectangular arrangement of numbers. Yet when equipped with operations such as matrix-vector multiplication or other operations (to be described in a moment), it becomes a very rich mathematical object. Its treatment is covered by a special section in mathematical analysis called *matrix theory*. Due to the relationship between matrices and linear operators, matrix theory is particularly important in the study of linear equations, linear systems, linear algebra, combinatorics, statistical analysis, and many parts of mathematics that are associated with engineering sciences. This section is not intended to cover all of matrix theory, just the material related to the analysis used in the following chapters. For an excellent treatment of matrix theory we recommend the books by Horn and Johnson [21, 22].

We denote by $\mathbb{R}^{m \times n}$ the set of all $m \times n$ matrices with real entries (similarly $\mathbb{C}^{m \times n}$ the set of all $m \times n$ matrices with complex entries). $\mathbb{R}^{m \times n}$ is a linear space (over the real field) if we define **matrix addition** and **scalar-matrix multiplication** as follows:

$$
\begin{bmatrix} x_{11} & x_{12} & \cdots & x_{1n} \\ x_{21} & x_{22} & \cdots & x_{2n} \\ \vdots & & & \vdots \\ x_{m1} & x_{m2} & \cdots & x_{mn} \end{bmatrix} + \begin{bmatrix} y_{11} & y_{12} & \cdots & y_{1n} \\ y_{21} & y_{22} & \cdots & y_{2n} \\ \vdots & & & \vdots \\ y_{m1} & y_{m2} & \cdots & y_{mn} \end{bmatrix}
$$

$$
= \begin{bmatrix} x_{11} + y_{11} & x_{12} + y_{12} & \cdots & x_{1n} + y_{1n} \\ x_{21} + y_{21} & x_{22} + y_{22} & \cdots & x_{2n} + y_{2n} \\ \vdots & & & \vdots \\ x_{m1} + y_{m1} & x_{m2} + y_{m2} & \cdots & x_{mn} + y_{mn} \end{bmatrix}
$$

and

$$
a \begin{bmatrix} x_{11} & x_{12} & \cdots & x_{1n} \\ x_{21} & x_{22} & \cdots & x_{2n} \\ \vdots & & & \vdots \\ x_{m1} & x_{m2} & \cdots & x_{mn} \end{bmatrix} = \begin{bmatrix} ax_{11} & ax_{12} & \cdots & ax_{1n} \\ ax_{21} & ax_{22} & \cdots & ax_{2n} \\ \vdots & & & \vdots \\ ax_{m1} & ax_{m2} & \cdots & ax_{mn} \end{bmatrix} .
$$

The dimension of the vector space $\mathbb{R}^{m \times n}$ is $m \cdot n$. Special cases are $\mathbb{R}^{n \times 1}$ and $\mathbb{R}^{1 \times n}$ (column vectors and row vectors) both of which, as we have already seen, are vector spaces with dimension $n \cdot 1 = n$.

We furthermore define **matrix multiplication** in extension to matrix-vector multiplication as follows:

$$\begin{bmatrix} x_{11} & \cdots & x_{1k} \\ \vdots & & \vdots \\ x_{m1} & \cdots & x_{mk} \end{bmatrix} \begin{bmatrix} y_{11} & \cdots & y_{1n} \\ \vdots & & \vdots \\ y_{k1} & \cdots & y_{kn} \end{bmatrix}$$

$$= \begin{bmatrix} \sum_{j=1}^{k} x_{1j} y_{j1} & \cdots & \sum_{j=1}^{k} x_{1j} y_{jn} \\ \vdots & & \vdots \\ \sum_{j=1}^{k} x_{mj} y_{j1} & \cdots & \sum_{j=1}^{k} x_{mj} y_{jn} \end{bmatrix}.$$

So, if $C = [c_{ij}] \in \mathbb{R}^{n \times m}$ is the product of the matrices $A \in \mathbb{R}^{n \times k}$, $B \in \mathbb{R}^{k \times m}$, then $c_{ij} = \sum_{l=1}^{k} a_{il} b_{lj}$. Notice that in order for the matrix product AB to be defined it is necessary that the number of columns in A be equal to the number of rows in B, in which case the matrices A and B are called **conformal**. The result C has the same number of rows as A and the same number of columns as B.

The Euclidean inner product between two (column) vectors x and y can be expressed as the product of the $1 \times n$ "matrix" x^T and the $n \times 1$ "matrix" y:

$$x \cdot y = x^T y.$$

Therefore, the Euclidean inner product between two vectors is a special case of matrix multiplication. The result, of course, is a 1×1 matrix, i.e., a scalar number.

It is important to note that, unlike scalar multiplication, matrix multiplication is not commutative; i.e., in general $AB \neq BA$. However, matrix multiplication is associative:

$$(AB)C = A(BC);$$

distributive over addition:

$$A(B + C) = AB + AC, \qquad (B + C)A = BA + CA;$$

and has a null element for every n, called the **identity matrix**:

$$I = \begin{bmatrix} 1 & 0 & \cdots & 0 \\ 0 & 1 & & 0 \\ \vdots & & \ddots & \vdots \\ 0 & 0 & \cdots & 1 \end{bmatrix} \in \mathbb{R}^{n \times n},$$

such that $AI = A$ if $A \in \mathbb{R}^{k \times n}$, and $IA = A$ if $A \in \mathbb{R}^{n \times k}$ for all A and k.

2.2.1 Partitioning, Inverse, and Transposition

A matrix may be considered as (1) a rectangular array of numbers, (2) a horizontal arrangement of column vectors, (3) a vertical arrangement of row vectors, or, most generally, (4) a rectangular arrangement of smaller submatrices. After all, numbers, columns, or rows are special cases of matrices with dimensions 1×1, $n \times 1$, and $1 \times n$, respectively.

Writing a matrix as an arrangement of smaller submatrices is called **partitioning** the matrix. It is easy to verify that the rules of matrix addition and matrix multiplication for partitioned matrices take the following form:

$$X = \begin{bmatrix} X_{11} & \cdots & X_{1k} \\ \vdots & & \vdots \\ X_{l1} & \cdots & X_{lk} \end{bmatrix}, \qquad Y = \begin{bmatrix} Y_{11} & \cdots & Y_{1k} \\ \vdots & & \vdots \\ Y_{l1} & \cdots & Y_{lk} \end{bmatrix},$$

$$X + Y = \begin{bmatrix} X_{11} + Y_{11} & \cdots & X_{1k} + Y_{1k} \\ \vdots & & \vdots \\ X_{l1} + Y_{l1} & \cdots & X_{lk} + Y_{lk} \end{bmatrix},$$

$$XY = \begin{bmatrix} \sum_{j=1}^{k} X_{1j} Y_{j1} & \cdots & \sum_{j=1}^{k} X_{1j} Y_{jm} \\ \vdots & & \vdots \\ \sum_{j=1}^{k} X_{lj} Y_{j1} & \cdots & \sum_{j=1}^{k} X_{lj} Y_{jm} \end{bmatrix}.$$

The **inverse** of a square matrix $A \in \mathbb{R}^{n \times n}$ is a matrix $X \in \mathbb{R}^{n \times n}$ such that $AX = I$. We denote the inverse by A^{-1}, but it does not always exist. If it does exist, the matrix A is called **nonsingular**; otherwise it is called **singular**. The product $P = A_1 A_2 \cdots A_l$ is nonsingular *iff* A_1, A_2, $\ldots$ and A_l are nonsingular. It is easy to show that

$$(AB)^{-1} = B^{-1} A^{-1}$$

provided that A and B are nonsingular.

Lemma 2.1 (Partitioned Matrix Inverse). The inverse of a partitioned matrix[2]

$$A = \begin{array}{c} \\ n \\ m \end{array} \begin{matrix} \overset{\displaystyle n \quad m}{\begin{bmatrix} P & Q \\ R & S \end{bmatrix}} \end{matrix}$$

[2] The notation $\begin{array}{c} \\ r_1 \\ r_2 \\ \vdots \\ r_l \end{array} \overset{\displaystyle c_1 \ c_2 \ \cdots \ c_k}{\begin{bmatrix} \\ \\ \\ \\ \end{bmatrix}}$ denotes that the matrix is partitioned horizontally into $r_1, r_2, \ldots, r_l$ rows and vertically into $c_1, c_2, \ldots, c_k$ columns.

can be written as follows:

$$A^{-1} = \begin{bmatrix} (P - QS^{-1}R)^{-1} & -P^{-1}Q(S - RP^{-1}Q)^{-1} \\ -(S - RP^{-1}Q)^{-1}RP^{-1} & (S - RP^{-1}Q)^{-1} \end{bmatrix} \qquad (2.5)$$

$$= \begin{bmatrix} P^{-1} & 0 \\ 0 & 0 \end{bmatrix} + \begin{bmatrix} -P^{-1}Q \\ I \end{bmatrix} [S - RP^{-1}Q]^{-1} [-RP^{-1} \quad I], \qquad (2.6)$$

assuming that all the involved inverses exist.

This formula gives rise to the following

Lemma 2.2 (Matrix Inversion Lemma).

$$(A + BCD)^{-1} = A^{-1} - A^{-1}B(C^{-1} + DA^{-1}B)^{-1}DA^{-1}, \qquad (2.7)$$

where $A \in \mathbb{R}^{n \times n}$, $C \in \mathbb{R}^{m \times m}$, $B \in \mathbb{R}^{n \times m}$, and $D \in \mathbb{R}^{m \times n}$.

Indeed, consider the matrix expression

$$\left(\begin{matrix} & n & m \\ n & \begin{bmatrix} I & B \\ 0 & I \end{bmatrix} \end{matrix} \begin{matrix} & n & m \\ n & \begin{bmatrix} A & 0 \\ 0 & C \end{bmatrix} \end{matrix} \begin{matrix} & n & m \\ n & \begin{bmatrix} I & 0 \\ D & I \end{bmatrix} \end{matrix} \right)^{-1}$$

$$= \begin{bmatrix} A + BCD & BC \\ CD & C \end{bmatrix}^{-1}$$

$$= \begin{bmatrix} I & 0 \\ D & I \end{bmatrix}^{-1} \begin{bmatrix} A & 0 \\ 0 & C \end{bmatrix}^{-1} \begin{bmatrix} I & B \\ 0 & I \end{bmatrix}^{-1}$$

$$= \begin{bmatrix} I & -D \\ 0 & I \end{bmatrix} \begin{bmatrix} A^{-1} & 0 \\ 0 & C^{-1} \end{bmatrix} \begin{bmatrix} I & 0 \\ -B & I \end{bmatrix}$$

$$= \begin{bmatrix} A^{-1} & -A^{-1}B \\ -DA^{-1} & C^{-1} + DA^{-1}B \end{bmatrix}.$$

Therefore,

$$\begin{bmatrix} A^{-1} & -A^{-1}B \\ -DA^{-1} & C^{-1} + DA^{-1}B \end{bmatrix}^{-1} = \begin{bmatrix} A + BCD & BC \\ CD & C \end{bmatrix}.$$

Using (2.5) we obtain

$$\begin{bmatrix} (A^{-1} - A^{-1}B[C^{-1} + DA^{-1}B]^{-1}DA^{-1})^{-1} & \cdots \\ \cdots & \cdots \end{bmatrix} = \begin{bmatrix} A + BCD & BC \\ CD & C \end{bmatrix},$$

from which (2.7) follows immediately.

We have already defined the transpose T for vectors as the operator that transforms a column vector into a row vector, and vice versa. For matrices the transpose operator swaps rows with columns; thus vector transposition is just a special case. We say that the matrix $B = [b_{ij}] \in \mathbb{R}^{m \times n}$ is the **transpose** of the matrix $A = [a_{ij}] \in \mathbb{R}^{n \times m}$, and we write $B = A^T$, iff $b_{ij} = a_{ji}$ for all i, j. The **Hermitian transpose** $A^* \in \mathbb{C}^{m \times n}$ of a complex matrix $A \in \mathbb{C}^{n \times m}$ is the complex conjugate transpose of A: $A^* = [b_{ij}] = [\bar{a}_{ji}] = \bar{A}^T \in \mathbb{C}^{m \times n}$.

Important properties of transposition are

- $(A^T)^T = A$, $(A^*)^* = A$.
- $(AB)^T = B^T A^T$, $(AB)^* = B^* A^*$.
- $(A^T)^{-1} = (A^{-1})^T \equiv A^{-T}$, $(A^*)^{-1} = (A^{-1})^* \equiv A^{-*}$.

2.2.2 Special Matrices

An $n \times n$ matrix is called **square**. A matrix $A \in \mathbb{R}^{m \times n}$ is called **diagonal** if $m = n$ and $a_{ij} = 0$ if $i \neq j$. If $m \neq n$ and still $a_{ij} = 0$ if $i \neq j$, then A is called **pseudodiagonal**. For example, the matrix D is diagonal, but the matrices P_1 and P_2 are pseudodiagonal:

$$
D = \begin{bmatrix} -4 & 0 & 0 \\ 0 & 1 & 0 \\ 0 & 0 & 6 \end{bmatrix}, \qquad
P_1 = \begin{bmatrix} -1 & 0 & 0 & 0 \\ 0 & 3 & 0 & 0 \end{bmatrix}, \qquad
P_2 = \begin{bmatrix} 2 & 0 \\ 0 & -5 \\ 0 & 0 \end{bmatrix}.
$$

A real square matrix $U \in \mathbb{R}^{n \times n}$ is called **orthogonal** if $U^T U = I$. The columns of an orthogonal matrix form an orthonormal set of vectors, and we have $U^T = U^{-1}$, which implies $U U^T = I$; i.e., the rows of U also form an orthonormal set.

A real square matrix $A \in \mathbb{R}^{n \times n}$ is called **symmetric** if $A = A^T$. A is called **skew-symmetric** if $A = -A^T$, implying $a_{ii} = 0$ for all i and $a_{ij} = -a_{ji}$ for all $i \neq j$. For example, matrix S is symmetric while K is skew-symmetric:

$$
S = \begin{bmatrix} 5 & -2 & 1 \\ -2 & -4 & 3 \\ 1 & 3 & 7 \end{bmatrix}, \qquad
K = \begin{bmatrix} 0 & -2 & 1 \\ 2 & 0 & 3 \\ -1 & -3 & 0 \end{bmatrix}.
$$

A square matrix $A \in \mathbb{R}^{n \times n}$ is called **column (row) stochastic** if $a_{ij} \geq 0 \; \forall i, j$, and the sum of each column (row) is 1: $\forall j \; \sum_{i=1}^{n} a_{ij} = 1$ ($\forall i \; \sum_{j=1}^{n} a_{ij} = 1$). A is **doubly stochastic** if it is both row and column stochastic.

We shall call a matrix $A \in \mathbb{R}^{m \times n}$, $m \neq n$, **strictly row (column) stochastic** if there is a matrix B such that $M = \begin{bmatrix} A \\ B \end{bmatrix}$ ($M = [A \mid B]$) is doubly stochastic. Clearly, the rows (columns) of a strictly row (column) stochastic matrix sum up to 1, while the columns (rows) sum up to something less or equal to 1.

Let the elementwise product $A \circ B = [a_{ij} b_{ij}]$ between two matrices of the same size be called the **Hadamard matrix product**. If U is orthogonal then the matrix

$U \circ U = [u_{ij}^2]$ is doubly stochastic since $\sum_{i=1}^{n} u_{ij}^2 = \sum_{j=1}^{n} u_{ij}^2 = 1$ (remember that the rows and columns of an orthogonal matrix have unit length).

A **permutation matrix** $P \in \mathbb{R}^{n \times n}$ is a matrix that has exactly one element equal to 1 in each row and each column with all other elements 0. An example of a permutation matrix is

$$P = \begin{bmatrix} 0 & 1 & 0 & 0 \\ 0 & 0 & 0 & 1 \\ 1 & 0 & 0 & 0 \\ 0 & 0 & 1 & 0 \end{bmatrix}.$$

The result of multiplying a matrix $A \in \mathbb{R}^{n \times 4}$ from the right by P is to permute the columns of A in the following fashion:

$$column\ 1 \rightarrow column\ 2$$

$$column\ 2 \rightarrow column\ 4$$

$$column\ 3 \rightarrow column\ 1$$

$$column\ 4 \rightarrow column\ 3$$

The result of multiplying a matrix $A \in \mathbb{R}^{4 \times n}$ from the left by P is to permute the rows of A in the following fashion:

$$row\ 1 \rightarrow row\ 3$$

$$row\ 2 \rightarrow row\ 1$$

$$row\ 3 \rightarrow row\ 4$$

$$row\ 4 \rightarrow row\ 2$$

Clearly every permutation matrix is doubly stochastic since the sum of any row and any column is 1.

A **row (column) selection matrix** $S \in \mathbb{R}^{m \times n}$, $m \le n$ ($m \ge n$), is a matrix that has exactly one entry equal to 1 in each row (column), has at most one entry equal to 1 in each column (row), while all other elements are 0. For example,

$$S_r = \begin{bmatrix} 0 & 0 & 1 & 0 \\ 1 & 0 & 0 & 0 \end{bmatrix}$$

is a row selection matrix.

Applying a row selection matrix S_r to a matrix A produces a matrix $B_r = S_r A$ whose rows are a subset of the rows of A (not necessarily in the order in which they appear in A) without any row being repeated twice. Similarly, multiplying from the right with a column selection matrix S_c results in a matrix $B_c = A S_c$ whose columns are a (not ordered) subset of the columns of A. Clearly, if S is row selective, then S^T is column selective.

The diagonals of a **Toeplitz** matrix have constant elements

$$
A = \begin{bmatrix}
a_1 & a_2 & \ddots & a_{n-1} & a_n \\
b_2 & a_1 & \ddots & a_{n-2} & a_{n-1} \\
\ddots & \ddots & \ddots & \ddots & \ddots \\
b_{n-1} & b_{n-2} & \ddots & a_1 & a_2 \\
b_n & b_{n-1} & \ddots & b_2 & a_1
\end{bmatrix}.
$$

Toeplitz matrices arise naturally in problems that involve covariances of stationary signals, such as the normal or Yule-Walker equations in spectral estimation [23].

The antidiagonals of a **Hankel matrix** (i.e., the diagonals from top right to bottom left) have constant elements:

$$
A = \begin{bmatrix}
a_1 & a_2 & \cdots & a_{n-1} & a_n \\
a_2 & a_3 & \cdots & a_n & a_{n+1} \\
\ddots & \ddots & \ddots & \ddots & \ddots \\
a_{n-1} & a_n & \cdots & a_{2n-3} & a_{2n-2} \\
a_n & a_{n+1} & \cdots & a_{2n-2} & a_{2n-1}
\end{bmatrix}.
$$

Hankel matrices arise in linear systems. Consider, for example, the state-space equations of a system

$$
x_{k+1} = Ax_k + Bu_k,
$$

$$
y_k = Cx_k,
$$

where, for all k, $x_k, B, C^T \in \mathbb{R}^n$, $u_k, y_k \in \mathbb{R}$, and $A \in \mathbb{R}^{n \times n}$. Let the system start at a zero initial condition $x_0 = 0$ and the input be the impulse function $u_0 = a$, $u_k = 0$, $k = 1, 2, \ldots$. Then

$$
Y = \begin{bmatrix}
y_1 & y_2 & \cdots & y_L \\
y_2 & y_3 & \cdots & y_{L+1} \\
\vdots & & & \vdots \\
y_L & y_{L+1} & \cdots & y_{2L-1}
\end{bmatrix}
$$

$$
= \begin{bmatrix}
CB & CAB & \cdots & CA^{L-1}B \\
CAB & CA^2B & \cdots & CA^L B \\
\vdots & & & \vdots \\
CA^{L-1}B & CA^L B & \cdots & CA^{2(L-1)}B
\end{bmatrix}
\begin{bmatrix}
a & 0 & \cdots & 0 \\
0 & a & \cdots & 0 \\
\vdots & & & \vdots \\
0 & 0 & \cdots & a
\end{bmatrix}
$$

$$
= aH.
$$

The matrix H comprising the entries $CA^l B$ (*Markov parameters*) is called the *system Hankel matrix*.

2.2.3 Similarity, Orthogonal Equivalence

A matrix $A \in \mathbb{R}^{n \times n}$ is called **similar** to a matrix $B \in \mathbb{R}^{n \times n}$ if there exists a nonsingular matrix $S \in \mathbb{R}^{n \times n}$ such that

$$A = S^{-1}BS.$$

S is called a **similarity matrix**.

Similarity is an equivalence relationship, namely, it is reflexive, symmetric, and transitive. Indeed, for any matrices $A, B, C \in \mathbb{R}^{n \times n}$

- A is similar to itself *(reflexivity)* since $A = I^{-1}AI$.
- If A is similar to B then B is also similar to A *(symmetry)* since $A = S^{-1}BS$ for some S implies $B = P^{-1}AP$ with $P = S^{-1}$.
- If A is similar to B and B similar to C then A is similar to C *(transitivity)* since $A = S_1^{-1}BS_1$ and $B = S_2^{-1}CS_2$ implies $A = P^{-1}CP$ with $P = S_2 S_1$.

If the similarity matrix S is orthogonal then A and B are called **orthogonally equivalent** and

$$A = S^T BS.$$

2.2.4 Span, Null Space, Rank, Determinant, Trace

The **column span** of a matrix $A \in \mathbb{R}^{m \times n}$ is the subspace spanned by its columns and it is denoted by span(A). In other words, span(A) $= \{y \in \mathbb{R}^m : y = Ax, \text{ for some } x \in \mathbb{R}^n\}$. The **null space** of A is defined as follows: null(A) $= \{x \in \mathbb{R}^n : Ax = 0\}$. It is easy to show that both span(A) and null(A) are linear subspaces (according to the definition of a subspace).

The **rank** of a matrix $A \in \mathbb{R}^{m \times n}$ is the maximum number of columns in A that are linearly independent. Clearly then rank(A) $=$ dim(span(A)). It turns out that the rank is also equal to the maximum number of rows in A that are linearly independent, so rank(A) $=$ rank(A^T) and rank(A) $\leq \min(m, n)$. The rank of a matrix is not changed by pre- or postmultiplication with a square nonsingular matrix. In fact for all matrices $A \in \mathbb{R}^{n \times m}, B \in \mathbb{R}^{n \times k}$,

$$\text{rank}(AB) \leq \text{rank}(A)\,\text{rank}(B). \tag{2.8}$$

Square matrices have special properties that deserve further attention. The **determinant** is a characteristic number defined only for square matrices. Let $A = [a_{ij}] \in \mathbb{R}^{n \times n}$. The determinant of A, denoted by $|A|$ or det(A), is defined as

$$|A| \equiv \det(A) = \sum_{\pi} (-1)^{s(\pi)} \prod_{i=1}^{n} a_{i,\pi(i)}, \tag{2.9}$$

where the sum is over all permutations π of the numbers $1, 2, \ldots, n$, and $s(\pi)$ is the number of *inversions* in a permutation π. An inversion is an ordered pair $[\pi(i), \pi(j)]$, $i < j$, of numbers in the permutation sequence such that $\pi(i) > \pi(j)$. For example, in the permutation $\{4, 2, 5, 3, 1\}$ the number of inversions is 6: $[4, 2]$, $[4, 3]$, $[4, 1]$, $[2, 1]$, $[5, 3]$, $[5, 1]$.

For example, the determinant of a 2×2 matrix is

$$\begin{vmatrix} a & b \\ c & d \end{vmatrix} = ad - bc.$$

Except for (2.9), an alternative way for computing the determinant is the *Lagrange expansion*. This approach inductively defines the determinant of $n \times n$ matrices assuming that we have already defined the determinant of $(n-1) \times (n-1)$ matrices. Let A_{ij} be the submatrix resulting from deletion of the ith row and the jth column of A. Then

$$\det(A) = \sum_{i=1}^{n} (-1)^{i+j} a_{ij} \det(A_{ij}) = \sum_{j=1}^{n} (-1)^{i+j} a_{ij} \det(A_{ij}).$$

For example,

$$\begin{vmatrix} a_{11} & a_{12} & a_{13} \\ a_{21} & a_{22} & a_{23} \\ a_{31} & a_{32} & a_{33} \end{vmatrix} = a_{11} \begin{vmatrix} a_{22} & a_{23} \\ a_{32} & a_{33} \end{vmatrix} - a_{21} \begin{vmatrix} a_{12} & a_{13} \\ a_{32} & a_{33} \end{vmatrix} + a_{31} \begin{vmatrix} a_{12} & a_{13} \\ a_{22} & a_{23} \end{vmatrix}.$$

The determinant has many important properties. Some of them will be more useful to us here.

- For all $A \in \mathbb{R}^{n \times n}$

$$\det(A) = 0 \Leftrightarrow A = \text{singular}$$

$$\Leftrightarrow \text{columns of } A \text{ linearly dependent}$$

$$\Leftrightarrow \text{rows of } A \text{ linearly dependent}$$

$$\Leftrightarrow \text{rank}(A) < n.$$

- For all $A \in \mathbb{R}^{n \times n}$

$$\det(A) = \det(A^T).$$

- If $A, B \in \mathbb{R}^{n \times n}$

$$\det(AB) = \det(A)\det(B).$$

The **trace** of a square matrix $A \in \mathbb{R}^{n \times n}$ is defined as follows:

$$\text{tr}(A) = \sum_{i=1}^{n} a_{ii}.$$

It has the following important properties:

- For all matrices $A \in \mathbb{R}^{n \times m}$, $B \in \mathbb{R}^{m \times n}$

$$\mathrm{tr}(AB) = \sum_{i=1}^{n} \left(\sum_{j=1}^{m} a_{ij}b_{ji} \right) = \sum_{j=1}^{m} \left(\sum_{i=1}^{n} b_{ji}a_{ij} \right) = \mathrm{tr}(BA).$$

- If $S \in \mathbb{R}^{n \times n}$ is a nonsingular matrix

$$\mathrm{tr}(S^{-1}AS) = \mathrm{tr}(SS^{-1}A) = \mathrm{tr}(A);$$

namely the trace is invariant under a similarity transformation.

2.2.5 Eigenvalue Decomposition

Let $A \in \mathbb{R}^{n \times n}$. If a nonzero vector $x \in \mathbb{C}^n$ and a scalar $\lambda \in \mathbb{C}$ satisfy the equation

$$Ax = \lambda x, \tag{2.10}$$

then we say that x is an **eigenvector** and λ is an **eigenvalue** of A. If x was equal to 0 the equation would have been trivially satisfied for any λ. We *do not* consider the 0-vector to be an eigenvector. If x is an eigenvector with eigenvalue λ then all scaled vectors αx with $\alpha \neq 0$ are also eigenvectors corresponding to the same eigenvalue λ.

The **eigenvalue equation** (2.10) can also be written as

$$(\lambda I - A)x = 0. \tag{2.11}$$

For this equation to have a nontrivial solution in x (i.e., a solution other than $x = 0$), it is necessary and sufficient that $(\lambda I - A)$ be singular; i.e.,

$$\det(\lambda I - A) = 0.$$

For an $n \times n$ matrix the expression on the left-hand side is a polynomial of degree n, called the **characteristic polynomial** of A:

$$p_A(\lambda) = \det(\lambda I - A),$$

the roots of which are the eigenvalues of A. From the fundamental theorem of algebra, $p_A(\lambda)$ has exactly n roots in $\mathbb{C}$, counting multiplicities. Therefore, every $n \times n$ matrix has exactly n eigenvalues in $\mathbb{C}$, counting multiplicities. The set of all the eigenvalues of A is called the **spectrum** of A and is denoted by $\lambda(A)$.

Observe that

$$p_{A^T}(\lambda) = \det(\lambda I - A^T) = \det(\lambda I - A) = p_A(\lambda),$$

so A and A^T have the same eigenvalues.

The eigenvalues of a real matrix may not be all real, although the complex eigenvalues must come in conjugate pairs. In fact it is possible that none of the eigenvalues is real. For example, consider the matrix

$$\begin{bmatrix} 0 & -1 \\ 1 & 0 \end{bmatrix}.$$

Its characteristic polynomial is

$$p(\lambda) = \begin{vmatrix} \lambda & 1 \\ -1 & \lambda \end{vmatrix} = \lambda^2 + 1,$$

which has only complex roots: $\lambda_1 = i$, $\lambda_2 = -i$.

If a matrix $A \in \mathbb{R}^{n \times n}$ has n linearly independent eigenvectors $x_1, \ldots, x_n \in \mathbf{C}^n$ corresponding to the eigenvalues $\lambda_1, \ldots, \lambda_n \in \mathbf{C}$, then

$$A = X\Lambda X^{-1}, \tag{2.12}$$

where $X = [x_1 \quad \cdots \quad x_n]$, $\Lambda = \mathrm{diag}\{\lambda_1, \ldots, \lambda_n\}$. Equation (2.12) is called the **spectral factorization** of A. We mention, however, that not all matrices have a spectral factorization. Although all matrices have n eigenvalues, counting multiplicities, not all matrices have n linearly independent eigenvectors. For example, the matrix

$$L = \begin{bmatrix} 1 & 0 & 0 \\ -2 & 1 & 0 \\ 4 & 3 & 1 \end{bmatrix}$$

doesn't have a spectral factorization. L has a single eigenvalue 1 with multiplicity 3 (can be easily verified by computing $\det(\lambda I - A)$). Therefore, if L could be factored we should have $\Lambda = \mathrm{diag}[1, 1, 1] = I$ and $L = XX^{-1} = I$, which is obviously wrong.

A symmetric matrix $A \in \mathbb{R}^{n \times n}$ is called **positive definite** if for all nonzero $x \in \mathbb{R}^n$ we have

$$x^T A x > 0.$$

The symmetry of A is essential. If A is just a real matrix that satisfies the condition $x^T A x > 0$ for all nonzero $x \in \mathbb{R}^n$, it may not be positive definite! For example, if M is a real skew-symmetric matrix we have $x^T M x = (x^T M x)^T = x^T M^T x = -x^T M x$, so $x^T M x = 0$ for all $x \neq 0$. Then any matrix $C = \alpha I + M$ with

$\alpha > 0$ satisfies the condition

$$x^T C x = x^T (\alpha I + M) x = \alpha \, \|x\|^2 > 0$$

for all nonzero $x \in \mathbb{R}^n$. However, C is not symmetric, and therefore, not positive definite.

A symmetric matrix A is called **negative definite, positive semidefinite,** or **negative semidefinite** if

$$x^T A x <, \ \geq, \ \text{or} \ \leq 0, \quad \forall x \in \mathbb{R}^n, \ x \neq 0$$

respectively. A is called **indefinite** if

$$x^T A x > 0 \text{ for some } x \in \mathbb{R}^n \quad and \quad y^T A y < 0 \text{ for some } y \in \mathbb{R}^n.$$

If A is an $n \times n$ matrix then the condition $\text{rank}(A) < n$ implies that there is a linear combination of the columns of A that is equal to 0; i.e., if $a_1, a_2, \ldots, a_n$, are the columns of A then there exist coefficients $\xi_1, \xi_2, \ldots, \xi_n$, not all zero, such that

$$\sum_{i=1}^{n} \xi_i a_i = 0$$

or

$$[a_1 \quad a_2 \quad \cdots \quad a_n] \begin{bmatrix} \xi_1 \\ \xi_2 \\ \vdots \\ \xi_n \end{bmatrix} = \begin{bmatrix} 0 \\ 0 \\ \vdots \\ 0 \end{bmatrix},$$

$$A \, \xi = 0 = 0 \, \xi,$$

where $\xi = [\xi_1, \ldots, \xi_n]^T$, and $[a_1 \quad a_2 \quad \cdots \quad a_n]$ is the column partition of A. Therefore, if $\text{rank}(A) < n$ at least one of the eigenvalues of A is 0. In fact, if $\text{rank}(A) = n - k, \ k > 0$, then the eigenvalue 0 has multiplicity k.

The trace is the sum of the eigenvalues of A, the first coefficient c_{n-1} in the characteristic polynomial $p(A)$, and it is real for real matrices since the eigenvalues are either real or come in conjugate pairs.

The determinant equals $(-1)^n$ times the last coefficient c_0 (i.e., the constant term) of the characteristic polynomial $p(\lambda)$ of A. Since the roots of the characteristic polynomial are the eigenvalues of A, we can write $p(\lambda) = (\lambda - \lambda_1)(\lambda - \lambda_2) \cdots (\lambda - \lambda_n)$. After we perform the expansion of the product it becomes clear that $c_0 = (-1)^n \lambda_1 \lambda_2 \cdots \lambda_n$; therefore,

$$\det(A) = \lambda_1 \lambda_2 \cdots \lambda_n.$$

Similar matrices have the same eigenvalues including the same multiplicities.

2.2.6 Functions of Matrices

Scalar functions, such as e^x, $\log(x)$, $x^{1/2}$, etc., can be extended to operate on square matrices that have a spectral factorization. If $A \in \mathbb{R}^{n \times n}$ is a matrix with spectral decomposition $X \Lambda X^{-1}$, where $\Lambda = \text{diag}[\lambda_1, \ldots, \lambda_n] \in \mathbf{C}^{n \times n}$, $X \in \mathbf{C}^{n \times n}$, $XX^* = I$, the function $f(A)$ is defined as

$$f(A) \equiv X \begin{bmatrix} f(\lambda_1) & & \\ & \ddots & \\ & & f(\lambda_n) \end{bmatrix} X^{-1} .$$

We often write $f(A) = X f(\Lambda) X^{-1}$. For example,

$$A^{1/2} = X \Lambda^{1/2} X^{-1} = X \text{ diag} \left[\lambda_1^{1/2}, \ldots, \lambda_n^{1/2} \right] X^{-1}.$$

Observe that if the scalar function has a convergent Taylor expansion

$$f(x) = \sum_{i=0}^{\infty} c_i x^i,$$

then

$$f(A) = \sum_{i=0}^{\infty} c_i A^i.$$

Indeed,

$$\sum_i c_i A^i = X \left(\sum_i c_i \Lambda^i \right) X^{-1} = X \text{ diag} \left[\sum_i c_i \lambda_1^i, \ldots, \sum_i c_i \lambda_n^i \right] X^{-1}$$

$$= X \text{ diag}[f(\lambda_1), \ldots, f(\lambda_n)] X^{-1} = f(A).$$

So, for example,

$$e^A = \sum_{m=0}^{\infty} \frac{1}{m!} A^m.$$

2.2.7 Symmetric Matrices

Symmetric matrices have a lot of interesting and aesthetically pleasing properties with respect to eigenvalue decomposition. A sample of the most important results that form the background for our analysis is given here.

Theorem 2.2. Real symmetric matrices have real eigenvalues. If (λ_1, x_1), (λ_2, x_2) are two eigenvalue/eigenvector pairs such that $\lambda_1 \neq \lambda_2$ then $x_1^T x_2 = 0$.

Proof. Indeed, if $Ax = \lambda x$ for some $\lambda \in \mathbb{C}$ and some nonzero $x \in \mathbb{C}^n$, then $x^*A^* = x^*A = x^*\overline{\lambda}$ and $x^*Ax = \lambda x^*x = \overline{\lambda}x^*x$, implying $\lambda = \overline{\lambda}$ thus $\lambda \in \mathbb{R}$. So we can assume that $x_i \in \mathbb{R}^n$, for all eigenvectors x_i, for if $[x, \bar{x}]$ is a pair of complex conjugate eigenvectors we can replace them by the real pair $[\text{Re}(x), \text{Im}(x)]$.

Also the equations $Ax_1 = \lambda_1 x_1$ and $Ax_2 = \lambda_2 x_2$ imply $x_1^T Ax_2 = \lambda_1 x_1^T x_2 = \lambda_2 x_1^T x_2$ so $(\lambda_1 - \lambda_2)x_1^T x_2 = 0$. If $(\lambda_1 - \lambda_2) \neq 0$ then $x_1^T x_2 = 0$. ∎

Theorem 2.3 (Spectral Theorem). Every symmetric matrix A has a spectral factorization and is orthogonally similar to a diagonal matrix Λ:

$$A = X\Lambda X^T = \sum_{i=1}^{n} \lambda_i x_i x_i^T,$$

where $\lambda_1, \ldots, \lambda_n$, are the eigenvalues of A repeated according to their multiplicities and $x_1, \ldots, x_n$, are the corresponding orthonormal eigenvectors.

Theorem 2.4. Let $A, B \in \mathbb{R}^{n \times n}$ be two symmetric matrices, and assume that A has n distinct eigenvalues. If $AB = BA$, then the eigenvectors of A are also eigenvectors of B.

Proof. Let x be an eigenvector of A corresponding to the eigenvalue λ_a. Then

$$A(Bx) = \lambda_a(Bx).$$

Therefore, Bx is also an eigenvector of A corresponding to λ_a. Since the eigenvalues of A are distinct, $Bx \in \text{span}(x)$, namely, there exists a scalar λ_b such that $Bx = \lambda_b x$. ∎

Theorem 2.5 (Rayleigh-Ritz). Let $\lambda_1 \geq \lambda_2 \geq \cdots \geq \lambda_n$ be the eigenvalues of a real symmetric matrix A. Then

$$\lambda_1 = \max_{x \neq 0, \, x \in \mathbb{R}^n} \frac{x^T Ax}{x^T x} = \max_{\substack{x \in \mathbb{R}^n \\ \|x\|_2 = 1}} (x^T Ax),$$

$$\lambda_n = \min_{x \neq 0, \, x \in \mathbb{R}^n} \frac{x^T Ax}{x^T x} = \min_{\substack{x \in \mathbb{R}^n \\ \|x\|_2 = 1}} (x^T Ax).$$

The eigenvalues are the stationary values of the *Rayleigh quotient*

$$r(x) = \frac{x^T Ax}{x^T x}.$$

Indeed, x_s is a stationary point *iff*

$$\frac{\partial r(x)}{\partial x} = 2Ax_s - r(x_s)x_s = 0,$$

so

$$Ax_s = r(x_s)x_s;$$

i.e., $r(x_s)$ is the eigenvalue associated with the eigenvector x_s.

Theorem 2.6 (Courant-Fischer). Let $\lambda_1 \geq \lambda_2 \geq \cdots \geq \lambda_n$ be the eigenvalues of a real symmetric matrix A. Then

$$\min_{\substack{w_1,\ldots,w_{n-k} \in \mathbb{C}^n}} \max_{\substack{x \neq 0, \, x \in \mathbb{C}^n \\ x \perp w_1,\ldots,w_{n-k}}} \frac{x^* A x}{x^* x} = \max_{\substack{w_1,\ldots,w_{k-1} \in \mathbb{C}^n}} \min_{\substack{x \neq 0, \, x \in \mathbb{C}^n \\ x \perp w_1,\ldots,w_{k-1}}} \frac{x^* A x}{x^* x} = \lambda_k. \quad (2.13)$$

Ellipsoid Representation of Symmetric Matrices. Let us consider the image of the unit ball in $\mathbb{R}^n$ under the linear transformation with a real symmetric matrix A, i.e., the locus of the points $y = Ax$ for $\|x\|^2 = 1$. What is the shape the unit ball after this transformation? To answer this assume for the moment that A has no zero eigenvalues; hence it is invertible. Then $x = A^{-1}y$, and the unit length condition for x becomes

$$y^T A^{-2} y = 1.$$

This equation describes an ellipsoid in $\mathbb{R}^n$. Indeed, if $A = U\Lambda U^T$ is the orthogonal spectral decomposition of A we can write $(y^T U)\Lambda^{-2}(U^T y) = 1$. Define $\hat{y} = U^T y$ to obtain

$$\sum_i \frac{1}{\lambda_i^2} \hat{y}_i^2 = 1. \quad (2.14)$$

The orthogonal transform $\hat{y} = U^T y$ preserves the norm of the vector y and simply rotates it. Thus (2.14) describes a rotated ellipsoid with axes $|\lambda_1|, |\lambda_2|, \ldots, |\lambda_n|$ (see Fig. 2.3).

In the case where some eigenvalues are zero, (2.14) describes a degenerate ellipsoid which is flattened; i.e., some of its axes have zero length.

2.2.8 Projections and Deflation

A matrix P is called a **projector** if $P^2 = P$. It is called an **orthogonal projector** if, in addition, we have $P^T = P$.

For example, if the columns of $U \in \mathbb{R}^{n \times m}$ $(m < n)$ form an orthogonal set of vectors, then $P = UU^T$ is an orthogonal projector since $P^2 = UU^TUU^T = UU^T =$

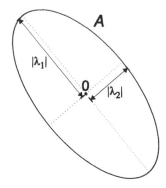

Figure 2.3. The ellipsoid corresponding to the real symmetric matrix A. The axes of the ellipsoid have sizes equal to the eigenvalues of A.

P and $(UU^T)^T = UU^T$. For every vector $x \in \mathbb{R}^n$, $Px = U(U^T x) \in \text{span}(U)$. In particular:

- If $x \in \text{span}(U)$ there exists some vector θ such that $x = U\theta$ so $Px = UU^T U\theta = U\theta = x$. So all vectors in the subspace spanned by the columns of U are mapped to themselves.
- If $x \in U^\perp$ then x is orthogonal to all the columns of U; therefore, $Px = UU^T x = 0$. So all vectors orthogonal to the subspace spanned by the columns of U are mapped to zero.

We say that UU^T *projects* all vectors onto the subspace $\text{span}(U)$.

As another example, consider the matrix $P = (I - UU^T)$. Notice that P is also an orthogonal projector since $P^2 = P$ and $P^T = P$. However, now

- If $x \in \text{span}(U)$ then $Px = U\theta - UU^T U\theta = 0$. So all vectors in the subspace spanned by the columns of U are mapped to zero.
- If $x \in U^\perp$ then $Px = x - UU^T x = x$. So all vectors orthogonal to the subspace spanned by the columns of U are mapped to themselves.

We say that $(I - UU^T)$ *projects* all vectors onto the subspace orthogonal to $\text{span}(U)$.

When computing the eigenvectors/eigenvalues of a matrix one by one, it is often useful to remove each eigenvector immediately after it is found. This way we avoid recomputing the same quantities over and over again. This eigenvector-removing process is commonly called **deflation**.

Consider, for example, a symmetric matrix $A \in \mathbb{R}^{n \times n}$. According to the spectral theorem 2.3, $A = \sum_{k=1}^{n} \lambda_k x_k x_k^T$, where $x_1, x_2, \ldots, x_n$ is an orthonormal set of eigenvectors of A. For the matrix

$$\tilde{A} = A - \lambda_i x_i x_i^T = (I - x_i x_i^T)A$$

the eigenvalue/eigenvector pairs now are $(\lambda_1, x_1), \ldots, (\lambda_{i-1}, x_{i-1}), (0, x_i),$ $(\lambda_{i+1}, x_{i+1}), \ldots, (\lambda_n, x_n)$. The ith eigenvalue has vanished, but all the other eigenvalues are intact, and none of the eigenvectors has changed. Notice that $(I - x_i x_i^T)$, which operates on A, is nothing but the projection matrix to the subspace orthogonal to x_i. Figure 2.4 depicts the situation for a 2×2 matrix. The 2-D ellipse spanned by A has been reduced to a line segment—a 1-D ellipsoid—after collapsing (i.e., deflating) along the x_2 direction.

Multiple deflation is also possible: for example, the matrix

$$\tilde{A} = A - \sum_{i=1}^{k} \lambda_i x_i x_i^T = (I - X_k X_k^T)A,$$

where $X_k = [x_1, \ldots, x_k] \in \mathbb{R}^{n \times k}$, $k < n$, is the projection of A onto the subspace orthogonal to $\text{span}(x_1, \ldots, x_k)$. As a result the new eigenvalue/eigenvector pairs are $(0, x_1), \ldots, (0, x_{k-1}), (\lambda_k, x_k), \ldots, (\lambda_n, x_n)$, so that all the eigenvalues from λ_1 to λ_k have vanished, while the rest of the eigenvalues and all the eigenvectors have remained intact. Moreover, $\tilde{A}$ can also be seen as the result of a sequence of deflations on A since

$$I - X_k X_k^T = (I - x_1 x_1^T)(I - x_2 x_2^T) \cdots (I - x_k x_k^T).$$

2.2.9 Gram-Schmidt Orthonormalization

Given a set of vectors $x_1, x_2, \ldots, x_m$, in $\mathbb{R}^n$, $m < n$, a question that often arises is whether we can construct an orthonormal basis of the space $S = \text{span}(x_1, x_2, \ldots, x_m)$. In this situation, we seek to rotate the vectors x_i so that they become mutually orthogonal yet still span the same space. Once this orthogonalizing rotation is achieved it is trivial to achieve normalization (i.e., making the vectors of unit length) via simple scaling.

The Gram-Schmidt orthogonalization procedure solves this problem in a recursive way: once k vectors have become orthonormal spanning a subspace $S_k \subset S$,

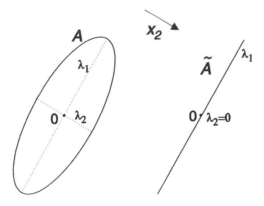

Figure 2.4. Deflation of the matrix A along the direction x_2.

we project x_{k+1} onto the subspace orthogonal to S_k. We start by normalizing the first vector x_1 and at the end we will have $S_m = S$:

Initial Step

$$v_1 = \frac{x_1}{\|x_1\|_2}.$$

Recursion Step

$$\tilde{v}_{k+1} = \left[\prod_{i=1}^{k} (I - v_i v_i^T) \right] x_{k+1},$$

$$v_{k+1} = \frac{\tilde{v}_{k+1}}{\|\tilde{v}_{k+1}\|}.$$

Since the vectors $v_1, \ldots, v_k$, are already orthonormal the cross-terms in the product $\prod_{i=1}^{k} (I - v_i v_i^T)$ disappear and we can write equivalently

$$v_{k+1} = \left(I - \sum_{i=1}^{k} v_i v_i^T \right) x_{k+1}$$

$$= x_{k+1} - \sum_{i=1}^{k} (v_i^T x_{k+1}) v_i. \tag{2.15}$$

2.2.10 Matrix Norms

Since matrices form vector spaces[3] it is possible (and useful) to define norms for them. Common norms for a matrix $A = [a_{ij}] \in \mathbb{R}^{m \times n}$ include

The Frobenius Norm

$$\|A\|_F = \left(\sum_{i=1}^{m} \sum_{j=1}^{n} a_{ij}^2 \right)^{1/2}.$$

The Frobenius norm has the following properties:

- $\|A\|_F^2 = \text{tr}\{AA^T\} = \text{tr}\{A^T A\}$.
- Let's assume without loss of generality that $n < m$. If $\lambda_1, \lambda_2, \ldots, \lambda_n$ are the eigenvalues of $A^T A$ then

$$\|A\|_F^2 = \sum_{i=1}^{n} \lambda_i.$$

---

[3]However, we shall rarely refer to matrices as vectors to avoid confusion with the usual meaning of a vector as an ordered n-tuple of numbers.

The eigenvalues of AA^T are $\lambda_1, \lambda_2, \ldots, \lambda_n, 0, \ldots, 0$; i.e. they are the same as the matrix $A^T A$ with the addition of some zero eigenvalues. Similarly we can write $\|A\|_F^2 = \sum_{i=1}^m \lambda_i$, if we define $\lambda_{n+1} = \cdots = \lambda_m = 0$. Notice that both matrices AA^T and $A^T A$ are real and symmetric, so their eigenvalues are real and nonnegative.

The Sum Norm

$$\|A\|_1 = \sum_{i=1}^m \sum_{j=1}^n |a_{ij}|.$$

The Spectral Norm

$$\|A\|_2 = \max_{\forall x \in \mathbb{R}^n, \|x\|=1} \{ \|Ax\|_2 \}.$$

An alternative definition is

$$\|A\|_2 = \max_{\forall x \in \mathbb{R}^n} \left\{ \frac{\|Ax\|_2}{\|x\|_2} \right\}$$

so

$$\|Ax\|_2 \leq \|A\|_2 \|x\|_2.$$

If $\lambda_1, \ldots, \lambda_n$ are the eigenvalues of $A^T A$ then

$$\|A\|_2^2 = \max\{\lambda_1, \ldots, \lambda_n\}.$$

An important property relating the Frobenius and the spectral norm is

$$\|AB\|_F^2 \leq \|A\|_F^2 \|B\|_2^2,$$
$$\|AB\|_F^2 \leq \|A\|_2^2 \|B\|_F^2$$

for any matrices $A \in \mathbb{R}^{n \times m}$, $B \in \mathbb{R}^{m \times k}$. Indeed, if we denote by a_i^T and b_i the rows of A and the columns of B, respectively, we get

$$\|AB\|_F^2 = \sum_{i=1}^n \|a_i^T B\|_2^2 \leq \sum_{i=1}^n \|a_i^T\|_2^2 \|B\|_2^2 = \|A\|_F^2 \|B\|_2^2$$
$$= \sum_{i=1}^m \|A b_i\|_2^2 \leq \sum_{i=1}^m \|A\|_2^2 \|b_i\|_2^2 = \|A\|_2^2 \|B\|_F^2.$$

2.2.11 Birkhoff's Theorem

The following nontrivial result is essential to our analysis in the following chapters. For this reason we present it complete with its proof.

Theorem 2.7 (Birkhoff). A matrix A is doubly stochastic if and only if it can be written as a convex combination of some permutation matrices $P_1, \ldots, P_N$; i.e., there are positive reals $\alpha_1, \ldots, \alpha_N$ such that $\alpha_1 + \cdots + \alpha_N = 1$ and $A = \sum_{i=1}^{N} \alpha_i P_i$.

Proof. Our proof is patterned according to the one given in [21]. The *if* part is obvious. For the *only if* part, we must show three things:

(a) The set $\mathcal{D}$ of doubly stochastic matrices is convex and compact.

(b) All permutation matrices are extreme points of $\mathcal{D}$.

(c) If P is not a permutation matrix it cannot be an extreme point of $\mathcal{D}$.

If we can show (a), (b), and (c) the only if part of the theorem follows from the fact that all the elements of a compact convex set can be written as convex combinations of its extreme points (see Appendix C; also see the same appendix for the definitions of compactness, convex sets, extreme points, etc.).

(a) Clearly if Q and S are doubly stochastic then so is $K = \alpha_1 Q + \alpha_2 S$, for any α_1, α_2 such that $0 \leq \alpha_1, \alpha_2 \leq 1$, $\alpha_1 + \alpha_2 = 1$, so $\mathcal{D}$ is convex.

Since $\mathbb{R}^{n \times n}$ is isomorphic to the Euclidean space $\mathbb{R}^{n^2}$, $\mathcal{D} \subset \mathbb{R}^{n \times n}$ is compact, according to the Heine-Borel Theorem C.1, if it is closed and bounded.

$\mathcal{D}$ is closed because its complement $\mathcal{D}^c$ is open. Indeed, it is easy to show that for every matrix A which is not doubly stochastic there is a ball $\mathsf{B}_\varepsilon = \{K : \|A - K\|_2 < \varepsilon\}$ which contains only non-doubly-stochastic matrices. $\mathcal{D}$ is also bounded, since for any doubly stochastic matrix A and any vector x, $\|x\|_2 = 1$, we have

$$\|Ax\|_2^2 = \sum_{i=1}^{n} \left(\sum_{j=1}^{n} a_{ij} x_j \right)^2 \leq \sum_{i=1}^{n} \sum_{j=1}^{n} a_{ij}^2 x_j^2 \leq n^2,$$

so $\|A\|_2 \leq n^2$.

(b) Let $P \in \mathbb{R}^{n \times n}$ be a permutation matrix. Assume that it can be written as a convex combination of two doubly stochastic matrices Q and S: $P = \alpha_1 Q + \alpha_2 S$, $0 < \alpha_1, \alpha_2 < 1$, $\alpha_1 + \alpha_2 = 1$. Take any zero entry $p_{ij} = 0$ of P. We have $p_{ij} = \alpha_1 q_{ij} + \alpha_2 s_{ij} = 0$, and since q_{ij} and s_{ij} are nonnegative we must have $q_{ij} = s_{ij} = 0$. Therefore Q and S have zero entries at the same positions where P has its zero entries. Since Q and S are doubly stochastic, all the rows and columns must sum to 1, and thus all the remaining entries must be filled with 1's. But these are exactly the same entries where $p_{ij} = 1$. Hence, we must have $P = Q = S$. Thus P is an extreme point.

(c) If $A \in \mathcal{D}$ is not a permutation matrix then there is a row $i(1)$ which has at least two nonzero entries. Pick one of them and observe that it must be strictly less than 1: $0 < a_{i(1)j(1)} < 1$. This implies that in the column $j(1)$ there must also be at least another nonzero entry because the sum in this column must be 1. Pick one of the other nonzero entries in this column, $0 < a_{i(2)j(1)} < 1$, $i(2) \neq i(1)$, and continue the argument for row $i(2)$, etc. After a certain number of steps the sequence of entries chosen by this process will visit some entry for a second time, in which case we stop. Let $a_{i',j'}$ be the smallest entry in this sequence and construct a matrix B such that $b_{i(1)j(1)} = 1$, $b_{i(2)j(1)} = -1$, $b_{i(2)j(2)} = 1$, $b_{i(3)j(2)} = -1$, etc. (i.e., put alternating 1's and -1's in the positions of the entries in the sequence) and let all other b_{ij} be equal to zero. Now all row and column sums of B are zero and the matrices $A_1 = A + a_{i'j'}B$, $A_2 = A - a_{i'j'}B$, are doubly stochastic (all the entries of A_1, A_2 are nonnegative because $a_{i'j'}$ is the smallest element in the sequence). But $A = \frac{1}{2}A_1 + \frac{1}{2}A_2$ and $A_1 \neq A \neq A_2$. So A is a convex combination of two other doubly stochastic matrices and therefore is not an extreme point. ∎

Birkhoff's theorem is very useful for optimizing functions involving orthogonal matrices. If a matrix $A = [a_{ij}]$ is orthogonal, then as we have seen, $A \circ A$ is doubly stochastic. The usefulness of the theorem will become apparent in later chapters.

Birkhoff's theorem results in the following

Corollary 2.1. A matrix $M_1 \in \mathbb{R}^{m \times n}$ is strictly row stochastic if and only if it can be written as a convex combination of some row selection matrices $S_1, \ldots, S_N$; i.e., there are positive reals $\alpha_1, \ldots, \alpha_N$ such that $\alpha_1 + \cdots + \alpha_N = 1$ and $M_1 = \sum_{i=1}^{N} \alpha_i S_i$.

In other words the set of strictly row stochastic matrices of size $m \times n$ is the convex hull of the $m \times n$ row selective matrices. Similarly the set of strictly column stochastic matrices of size is the convex hull of the corresponding column selective matrices.

Proof. The corollary readily follows from Theorem 2.7 if we notice that there is a doubly stochastic matrix $M = \begin{bmatrix} M_1 \\ M_2 \end{bmatrix}$, which can be written as a convex combination of N' permutation matrices P_j:

$$M = \sum_{j=1}^{N'} \beta_j P_j = \sum_{j=1}^{N'} \beta_j \begin{bmatrix} P_{j1} \\ P_{j2} \end{bmatrix},$$

and that P_{j1}, $j = 1, \ldots, N'$, are row selection matrices. If we partition the indices $j = 1, \ldots, N'$ into N equivalence classes ω_i, $i = 1, \ldots, N$, such that $P_{j_1 1} = P_{j_2 1}$ for all $j_1, j_2 \in \omega_i$, then

$$M_1 = \sum_{i=1}^{N} \alpha_i S_i,$$

where $\alpha_i = \sum_{j \in \omega_i} \beta_j$, and $S_i = P_j$, any $j \in \omega_i$. ∎

3

PRINCIPAL COMPONENT ANALYSIS

Principal component analysis (PCA) [24] is a statistical technique falling under the general title of *factor analysis*. The purpose of PCA is to identify the dependence structure behind a multivariate stochastic observation in order to obtain a compact description of it. When there is nonzero correlation between the observed variables the dimensionality, n, of the data space (i.e., the number of observed variables) does not represent the number of independent variables, m, that are really needed to describe the data. We may liken m to the number representing the degrees of freedom of a physical system. In the statistical context the number n is called the *superficial dimensionality* of the data, whereas m is called the *intrinsic dimensionality* of the data. The stronger the correlation between the observed variables, the smaller the number of independent variables that can adequately describe them.

The n observed variables are thus represented as functions of m latent variables called *factors*, where $m < n$ and often $m \ll n$. The simpler the mathematical form of the representation functions the more economical is the description of the dependence structure between the variables. Traditional PCA is associated with linear transformations, which are the simplest and most mathematically tractable functional forms for representation. The factor variables are also called *features* of the multivariate random signal, and the vector they form is a member of the *feature space*.

The idea behind PCA is quite old. It originated from Pearson [25] in 1901 as a methodology for fitting planes in the least-squares sense (what is called *linear regression*). It was Hotelling (1933) [24] who proposed this technique for the purpose of analyzing the correlation structure between many random variables.

Consider a random vector $x = [x_1, \ldots, x_n]^T$ with mean $E\{x\} = 0$ and covariance matrix $R_x = E\{xx^T\} \in \mathbb{R}^{n \times n}$. In PCA the feature vector, y, is an orthogonal, linear transformation of the data:

$$y = Wx,$$

where the columns of W form an *orthonormal basis* of a subspace $\mathcal{L}$, namely, $WW^T = I$ and $\mathcal{L} = \text{span}(W)$. The projection of x onto $\mathcal{L}$ is the reconstruction of x from y:

$$\hat{x} = W^T y = W^T W x. \tag{3.1}$$

PCA seeks to minimize the mean square reconstruction error

$$\begin{aligned}
J_e &= E\{\|x - \hat{x}\|^2\} \\
&= E\left\{\text{tr}\left[(x - \hat{x})(x - \hat{x})^T\right]\right\} \\
&= \text{tr}(R_x) - \text{tr}(WR_xW^T), \tag{3.2}
\end{aligned}$$

where we used the facts $\text{tr}(A) = \text{tr}(A^T)$, and

$$\begin{aligned}
\text{tr}\left(E\{W^T W x x^T W^T W\}\right) &= \text{tr}(WW^T WR_xW^T) \\
&= \text{tr}(WR_xW^T).
\end{aligned}$$

Observe that the last term (call it J_v) in (3.2) is equal to the variance of y, which is also equal to the variance of the projection $\hat{x}$:

$$J_v \equiv \text{tr}(WR_xW^T) = E\left\{\text{tr}(yy^T)\right\} = \sum_{i=1}^{m} y_i^2 \tag{3.3}$$

$$= \text{tr}(W^T WR_xW^T W) = E\left\{\text{tr}(\hat{x}\hat{x}^T)\right\} = \sum_{i=1}^{n} \hat{x}_i^2. \tag{3.4}$$

Thus, maximization of the projection variance is equivalent to minimization of the mean square reconstruction error. PCA can be seen equivalently as either a variance maximization technique or a least-mean-squares technique.

Theorem 3.1 (PCA). Let the eigenvalues $\lambda_1, \lambda_2, \ldots, \lambda_n$, of R_x be arranged in decreasing order, and let their corresponding normalized eigenvectors be $e_1, e_2, \ldots, e_n$. Then the minimizer of the mean square reconstruction error J_e (equivalently the maximizer of the projection variance J_v), under the constraint $WW^T = I$, has the form

$$W_{opt} = T[\pm e_1 \cdots \pm e_m]^T,$$

where T is any square orthogonal matrix.

The minimal reconstruction error is

$$\min J_e = \sum_{i=m+1}^{n} \lambda_i \tag{3.5}$$

and the maximum variance is

$$\max J_v = \sum_{i=1}^{m} \lambda_i. \tag{3.6}$$

Before proceeding to the proof we remark that R_x is symmetric and semipositive definite, so all the eigenvalues are real and nonnegative. Thus, the right-hand side of (3.5) is a nonnegative quantity consistent with the square error in the left-hand side, which is clearly also nonnegative.

Proof. We want to maximize J_v under the constraint $WW^T = I$. Let $U\Lambda U^T$ be the spectral factorization of R_x, where $U = [e_1, \ldots, e_n]$ and $\Lambda = \text{diag}[\lambda_1, \ldots, \lambda_n]$. Then

$$J_v = \text{tr}(T^T W R_x W^T T)$$

for any orthogonal $T \in \mathbb{R}^{m \times m}$. So

$$J_v = \text{tr}(T^T W U \Lambda U^T W^T T) = \text{tr}(\tilde{W} \Lambda \tilde{W}^T),$$

where $\tilde{W} = [\tilde{w}_{ij}] = T^T W U$. We have

$$J_v = \sum_{i=1}^{m} \lambda_j \sum_{j=1}^{n} \tilde{w}_{ij}^2,$$

where $M = [\tilde{w}_{ij}^2]$ is a strictly row stochastic matrix. From Corollary 2.1 the set $\mathcal{A}$ of strictly row stochastic matrices is convex. Since J_v is a linear function with respect to M, the optimum is attained at a vertex of $\mathcal{A}$ (see Appendix C). Thus the optimal M is a row selection matrix S and $\tilde{W} = [\pm\sqrt{s_{ij}}]$. Hence $W = T\tilde{W}U^T = T[\pm e_{i(1)} \cdots \pm e_{i(m)}]^T$ for some set of indices $i(1), \ldots, i(m)$, and $J_v = \sum_{k=1}^{m} \lambda_{i(k)}$. The maximum is clearly attained for the set $i(1) = 1, \ldots, i(m) = m$; therefore,

$$W_{\text{opt}} = T[\pm e_1 \cdots \pm e_m]^T,$$

$$\max J_v = \sum_{i=1}^{m} \lambda_i,$$

$$\min J_e = \sum_{i=m+1}^{n} \lambda_i. \qquad \blacksquare$$

The (normal) eigenvectors of R_x corresponding to its largest eigenvalues (i.e., the rows of W_{opt}) are called *principal eigenvectors*.

The features $y_1, \ldots, y_m$, elements of the random vector y, are called the *principal components* of x. They are statistically uncorrelated:

$$E\{y_i y_j\} = e_i^T R_x e_j = 0,$$

their variances are equal to the eigenvalues of R_x:

$$E\{y_i^2\} = e_i^T R_x e_i = \lambda_i,$$

and are arranged in order of decreasing variance $E\{y_1^2\} \geq E\{y_2^2\} \geq \cdots \geq E\{y_m^2\}$.

An alternative criterion maximized by the principal eigenvectors is the constrained output variance

$$J_v' = \text{var}\{w^T x\} = E\{(w^T x)^2\} = w^T R_x w \qquad \text{under } \|w\| = 1. \qquad (3.7)$$

The first feature (principal component) y_1 is a linear combination of the observed variables

$$y_1 = w_{11} x_1 + \cdots + w_{1n} x_n = w_1^T x$$

such that its variance

$$E\{y_1^2\} = w_1^T E\{xx^T\} w_1 = w_1^T R_x w_1 \qquad (3.8)$$

is maximum under the constraint that the coefficient vector is normalized $\|w_1\| = 1$. According to the Rayleigh-Ritz theorem (Theorem 2.5) $w_1 = e_1$ and the maximum eigenvalue λ_1 is equal to the variance of the first component.

The second feature (principal component) $y_2 = w_2^T x$ is also a linear combination of the observed variables. It also maximizes the variance of y, but this time under the constraint $\|w_2\| = 1$ and $w_2 \perp e_1$.

To summarize, for $w = e_1$, the constrained output variance is maximum, while in general, for $w = e_p$, $p > 1$, the variance is maximized under the additional constraint that w is orthogonal to all prior eigenvectors $e_1, \ldots, e_{p-1}$. Figure 3.1 shows a geometric interpretation of the principal component subspaces: based on the variance criterion the principal component direction should be the one where the signal has more energy (i.e., projection variance); the least principal direction is the one with the least energy. If the signal is zero mean then the maximum energy direction is also the direction of maximum spread or, in information-theoretical parlance, the direction that contains the most information of the signal (assuming it is Gaussian). It should be also intuitively clear from the same figure that the principal direction is the one corresponding to the minimum reconstruction error.

The principal components are also related to the maximization of the determinant as shown by the following result.

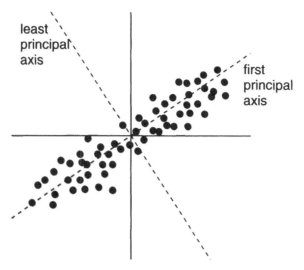

Figure 3.1. The principal component (1) contains most of the energy of the signal, (2) has the minimum signal projection error, and (3) keeps the maximum information of the signal, if the latter is zero mean and Gaussian. The least principal axis has just the opposite properties.

Theorem 3.2. Let A be a square symmetric $n \times n$ matrix with eigenvalues $\lambda_1 \geq \lambda_2 \geq \cdots \geq \lambda_n > 0$, and let $V \in \mathbb{R}^{p \times n}$, $p < n$. Then

$$\max_{VV^T = I} \left\{ \det(VAV^T) \right\} = \prod_{i=1}^{p} \lambda_i,$$

and the maximum is attained for $V = M[e_1, \ldots, e_p]$, where M is any square orthogonal matrix.

3.1   THE INTERPRETATION OF THE PRINCIPAL COMPONENTS

Principal components reveal the structure behind the correlation of many variables. It is often the case that knowing the values of one or few variables is sufficient to predict the value of the others, depending of course on the level of correlation among them. If the variables are statistically uncorrelated prediction of any one based on the others is impossible.

Example 3.1. Consider first the case of a random vector $x = [x_1, x_2, \ldots, x_n]^T$ with a rank-1 autocorrelation matrix R_x. This implies that the first principal component explains all the variation of the multi-variate distribution. In other words, all the "action" in this particular distribution of n variables happens along a single one-dimensional direction. This is the direction of the principal component. This direction is described by the normalized principal eigenvector e_1. Knowing the value of one variable, say x_1, in the vector x leads to the precise estimation of the other variables by simple extrapolation (see Fig. 3.2 for a two-dimensional example). Algebraically, in n dimensions the principal component line is defined by the equation

$$Ax = 0, \tag{3.9}$$

where $A = (I - e_1 e_1^T) \in \mathbb{R}^{n \times n}$ spans the space orthogonal to e_1, so that the only real vectors satisfying (3.9) are $x = \alpha e_1$, for any $\alpha \in R$. Let us partition A into $[a_1 \mid \tilde{A}]$, where a_1 is the first column of A, and let $x^T = [x_1 \mid \tilde{x}^T]$, where $\tilde{x} = [x_2, \dots, x_n]^T$. With x_1 known we can write

$$[a_1 \mid \tilde{A}] \begin{bmatrix} x_1 \\ \tilde{x} \end{bmatrix} = 0,$$

$$\tilde{x} = [x_2 \quad \cdots \quad x_n]^T = -x_1 (\tilde{A}^T \tilde{A})^{-1} \tilde{A}^T a_1.$$

Thus, if (3.9) is always true all variables $x_2, \dots, x_n$ can be predicted from x_1.

Even in the more common case where, say, 90% of the variance of an n-variate distribution can be accounted for by, say, five components we know that this proportion of the variance happens along the hyperplane spanned by the eigenvectors e_1, e_2, e_3, e_4, e_5. Therefore, a reasonably good representation of the original n-dimensional vector can be obtained by a five-dimensional principal component vector $[y_1, y_2, y_3, y_4, y_5] = [e_1^T x, e_2^T x, e_3^T x, e_4^T x, e_5^T x]$. Not only dimensionality reduction is achieved (assuming $5 < n$) under a small approximation error, but also the coefficients of the principal eigenvectors indicate the relationship between the original variables in the derived components.

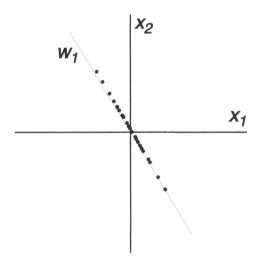

Figure 3.2. The direction w_1 accounts for all the variance of the random vector $x = (x_1, x_2)$. Therefore if we know the value of the variable x_1 we can predict with certainty the value of x_2.

Example 3.2 (Characterization of Turtle Shells). The following example, taken from D. Morrison [26, Chapter 8], explains the meaning of principal components. Jolicoeur and Mosimann [27] studied the statistical analysis of turtle shells with respect to size. Three variables were analyzed: shell length, width, and height, all in millimeters. The covariance matrix for a sample of 24 female turtles was

$$R = \begin{array}{c} \\ L \\ W \\ H \end{array} \begin{array}{ccc} L & W & H \\ \begin{bmatrix} 451.33 & 271.17 & 168.70 \\ 271.17 & 171.73 & 103.29 \\ 168.70 & 103.29 & 66.65 \end{bmatrix} \end{array}$$

The three eigenvectors and associated variances are shown in Table 3.1. The first principal component

$$Y_1 = 0.81L + 0.50W + 0.31H$$

accounts for almost all (98.6%) of the variance of the joint distribution of the three variables. Thus the shape of the shell can be characterized by a weighted average of the length, the width, and the height of the shell with progressively diminishing emphasis on the variables in that order. We can think of the first component y_1 also as the logarithm of the volume of a box with volume $L^{0.81} \times W^{0.50} \times H^{0.31}$.

The other two components have minor significance and appear to indicate comparisons between length versus combined width and height (component 2) and between height versus length and width (component 3).

Example 3.3 (Handwritten Character Recognition). K. Fu [28] presents a feature selection procedure for the recognition of handwritten characters using PCA. The subjects of this experiment were asked to write the letters *a*, *b*, *c*, and *d* inside circles with diameters of 2 inches. The measurements for each character were 18 radial distances from the perimeter of the circle as shown in Figure 3.3.

The measurement vector $x = [x_1, \ldots, x_{18}]$ can be used directly to decide the class ω_i of the character under test. There are four classes corresponding to the letters *a*, *b*, *c*, and *d*, respectively. The Bayesian classifier was used with equal a priori probabilities and with equal penalties for wrong decisions. This translates into the following decision rule: choose the class i that maximizes the likelihood

$$l_i = P(x \mid \omega_i)$$

Table 3.1. Principal Component Coefficients for Turtle Shells

Variable	Component 1	2	3
Length (L)	0.8126	−0.5454	−0.2054
Width (W)	0.4955	0.8321	−0.2491
Height (H)	0.3068	0.1006	0.9465
Variance	680.4	6.5	2.9

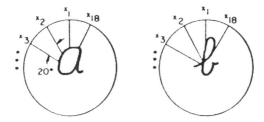

Figure 3.3. Measurements from samples of handwritten characters *a* and *b*. (From K. S. Fu, *Sequential Methods in Pattern Recognition and Machine Learning*, Academic Press, N.Y. 1968 (28).)

for the observation x. The recognition was first attempted using only the first 2 measurements out of the total 18. The recognition procedure was then repeated using the first 4, 6, 8 measurements, etc; until finally all 18 measurements were used. The results of this classification method are shown in Figure 3.4 under the title "Unordered Observations." The corresponding plot shows the percentage of correct recognition over 240 samples of characters.

The same recognition method was repeated with the raw measurement data replaced by the principal components of the correlation matrix $R_x = E\{xx^T\}$. The transformed vector $v = [e_1^T x, \ldots, e_{18}^T x]$ was used now, instead of x, to form the likelihoods

$$l_i' = P(v \mid \omega_i).$$

The same Bayesian classifier was used as the decision rule over the same 240 data samples. The results are shown in Figure 3.4 under the title "Ordered Observations."

We see that the "ordered" results are better than the "unordered" ones using any number of measurements, from 2 up to 18. We also note that using only the first 6 or 8 principal components is almost as good as using all 18 of them. It is also almost as good as using all 18 raw data measurements. Using more than eight components only marginally improves the performance. We may claim that intrinsically the dimensionality of the data is between 6 and 8. The 18 raw measurements thus have a high degree of redundancy. The exact degree of redundancy, however, is not immediately obvious and is revealed through PCA.

3.2 THE KARHUNEN-LOÈVE TRANSFORM (KLT)

During the 1940s, Karhunen [29] and Loève [30] independently developed a theory regarding optimal series expansions of continuous-time stochastic processes. Their results extend PCA in the case of infinite-dimensional spaces, such as the space of continuous-time functions. Their analysis uses single-parameter functions instead of vectors, two-parameter functions for representing autocorrelation instead

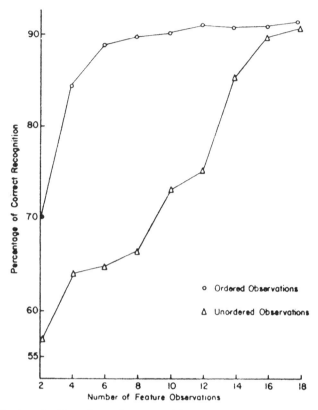

Figure 3.4. The handwritten character recognition performance based on six or eight principal components is nearly as good as using all 18 features. (From K. S. Fu, *Sequential Methods in Pattern Recognition and Machine Learning*, Academic Press, N.Y. 1968 (28).)

of matrices, and the following standard extension of the inner product:

$$g \cdot f \equiv \int_a^b g(t)f(t)\, dt$$

between two single-parameter functions $f(\cdot)$, $g(\cdot)$, in place of the Euclidean vector inner product.

The autocorrelation function of a zero-mean, continuous-time stochastic process $x(t) \in \mathbb{R}$, $t \in [a,b]$ $(a,b$ finite), is defined as

$$r_x(t,s) = E\{x(t)x(s)\}, \qquad a \le t, s \le b, \tag{3.10}$$

where r_x is symmetric, i.e., $r_x(t,s) = r_x(s,t)$, continuous, and positive semidefinite. Positive definiteness of a two-variable symmetric function $h(\cdot, \cdot)$ happens if, for any continuous function $f(\cdot)$,

$$f \cdot (h \cdot f) \ge 0.$$

Indeed, for r_x we have

$$
\begin{aligned}
f \cdot (r_x \cdot f) &= \int_a^b f(t) \int_a^b r_x(t, s) f(s) \, ds \, dt \\
&= E \left\{ \int_a^b \int_a^b f(t) x(t) f(s) x(s) \, ds \, dt \right\} \\
&= E \left\{ \left[\int_a^b f(t) x(t) \, dt \right]^2 \right\} \geq 0.
\end{aligned}
$$

This is clearly analogous to the corresponding definition in matrix theory where f is replaced by a vector, r_x by a matrix, and the inner product is the Euclidean inner product.

Not surprisingly, a similar result to Theorem 2.3 in linear algebra also exists in the theory of continuous functions.

Theorem 3.3 (Mercer). Every symmetric, continuous, and positive definite function $r_x(t, s)$, defined in the square $a \leq t, s \leq b$ $(a, b,$ finite$)$, can be expanded in the absolutely and uniformly convergent series

$$
r_x(t, s) = \sum_{k=1}^{\infty} \lambda_k e_k(t) e_k(s),
$$

where $e_k(t)$ and λ_k are the *eigenfunctions* and *eigenvalues* of the homogeneous integral equation

$$
\lambda e(t) = \int_a^b r_x(t, s) e(s) \, ds, \qquad t \in [a, b].
$$

(As with eigenvectors, the trivial solution $e(t) = 0$ of the integral equation is not considered an eigenfunction.)

Theorem 3.4 (Karhunen-Loève Expansion). Let $x(t)$ be a zero-mean continuous-time stochastic process with correlation $r_x(t, s) = E\{x(t) x(s)\}$. Then

$$
x(t) = \sum_{k=1}^{\infty} y_k e_k(t),
$$

where

$$
y_k = \int_a^b x(t) e_k(t) \, dt
$$

are uncorrelated random variables with zero mean and variance λ_k; i.e.,

$$
E\{y_i y_j\} = \begin{cases} 0, & i \neq j, \\ \lambda_i, & i = j. \end{cases}
$$

The series $\sum_{k=1}^{n} y_k e_k(t)$ converges in the mean square sense to $x(t)$; that is,

$$\lim_{n \to \infty} E \left\{ x(t) - \sum_{k=1}^{n} y_k e_k(t) \right\} = 0$$

uniformly for $t \in [a, b]$.

The transform of $x(t)$ into the coefficients

$$y_k = \int_a^b x(t) e_k(t) \, dt$$

is called the **Karhunen-Loève transform** of x, or KLT for short. Similarly, the series

$$x(t) = \sum_{k=1}^{\infty} y_k e_k(t)$$

is called the **Karhunen-Loève expansion** of x.

What was developed by Karhunen and Loève for continuous-time processes can be easily extended for discrete-time processes as well. There is no essential difference between the discrete-time and continuous-time results, except that integrals are replaced by sums. Let $x_k \in \mathbb{R}$, $k = 0, 1, \ldots$, be a stochastic process (i.e., random sequence) such that

$$E\{x_k\} = 0 \quad \text{and} \quad E\{x_k x_l\} = r_x(k, l).$$

If $r_x(k, l) = r_x(k - l)$, then the sequence x_k is called **wide-sense stationary** because its mean and variance are independent of time.[1]

The KL transform of x_k is now [31]

$$y_i = \sum_{k=0}^{\infty} e_i(k) x_k, \tag{3.11}$$

where the $e_i(k)$'s are the (infinite dimensional) eigenvectors of $r_x(k - l)$. In this situation an eigenvector $e(k)$ of r_x is defined by the property that there exists a scalar λ such that, for all k,

$$\lambda e(k) = \sum_{l=0}^{\infty} r_x(k - l) e(l).$$

[1] Stationarity in the strict sense occurs when the variables x_k, for all k, are identically distributed.

The inverse transform

$$x_k = \sum_{i=0}^{\infty} e_i(k) y_i \tag{3.12}$$

is the Karhunen-Loève expansion of x_k.

The relationship between KLT and PCA becomes obvious if the time parameter k has a limited range of values. For example, if $k = 1, \ldots, n$, the KLT of $\{x_k\}$ is the PCA of the random vector $x = [x_1, \ldots, x_n]^T$. Furthermore, the (k, l) element of the autocorrelation matrix R_x of the vector x is the value $r_x(k, l)$ of the autocorrelation function of the sequence x_k. Similarly, the kth element of the eigenvector e_i of R_x is the value $e_i(k)$ of the ith eigenfunction of the sequence x_k.

In general there is little difference between KLT and PCA, except that KLT typically refers to stochastic processes, whereas PCA refers to random vectors. Conceptually, both KLT and PCA extract the most important features of the data. Also in terms of optimality the partial KL expansion $\hat{x}_k = \sum_{i=1}^{p} y_{ik} e_i$ for $p < n$ has the same optimal properties of least-squares reconstruction and variance maximization as PCA. Similar to PCA the KL transform variables y_i, y_j are statistically independent and arranged in order of decreasing variance:

$$E\{y_i y_j\} = \begin{cases} 0, & \text{if } i \neq j, \\ \lambda_i, & \text{if } i = j. \end{cases}$$

3.3 THE SINGULAR VALUE DECOMPOSITION (SVD)

The singular value decomposition can be viewed as the extension of the eigenvalue decomposition for the case of nonsquare matrices: it shows that any real matrix can be diagonalized by using two orthogonal matrices. The eigenvalue decomposition, instead, works only on square matrices and uses only one matrix (and its inverse) to achieve diagonalization. If the matrix is square and symmetric, then the two orthogonal matrices of SVD become equal, and eigenvalue decomposition and SVD become one and the same thing. Because the SVD is much more general than the eigenvalue decomposition and intimately related to the matrix rank and reduced-rank least-squares approximations, it is a very important and useful tool in matrix theory, statistics, and signal analysis.

Theorem 3.5 (SVD). For any $A \in \mathbb{R}^{m \times n}$ there exist two orthonormal matrices, $U \in \mathbb{R}^{m \times m}$ and $V \in \mathbb{R}^{n \times n}$, and a pseudodiagonal matrix $D = \text{diag}[\sigma_1, \ldots, \sigma_p] \in \mathbb{R}^{m \times n}$, where $p = \min\{m, n\}$, such that

$$A = UDV^T. \tag{3.13}$$

If $m > n$ then

$$
D = \begin{bmatrix} \sigma_1 & & & \\ & \ddots & & \\ & & \sigma_n & \\ 0 & \cdots & 0 & \\ \vdots & & \vdots & \\ 0 & \cdots & 0 & \end{bmatrix},
$$

while for $m < n$

$$
D = \begin{bmatrix} \sigma_1 & & & 0 & \cdots & 0 \\ & \ddots & & \vdots & & \vdots \\ & & \sigma_m & 0 & \cdots & 0 \end{bmatrix}.
$$

If we denote by u_i, v_i the columns of the matrices U and V respectively, then we can also write

$$
A = \sum_{i=1}^{p} \sigma_i u_i v_i^T. \tag{3.14}
$$

The vectors u_i, v_i are called the **left** and **right singular vectors** of A, while the σ_i are called the **singular values** of A. Without loss of generality we can assume that all the singular values are nonnegative (if, say, σ_i is negative we can simply change the sign of either u_i or v_i and set σ_i positive).

3.3.1 SVD and Eigenvalue Decomposition

Like the eigenvalue decomposition, SVD is not a direct statistical technique but rather a matrix processing technique. The association of SVD with statistics arises only when the matrix to be processed is related to some statistical observations. To see the relation between SVD and eigenvalue decomposition note that from (3.13) we obtain

$$
AA^T U = U D D^T, \tag{3.15}
$$

$$
A^T A V = V D^T D. \tag{3.16}
$$

Both DD^T and $D^T D$ are square diagonal matrices. If $m > n$,

$$
DD^T = \mathrm{diag}[\sigma_1^2, \ldots, \sigma_n^2, \underbrace{0, \ldots, 0}_{m-n}]
$$

and $D^T D = \mathrm{diag}[\sigma_1^2, \ldots, \sigma_n^2]$, and if $m < n$,

$$D^T D = \mathrm{diag}[\sigma_1^2, \ldots, \sigma_m^2, \underbrace{0, \ldots, 0}_{n-m}]$$

and $DD^T = \mathrm{diag}[\sigma_1^2, \ldots, \sigma_m^2]$. It follows that the vectors u_i and v_i are eigenvectors of the matrices AA^T, $A^T A$, respectively:

$$AA^T u_i = \sigma_i^2 u_i, \qquad i = 1, \ldots, m,$$

$$A^T A v_i = \sigma_i^2 v_i, \qquad i = 1, \ldots, n.$$

where we define $\sigma_{p+1} = \sigma_{p+2} = \cdots = \sigma_{\max(m,n)} = 0$.

Furthermore, the nonzero eigenvalues of both matrices are the same and equal to σ_i^2, which are the nonzero diagonal entries of DD^T and $D^T D$.

Returning to PCA and the statistical description of a stationary signal x, we find that in many situations the autocorrelation matrix is not known in advance. However, it may be estimated by a time average (for example) over a sample sequence of input vectors

$$R_x \approx \frac{1}{N} \sum_{k=1}^{N} x_k x_k^T = \frac{1}{N} X_N X_N^T, \tag{3.17}$$

where $X_N = [x_1 \quad x_2 \quad \cdots \quad x_N]$ is the input data matrix. In this context, there is a straightforward asymptotic connection between PCA and SVD.

If

$$\bar{X}_N \equiv \frac{1}{\sqrt{N}} X_N = U_N \Sigma_N V_N^T$$

is the SVD of $\bar{X}_N$, then the principal components of $\{x\}$ are the columns of U_N as $N \to \infty$. The singular values of $\bar{X}_N$ are equal (in the limit) to the square roots of the eigenvalues λ_i.

3.3.2 SVD and the Matrix Rank

If $m > n$ (thus $p \equiv \min\{m, n\} = n$) the vectors u_i, $i = p + 1, \ldots, m$, do not participate in the sum in the left-hand side of (3.14); therefore

$$u_i^T A = 0, \qquad i = p + 1, \ldots, m.$$

If, in addition, some of the singular values are zero (e.g., if $\sigma_{r+1} = \sigma_{r+2} = \cdots = \sigma_p = 0$), then

$$u_i^T A = 0, \qquad i = r + 1, \ldots, m,$$

$$A v_i = 0, \qquad i = r + 1, \ldots, n.$$

Since v_i are linearly independent (in fact orthogonal) it follows that the null space of A has dimension $n - r$ and the rank of A is r. The vectors v_i, $i = r + 1, \ldots, n$, form an orthonormal basis of this null space. Conversely, if the rank is r, then only r of the singular values are nonzero.

The following theorem, originally due to Eckart and Young [32], is very useful for least-squares reduced-rank approximation problems.

Theorem 3.6. Let UDV^T be the SVD of an $m \times n$ matrix A with rank r. Let us also assume that the singular values are arranged in decreasing order $\sigma_1 \geq \sigma_2 \geq \cdots \geq \sigma_p$, where $p = \min\{m, n\}$. Then for any $l \leq r$,

$$\min_{\text{rank}(B)=l} \|A - B\|_F^2 = \|A - A_l\|_F^2 = \sum_{i=l+1}^{n} \sigma_i^2, \tag{3.18}$$

where

$$A_l = \sum_{i=1}^{l} \sigma_i u_i v_i^T.$$

Proof. For $l = r$ the theorem is obvious. If $l < r$ consider a matrix $B \in \mathbb{R}^{m \times n}$ with rank$(B) = l$ and let $X \in \mathbb{R}^{n \times (n-l)}$ be a matrix with orthonormal columns spanning null(B), namely $BX = 0$. So $(A - B)X = AX$, and

$$\|AX\|_F^2 = \|(A - B)X\|_F^2$$
$$\leq \|A - B\|_F^2 \|X\|_2^2 = \|A - B\|_F^2.$$

Hence,

$$\min_{\text{rank}(B)=l} \|A - B\|_F^2 \geq \min_{X^T X=I} \text{tr}(X^T A^T A X) = \sum_{i=l+1}^{n} \sigma_i^2$$

(the last equality from Theorem 3.1). Clearly this lower bound is achieved by the matrix $\sum_{i=1}^{l} \sigma_i u_i v_i^T$ and the theorem follows. ∎

A_l is the closest rank-l matrix to A (in the Frobenius norm sense), and the square distance is $\sum_{i=l+1}^{n} \sigma_i^2$. A_l is composed of the outer products of the l *principal singular vectors* weighted by the l *principal singular values*.

Corollary 3.1. Let $A \in \mathbb{R}^{n \times n}$ be a real symmetric matrix with eigenvalues $\lambda_1 \geq \lambda_2 \geq \cdots \geq \lambda_n$ and corresponding orthonormal set of eigenvectors $e_1, e_2, \ldots, e_n$. Then for any $l \leq r = \text{rank}(A)$,

$$\min_{\text{rank}(B)=l} \|A - B\|_F^2 = \|A - A_l\|_F^2 = \sum_{i=l+1}^{n} \lambda_i^2,$$

where

$$A_l = \sum_{i=1}^{l} \lambda_i e_i e_i^T.$$

Proof. Obvious since the eigenvalue decomposition $A = \sum_i \lambda_i e_i e_i^T$ is also the SVD of A. ∎

Returning to Theorem 3.6, σ_p is the smallest distance between A and the set of rank-deficient matrices. Clearly, if $\sigma_p = 0$, then the matrix is rank deficient. Also if $\sigma_p = \epsilon$, where ϵ is very small for some given computer accuracy, then it might make sense to consider the matrix to be rank deficient from the numerical point of view. This is particularly helpful when the inversion of the matrix is to be performed and we want to avoid numerical difficulties with inverting very small numbers. In fact, the SVD can be used directly to invert a square nonsingular matrix A as

$$A^{-1} = \sum_{i=1}^{p} \sigma_i^{-1} v_i u_i^T = V D^{-1} U^T,$$

or in compact form,

$$A^{-1} = V D^{-1} U^T.$$

3.3.3 SVD and Least Squares

Matrix inversion is the heart of the solution of the least-squares problem

$$\min_x \|Ax - b\|^2. \tag{3.19}$$

In the special case where the matrix A is square and has full rank, the solution is

$$x_{LS} = A^{-1} b \tag{3.20}$$

and the minimum error is 0.

A more interesting case arises when the matrix is noninvertible or nonsquare. Then it is useful to define the *pseudoinverse* of A as

$$A^+ = \sum_{i=1}^{p} \sigma_i^+ v_i u_i^T,$$

where

$$\sigma_i^+ = \begin{cases} \sigma_i^{-1} & \text{if } \sigma_i \neq 0, \\ 0 & \text{if } \sigma_i = 0, \end{cases}$$

or in more compact form,

$$A^+ = VD^+U^T,$$

where $D = \text{diag}[\sigma_1^+, \ldots, \sigma_p^+] \in \mathbb{R}^{n \times m}$.

An alternative representation of the pseudoinverse for the special cases of non-square, full-rank matrices is

$$A^+ = \begin{cases} A^T(AA^T)^{-1} & \text{if } m < n, \\ (A^T A)^{-1}A^T & \text{if } m > n. \end{cases}$$

Theorem 3.7. For any matrix $A \in \mathbb{R}^{m \times n}$ and vector $b \in \mathbb{R}^m$, the vector

$$x_{LS} = A^+ b$$

minimizes $\|Ax - b\|^2$. If $\text{rank}(A) = n$ this solution is unique. If $\text{rank}(A) < n$ the solution is not unique, but x_{LS} is the one with the smallest norm. Furthermore, the minimum error is

$$\sum_{i=\text{rank}(A)+1}^{m} (u_i^T b)^2.$$

Notice that if $m < n$ the rank cannot be equal to n (it can be at most m), so we have multiple solutions. In this case we have more unknowns than equations (i.e., the problem is underdetermined), and x_{LS} is the solution with the smallest norm. On the other hand, if $m > n$ (a case much more frequent in practice) we have more equations than unknowns and the problem is overdetermined. If, in addition, $\text{rank}(A) = n$, then x_{LS} is the unique solution to the problem.

3.4 INFORMATION-THEORETICAL VIEWPOINT

The primary objects of study in information theory are *messages* and *transmission channels*. Concepts such as *information, noise, capacity, rate*, etc; are all related to these primitive objects. These terms are commonly used by people working in telecommunications and related fields. We shall show that the maximization of information by a linear channel in the Gaussian setting is very closely related to PCA.

3.4.1 Elements of Information Theory

First we shall give some introductory material that will only go as far as explaining the concepts of entropy and mutual information, which will be used below. This part may be skipped by readers familiar with the subject.

The following material is covered in most introductory books on information theory, such as [33, 34]. The message x is considered to be the outcome of a probabilistic experiment. For illustration purposes we assume that x can take on a finite number of possible values $x_1, \ldots, x_N$, but this assumption is not essential and it will be relaxed later. Let $p_1 = \text{Prob}(x = x_1), \ldots, p_N = \text{Prob}(x = x_N)$. The **entropy** $H(x)$ of the message is a measure of the average uncertainty of the random variable x: $\sum_{i=1}^{N} p_i h(p_i)$, where $h(p_i)$ is the uncertainty removed, or the surprise expected, by revealing that x took on the value x_i as the result of some experiment. H is clearly a function of $p_1, \ldots, p_M$. For example, if x takes two values with probabilities $p_1 = 0.99$ and $p_2 = 0.01$, then 99% of the time the result will be hardly surprising and the entropy should be small. However, if $p_1 = p_2 = 0.5$ then the result will be quite unpredictable (50% probability that our prediction of the outcome will be wrong), so H should be high.

Also the number of possible outcomes should affect the value of H: more possible outcomes imply more uncertainty regarding the result of the experiment. Thus we have the first axiom of entropy:

[H-1] $H\left(p_1 = \frac{1}{N} \ldots, p_N = \frac{1}{N}\right)$ should be a monotonically increasing function of N.

If we have two independent experiments described by the variables x and y, taking on the values $x_1, \ldots, x_N$, with equal probability, and $y_1, \ldots, y_M$, also with equal probability, then the joint experiment has NM equally likely outcomes. Since the experiments are independent, revealing the outcome of one should not affect the expectation regarding the other. Therefore, the uncertainty of the joint experiment should be the sum of the uncertainties of x and y. This yields the second axiom of entropy:

[H-2] $H\left(p_1 = \frac{1}{NM}, \ldots, p_{NM} = \frac{1}{NM}\right)$

$$= H\left(p_1 = \frac{1}{N}, \ldots, p_N = \frac{1}{N}\right) + H\left(p_1 = \frac{1}{M}, \ldots, p_M = \frac{1}{M}\right).$$

The third axiom for entropy is obtained by partitioning the outcomes of an experiment into two sets $A = \{x_1, \ldots, x_r\}$ and $B = \{x_{r+1}, \ldots, x_N\}$, with probabilities $p_A = \text{Prob}(x \in A) = \sum_{i=1}^{r} p_i$ and $p_B = \text{Prob}(x \in B) = \sum_{i=r+1}^{N} p_i$. The conditional probabilities are $\text{Prob}(x = x_i \mid A) = p_i/p_A$, $i = 1, \ldots, r$, and $\text{Prob}(x = x_i \mid B) = p_i/p_B$, $i = r+1, \ldots, N$. The total average uncertainty of the experiment can be seen as the sum of three parts: (1) the uncertainty between A and B, (2) $p_A \times$ (uncertainty within A), (3) $p_B \times$ (uncertainty within B), or

[H-3] $H(p_1, \ldots, p_N) = H(p_A, p_B) + p_A H\left(\frac{p_1}{p_A}, \ldots, \frac{p_r}{p_A}\right) + p_B H\left(\frac{p_{r+1}}{p_B}, \ldots, \frac{p_N}{p_B}\right).$

Finally, the last axiom says simply that small changes in the probability distribution of x should result in small changes in H.

[H-4] $H(p, 1 - p)$ is a continuous function of p.

It is a fact that

$$H(x) = H(p_1, \ldots, p_N) = - \sum_{i=1}^{N} p_i \log(p_i) \tag{3.21}$$

is the only function that satisfies the four axioms [H-1]–[H-4] up to the basis of the logarithm, which is arbitrary. Typically we use base=2, in which case H is measured in **bits**. We use the convention that for $p_i = 0$ the term $p_i \log(p_i)$ is replaced by $\lim_{p_i \to 0} p_i \log(p_i) = 0$, so H is rendered computable for any probability distribution.

If x is a continuous variable with probability density function $p(x)$ the definition is naturally extended to

$$H(x) = - \int p(x) \log(p(x)) \, dx, \tag{3.22}$$

where the limits of integration are the infimum and supremum values of x.

The entropy can also be interpreted as the mean of the function $b(x) = -\log(p(x))$:

$$H(x) = -E\{ \log(p(x)) \}, \tag{3.23}$$

which is a unifying formula for both the discrete and continuous cases.

In the same spirit we may define the conditional entropy of y given x as the average of $-\log(y \mid x)$:

$$H(y \mid x) = -E\{ \log(p(y \mid x)) \}$$

$$= \begin{cases} - \sum_{i=1}^{N} \sum_{j=1}^{M} p(x_i, y_j) \log(y_j \mid x_i) & \text{(discrete case)} \\ - \int_x \int_y p(x, y) \log(y \mid x) \, dx \, dy & \text{(continuous case)}. \end{cases}$$

$H(y|x)$ is the remaining uncertainty about y after we are told the outcome x. If y and x are independent then $p(y \mid x) = p(y)$ and $H(y \mid x) = -E\{ \log(p(y)) \} = H(y)$. In that case the revelation of x tells us nothing about y, and therefore the uncertainty (entropy) of y does not change. We say that x *conveys no information about y* and the **mutual information** index

$$I(y \mid x) = H(y) - H(y \mid x) \tag{3.24}$$

is 0. It is a fact that $H(y \mid x) \leq H(y)$, so the mutual information is a nonnegative quantity. In simple words this means that the expected surprise from revealing y, after we are told the value of x, cannot be larger than the surprise about y without knowing x, whatever the relation between x and y may be. As x and y become more correlated, the revelation of x yields more information about y, and

$I(y \mid x)$ increases. The maximum information occurs, of course, for $x \equiv y$, whence $H(y \mid x) = 0$, $I(y \mid x) = H(y)$ in the discrete case or $H(y \mid x) = -\infty$, $I(y \mid x) = \infty$ in the continuous case.

We can also express the mutual information in terms of averages:

$$
\begin{aligned}
I(y \mid x) &= -E_{x,y}\{\log(p(y)) - \log(p(y \mid x))\} \\
&= -E_{x,y}\{\log(p(y)p(x)/p(x,y))\} \\
&= -E_{x,y}\{\log(p(x)) - \log(p(x \mid y))\} = I(x|y)
\end{aligned}
$$

with $E_{x,y}$ denoting expectation with respect to x and y. Thus the information about y conveyed by x is the same as the information conveyed about x by y. Because of this symmetry we define

$$
I(x, y) \equiv I(y \mid x) = I(x \mid y).
$$

3.4.2 Relation to PCA

Principal component analysis is related to information-theoretical questions regarding optimization of linear channels under the Gaussian assumption. To be more specific, consider a message $x \in \mathbb{R}^n$ with zero-mean Gaussian distribution and correlation $R_x = E\{xx^T\}$. Thus x follows the distribution

$$
p(x) = \frac{1}{\sqrt{(2\pi)^n |R_x|}} \exp\left\{ -\frac{1}{2}(x^T R_x^{-1} x) \right\}.
$$

Assume now that this message is sent through a linear channel which applies the transform

$$
y = Wx, \tag{3.25}
$$

$W \in \mathbb{R}^{m \times n}$, $y \in \mathbb{R}^m$, $m < n$. From the information-theoretical point of view we ask, "What is the optimal channel (3.25) which maximizes the mutual information $I(x, y)$ between x and y?" The answer is practically the same as the one given by standard PCA, as shown in the following

Theorem 3.8 [35]. The linear channel which maximizes $I(x, y)$ is

$$
W_{\text{opt}} = M[e_1 \ldots e_m]^T,
$$

where $M \in \mathbb{R}^{n \times n}$ is any invertible matrix.

Proof. Since y is a deterministic function of x we have $H(y \mid x) = 0$, so

$$
I(x, y) = H(y).
$$

Linear combinations of Gaussian variables are also Gaussian; hence y has a probability density function of the form

$$p(y) = \frac{1}{\sqrt{(2\pi)^m |R_y|}} \exp\left\{-\frac{1}{2}(y^T R_y^{-1} y)\right\},$$

where $R_y = WR_x W^T$ is the covariance matrix of y.

Computing the entropy

$$
\begin{aligned}
H(y) &= -E\left\{\log_2(p(y))\right\} \\
&= \frac{1}{2}\log_2((2\pi)^m |R_y|) + \frac{\log_2 e}{2} E\{y^T R_y^{-1} y\} \\
&= \frac{1}{2}\log_2((2\pi)^m |R_y|) + \frac{\log_2 e}{2} \operatorname{tr}(E\{R_y^{-1} yy^T\}) \\
&= \frac{1}{2}\log_2((2\pi)^m |R_y|) + \frac{m}{2}\log_2 e,
\end{aligned}
\tag{3.26}
$$

we see that the cost is proportional to the determinant of the matrix $WR_x W^T$. Using the result of Theorem 3.2 the proof follows immediately. ∎

3.5 EIGENVALUE COMPUTATION TECHNIQUES

Principal component analysis of a real input sequence can be approximated in a batch mode: first the data are collected and then an estimate of R_x is computed, since it is not known in advance. After that follows an eigenvalue decomposition of the estimate and a projection of the signal onto the principal component subspace of a desired dimension.

However, it is emphasized that this is an approximation to PCA since the statistical expectation in R_x is replaced by sample averaging. In the exact stochastic framework of PCA one has to work with infinitely long data sequences, in which case batch methods become nonapplicable simply because they have to wait until all the data are collected before they start the computations.

In this case one can use stochastic approximation techniques which yield the desired components in the limit when time tends to infinity. The idea is that the components are estimated every time a new input sample comes along, and the estimate becomes progressively better as time passes and in the limit it converges to the optimal solution. These are also called adaptive techniques, and most neural network algorithms fall in this category. Like most adaptive techniques, neural networks can work for infinitely long sequences of data and require less storage than batch methods since the data are used only as they arrive and need not be remembered for the future. Such methods are also useful when one wants to track the principal component subspaces in a slowly changing environment without having to do the eigenvalue decomposition every time from scratch.

In the following chapters we'll discuss different neural net approaches for the PC extraction problem. However, for now we shall make a brief exposition of the batch approach.

First, temporal averaging is used to estimate the autocorrelation matrix, as in (3.17). Weighted averaging can also be used to incorporate a forgetting factor $0 < \gamma \leq 1$ that determines the relative influence of past data into the current estimate:

$$R_x \approx \hat{R}_x(N) = (1 - \gamma) \sum_{k=1}^{N} \gamma^{N-k} x_k x_k^T . \tag{3.27}$$

The symmetric eigenvalue problem is a basic problem studied in numerical algebra for many decades. As a result there are a host of techniques to compute the eigenvalue decomposition of real symmetric matrices. The problem is also mathematically elegant. As Golub and VanLoan put it [36]: "Indeed, the symmetric eigenvalue problem with its rich mathematical structure is one of the most aesthetically pleasing problems in numerical algebra." In the following we'll make a brief exposition of the basic eigenvalue computation techniques starting from the simpler approaches, like the power method, and going to the more efficient and/or parallelizable algorithms like the QR method, Lanczos' algorithm, and Jacobi's iteration. A very good reference including in-depth analysis of the symmetric eigenvalue problem is a book of the same title by Parlett [37].

3.5.1 Power Method

Given a real symmetric matrix $A \in \mathbb{R}^{n \times n}$ and an initial estimate $q^{(0)}$ of the principal eigenvector of A the power method proceeds as follows:

for $k := 0, 1, \ldots$ do
    $p := A q^{(k)}$
    $q^{(k+1)} := p/\|p\|$
end

$q^{(k)}$ converges to the principal eigenvector e_1 of A as $k \to \infty$ with an exponential rate

$$|\lambda_1 - q^{(k)^T} A q^{(k)}| = O\left(\left|\frac{\lambda_2}{\lambda_1}\right|^k\right),$$

but the rate depends on the ratio of the two largest eigenvalues. If these eigenvalues are sufficiently separated then the algorithm converges extremely fast. However, if they are very close the algorithm has a disadvantage with respect to other methods. In addition, the eigenvectors can be extracted only one at a time. In order to extract the rest of the eigenvalues a deflation procedure must be followed, as described in

Section 2.2.8. The power method is very closely related to the normalized Hebbian rule for training neural connections, as studied in Chapter 4.

3.5.2   Orthogonal Iteration

In order to describe this technique we need to introduce the Householder transformation and the QR decomposition.

Householder Transformation   Given any vector $x \in \mathbb{R}^n$ we define the Householder vector $v = [v_1, v_2, \ldots, v_n]^T$ and the Householder matrix H as follows:

$$v_1 = \begin{cases} x_1 + \text{sign}(x_1)\|x\| & \text{if } x \neq 0, \\ 1 & \text{otherwise,} \end{cases}$$

$$v_i = x_i / v_1, \qquad i = 2, \ldots, n$$

$$H = \left[I - 2\frac{vv^T}{\|v\|^2} \right].$$

Then the vector resulting from the Householder transformation of x,

$$h(x) \equiv Hx,$$

has all elements zero except the first one, i.e.,

$$h(x) = [\times, 0, 0, \ldots, 0]^T.$$

Furthermore, the Householder matrix H is orthogonal and symmetric. Thus the Householder transformation is an orthogonal transformation which nullifies all the elements of a given vector, except for the first one, in one stroke.

QR Factorization   Every $m \times n$ matrix A, $m \geq n$, can be decomposed into a product of an orthogonal matrix $Q \in \mathbb{R}^{m \times m}$ times an upper triangular matrix $R \in \mathbb{R}^{m \times n}$ as

$$A = QR.$$

We'll describe two basic approaches in order to compute the QR factorization of a given matrix A: using the Householder transform, and using the Givens rotation.

Householder QR. This approach is particularly attractive for non-banded matrices, i.e., matrices whose diagonals are nonzero. In this method we make use of the Householder transformation property, which nullifies all the elements of a vector except the first one. The idea is to nullify, at iteration k, all the elements of the kth column of the matrix from row $k + 1$ onto the last row by multiplying from the left with an orthogonal matrix

$$Q^{(k)} = \begin{bmatrix} I_{k-1} & 0 \\ 0 & H^{(k)} \end{bmatrix},$$

where I_{k-1} is the $(k-1) \times (k-1)$ identity matrix and $H^{(k)}$ is the appropriate Householder matrix. For iteration $k = 1$ we simply have $Q^{(1)} = H^{(1)}$. After n iterations we will have transformed A into a totally upper triangular form R:

$$Q^{(n)} \cdots Q^{(1)} A = R.$$

Since the matrices $Q^{(k)}$ are orthogonal, so is their product. Clearly then the final matrix Q of the QR decomposition will be given by

$$Q = Q^{(1)^T} \cdots Q^{(n)^T}.$$

/* QR factorization (Householder method) */
$R := A$
$Q := I$
for $k := 1, 2, \ldots$ do
$$Q^{(k)} := \begin{bmatrix} I_{k-1} & 0 \\ 0 & H^{(k)} \end{bmatrix}$$
/* $H^{(k)}$ nullifies the elements $r_{k+1,k}, \ldots, r_{m,k}$ */
$R := Q^{(k)} R$
$Q := Q Q^{(k)^T}$
end

The total Householder-QR algorithm without the accumulation of the $Q^{(k)}$'s requires $2n(m - n/3)$ *floating-point operations (flops)*.

Givens QR. This approach is particularly attractive for banded matrices, especially for tridiagonal matrices which we'll encounter in the next section.

Given a matrix $A \in \mathbb{R}^{m \times n}$, the Givens rotation matrix

$$C_{ij} = \begin{array}{c} \\ \\ j \\ \\ i \\ \\ \\ \end{array} \overset{\begin{array}{cc} j & i \end{array}}{\begin{bmatrix} 1 & \cdots & 0 & \cdots & 0 & \cdots & 0 \\ \vdots & \ddots & \vdots & & \vdots & & \vdots \\ 0 & \cdots & c & \cdots & s & \cdots & 0 \\ \vdots & & \vdots & \ddots & \vdots & & \vdots \\ 0 & \cdots & -s & \cdots & c & \cdots & 0 \\ \vdots & & \vdots & & \vdots & \ddots & \vdots \\ 0 & \cdots & 0 & \cdots & 0 & \cdots & 1 \end{bmatrix}}, \quad (3.28)$$

where

$$c = \frac{a_{jj}}{\sqrt{a_{ij}^2 + a_{jj}^2}}, \qquad s = \frac{a_{ij}}{\sqrt{a_{ij}^2 + a_{jj}^2}},$$

is orthonormal and nullifies the element a_{ij} after the transformation

$$A \leftarrow C_{ij}A.$$

Notice that because of the special structure of C_{ij} only the rows i and j are affected after the transformation; therefore a full-blown matrix multiplication routine is not required to implement Givens rotations. The strategy to compute the QR decomposition based on Givens is simple: nullify the elements of A in the order $a_{21}, \ldots, a_{m1}, a_{32}, \ldots, a_{m2}, \ldots, a_{n+1,n}, \ldots, a_{m,n}$. The algorithm is summarized below:

```
/* QR factorization (Givens method) */
R := A
Q := I
for j := 1, 2, ..., n, do
    for i := j + 1, j + 2, ..., m, do
        R := C_{ij}R
        Q := QC_{ij}^T
    end
end
```

An efficient implementation of this algorithm on banded matrices with lower bandwidth p and upper bandwidth q requires $O(np(p + q))$ floating-point operations. In particular when the matrix is tridiagonal ($p = q = 1$) it takes $O(n)$ flops.

The Orthogonal Iteration Algorithm   This technique is a generalization of the power method to extract multiple eigenvectors in parallel. The role of the single vector q in the power method is now played by the matrix $Q \in \mathbb{R}^{n \times p}$. Indeed, if $p = 1$ the method degenerates into the power method.

```
Let Q^{(0)} ∈ R^{n×p} be orthogonal
for k := 0, 1, ... do
    P := AQ^{(k)}
    Q^{(k+1)}R := P  /* QR factorization of P
                       using Givens' or Householder's method */
end
```

The convergence is exponential based on the ratio $|\lambda_{p+1}/\lambda_p|$. Similar comments with the power method can be made regarding the convergence speed in relation to the distance between λ_{p+1} and λ_p.

3.5.3 Symmetric QR Method

This method starts by tridiagonalizing the original matrix A, i.e., transforming it into a matrix whose elements are 0 except for the main diagonal and the subdiagonals above and below it. The symmetric QR method is the best algorithm for implementation on sequential machines.

Tridiagonalization   Tridiagonalization can be performed using the Householder transformation described before. Let

$$A = A^{(1)} = \begin{bmatrix} a_1 & c_1^T \\ c_1 & A_1 \end{bmatrix} \in \mathbb{R}^{n \times n}$$

be the original matrix. Consider the orthogonal transformation

$$A^{(2)} \leftarrow Q^{(1)} A^{(1)} Q^{(1)}$$
$$= \begin{bmatrix} 1 & 0 \\ 0 & H^{(1)} \end{bmatrix} A^{(1)} \begin{bmatrix} 1 & 0 \\ 0 & H^{(1)} \end{bmatrix}$$
$$= \begin{bmatrix} a_1 & c_1^T H^{(1)} \\ H^{(1)} c_1 & H^{(1)} A_1 H^{(1)} \end{bmatrix},$$

where $H^{(1)}$ is the Householder matrix corresponding to c_1. After the transformation, $A^{(2)}$ is tridiagonal in its first column and row. In the next step we inspect the lower-right-corner matrix

$$H^{(1)} A_1 H^{(1)} = \begin{bmatrix} a_2 & c_2^T \\ c_2 & A_2 \end{bmatrix}$$

and use the orthonormal transformation

$$A^{(3)} \leftarrow Q^{(2)} A^{(2)} Q^{(2)},$$

where now

$$Q^{(2)} = \begin{bmatrix} 1 & 0 & 0 \\ 0 & 1 & 0 \\ 0 & 0 & H^{(2)} \end{bmatrix}$$

and $H^{(2)}$ is the Householder matrix for c_2. This transformation will leave the first column and row of $A^{(2)}$ untouched, but it will tridiagonalize the second column and row. Clearly, after $n - 1$ iterations of this procedure the whole matrix will have been tridiagonalized by an orthogonal transformation of the form

$$T = Q^T A Q$$
$$= Q^{(n)} Q^{(n-1)} \cdots Q^{(1)} A Q^{(1)} \cdots Q^{(n-1)} Q^{(n)}.$$

An efficient implementation of this approach will require $4n^3/3$ flops.

The Symmetric QR Algorithm   The following procedure summarizes the total algorithm. The shift parameter $\delta^{(k)}$ is used to accelerate the algorithm, but it is not theoretically necessary.

$T := Q^T A Q$ /* Householder Tridiagonalization */
for $k := 1, 2 \ldots$ do
    determine shift parameter $\delta^{(k)}$
    $QR := T - \delta^{(k)} I$ /* QR factorization */
    $T := RQ + \delta^{(k)} I$
end

There are many different strategies to select the shift parameter for fast convergence. A popular strategy is Wilkinson's shift, which guarantees convergence under any conditions and at the same time achieves very good performance. Other strategies with good performance, such as the Rayleigh quotient shift, converge *almost* always; i.e., they can fail under certain conditions. The Wilkinson $\delta^{(k)}$ at iteration k is given by [37, Chapter 8]

$$\delta^{(k)} = t_{11} - \text{sign}(d) \frac{t_{12}}{|d| + \sqrt{d^2 + t_{12}^2}},$$

where $d = (t_{11} - t_{12})/2$. With Wilkinson's shift not only is convergence guaranteed, but it is also asymptotically better than cubic almost always (i.e. the off-diagonal elements decay with a function of time that is higher than third order), while it is linear right from the start. However, there is a possibility that the convergence is asymptotically quadratic for some very special cases.

The algorithm requires few computations compared to other techniques: only $O(n)$ flops per iteration if the orthogonal matrices are not accumulated, and $O(n^2)$ if they are. Of course, there is also the one-time cost of tridiagonalization, which is $4n^3/3$, as we saw in the previous subsection. Both excellent convergence and computational efficiency make this the algorithm of choice for small- or medium-size nonsparse matrices when parallelism is not considered.

3.5.4 Lanczos' Method

Lanczos' method generates a sequence of tridiagonal matrices T_k, $k = 1, \ldots, n$, whose extreme eigenvalues are increasingly better estimates of the extreme eigenvalues of A. The convergence of these estimates to the true values is very fast and can be extremely close to the true values well before $k = n$. That is an attractive feature for problems with very large and sparse symmetric matrices, especially when few extreme eigenvalues are sought. However, in the context of the following chapters such cases will rarely arise. If the algorithm does not terminate before $k = n$, then the final tridiagonal matrix T_n can be used to determine *all* the eigenvalues of A, using any other eigenvalue method, such as the symmetric QR algorithm. In other words, one can view the Lanczos' technique as yet another tridiagonalizing method similar to Householder's tridiagonalization. However, it has been shown that Lanczos is numerically inferior to Householder in that capacity. We briefly outline the method. For a more thorough treatment refer to [36, Chapter 9] and [37, Chapter 13].

Let $q_0 := 0$, $\beta_0 := 1$, $r_0 :=$ any nonzero vector
for $k := 1, \ldots, n$ do
$\quad q_k := \frac{r_{k-1}}{\|r_{k-1}\|}$
$\quad \alpha_k := q_k^T A q_k$
$\quad r_k := (A - \alpha_k I)q_k - \beta_{k-1}q_{k-1}$
$\quad \beta_k := \|r_k\|$
$\quad$ If desired, form the tridiagonal matrix

$$T^{(k)} := \begin{bmatrix} \alpha_1 & \beta_1 & \cdots & & 0 \\ \beta_1 & \alpha_2 & \ddots & & \vdots \\ \vdots & \ddots & \ddots & & \beta_{k-1} \\ 0 & \cdots & & \beta_{k-1} & \alpha_k \end{bmatrix}$$

$\quad$ and compute the eigenvalue decomposition of $T^{(k)}$
$\quad$ using any standard method
end

Unfortunately, round-off errors affect the behavior of the algorithm in a significant way, especially in terms of orthogonality of the vectors $q_1, q_2, \ldots$. Such problems can be amended using some reorthogonalization procedures, but we will not dive into details here.

3.5.5 Jacobi's Method

The idea behind the Jacobi method is to nullify at each iteration k the biggest off-diagonal element of A by multiplying from both sides by a properly chosen orthogonal matrix $J^{(k)}$:

for $k = 1, 2, \ldots$ do
$\quad$ identify largest off-diagonal element a_{ij} of A
$\quad$ construct matrix $J^{(k)}$
$\quad A := J^{(k)^T} A J^{(k)}$
end

Other nullification strategies can also be followed: for example, instead of picking the largest off-diagonal element we may kill the off-diagonal elements in a certain prespecified order. The Jacobi transformation matrix

$$
J_{ij} = \quad
\begin{array}{c}
\\ \\ j \\ \\ i \\ \\ \\
\end{array}
\begin{bmatrix}
1 & \cdots & 0 & \cdots & 0 & \cdots & 0 \\
\vdots & \ddots & \vdots & & \vdots & & \vdots \\
0 & \cdots & c & \cdots & s & \cdots & 0 \\
\vdots & & \vdots & \ddots & \vdots & & \vdots \\
0 & \cdots & -s & \cdots & c & \cdots & 0 \\
\vdots & & \vdots & & \vdots & \ddots & \vdots \\
0 & \cdots & 0 & \cdots & 0 & \cdots & 1
\end{bmatrix}
\tag{3.29}
$$

nullifies both the (i, j)th and the (j, i)th elements of A after the transformation

$$A \leftarrow J_{ij}^T A J_{ij}.$$

The scalars c, s, are computed by the formula

$$c = \frac{1}{\sqrt{1 + t^2}}, \qquad s = \frac{t}{\sqrt{1 + t^2}},$$

$$t = \frac{\text{sign}(\theta)}{|\theta| + \sqrt{1 + \theta^2}},$$

$$\theta = \frac{a_{jj} - a_{ii}}{2a_{ij}}.$$

Compare this with the Givens rotation matrix C_{ij}, which is of similar form except for the different formulas for c and s. Remember however, that Givens' rotation is a left-side transform $A \leftarrow C_{ij}A$ which nullifies only the (i, j)th element of A, while Jacobi's rotation is a double-sided transform $A \leftarrow J_{ij}^T A J_{ij}$ which simultaneously nullifies both symmetric positions (i, j) and (j, i).

Of course, even if we nullify some element (i, j) at iteration k, it will be, in general, replaced with a nonzero value in the next iteration. However, it can be shown that the cumulative size of all the off-diagonal elements is shrinking at each iteration. So after many, say N, Jacobi iterations the off-diagonal elements of A almost vanish and thus A is reduced to almost diagonal form (up to a certain level of accuracy). Thus the eigenvector matrix of the original A is simply the product of the individual $J^{(k)}$'s:

$$U = J^{(1)}J^{(2)} \cdots J^{(N)},$$

while the eigenvalues are the diagonal elements of the final matrix A.

The Jacobi method converges quadratically. However, two iterations of the Jacobi algorithm require almost as many flops as the whole QR method (if we do not count the initial tridiagonalization), so it is inferior to the QR method. Yet, compared to the QR method, the Jacobi algorithm is more parallelizable. For that reason it has currently attracted a lot of attention.

4

PCA NEURAL NETWORKS

In this chapter, we establish the connection between neural networks and PCA. First, we discuss the Hebbian law and its relatives, such as Oja's model, Földiák's model, the GHA model, the APEX model, Rubner's model, etc., in detail. Theoretical analysis for each model will be provided. Finally, we explore the close relationship between the well-known back-propagation rule and PCA networks.

4.1 HEBB'S NEUROPHYSIOLOGICAL POSTULATE

In his seminal work, *The Organization of Behavior* [15, Chapter 4], Donald Hebb postulated the following assumption regarding the organization of a collection of neurons (cell assembly)

> When an axon of cell A is near enough to excite a cell B and repeatedly and persistently takes part in firing it, some growth process or metabolic change takes place in one or both cells such that A's efficiency, as one of the cells firing B, is increased.

Hebb assumed that the most probable way of increasing the efficiency of cell A in firing B is by increasing the area of contact between the incoming axon and the receiving soma or dendrite. So the axon of the first cell develops synaptic knobs or enlarges already existing ones in contact with the receiving cell. Such structural changes in the cell assembly constitute **learning**. Hebb put forward such an assumption to account for permanence in memory, i.e., the fact that some memories are acquired immediately and retained henceforth for long periods of time. He theorized that permanent memories can only be ascribed to permanent modifications of the connectivity structure of the cell assembly and not just to the patterns of

74

activations of those cells. Based on his assumptions he then proceeded to develop a theory of perception and behavior that deals the problems of expectancy, attention, learning, generalization, memory, volition, emotion, hunger, pain, and so on.

Although the Hebbian rule is quite vague to be useful for practical applications, a lot of artificial neural training methods are based on the above philosophy or an extension of it. A natural extension is the following [38]:

Adjust the strength of the connection between units A and B in proportion to the product of their simultaneous activation.

This extension covers the general case of the neurons having positive and negative activation values. It came to be known as the *Hebbian rule*, although it is not exactly what Hebb originally proposed. In Hebb's philosophy the synaptic weights are a measure of the *correlation* between the activations of the units: if A and B are often simultaneously positive or simultaneously negative then they are positively correlated and, according to Hebb, their connection strength should increase (become more excitatory). However, if their activation levels are often of opposite sign, then their correlation is negative and their connection strength should decrease (become more inhibitory).

Let $x_k \in \mathbb{R}^n$, $k = 0, 1, 2, \ldots$, be the input excitation or inhibition vector into a neuron at time k, and let $y_k \in \mathbb{R}$ be the output of the neuron. Assume that $\{x_k\}$ is a wide-sense stationary stochastic process with mean $\mu = E\{x_k\}$ and positive-definite correlation

$$E\{x_k x_k^T\} = R_x.$$

Using this notation, the realization of the Hebbian rule in its simplest form is

$$w_{k+1} = w_k + \beta_k(y_k x_k), \tag{4.1}$$

where β_k is a sequence of small step-size parameters. Indeed, the term $y_k x_k$ expresses the correlation between the signals of this neuron and the signals of the neurons that drive its input. However, Eq. (4.1) is numerically unstable if x_k and y_k are linearly related:

$$y = w^T x. \tag{4.2}$$

This is a special case of the McCulloch-Pitts model (1.1) for $f(x) = x$ and $\theta = 0$. In this linear case the Hebbian rule becomes

$$\frac{\Delta w_k}{\beta_k} = x_k x_k^T w_k. \tag{4.3}$$

According to the theory of stochastic recursive equations [39, 40] (elaborated in Appendix A), (4.3) can be approximated, for large k, by the deterministic ordinary differential equation (ODE)

$$\frac{dw(t)}{dt} = R_x w(t), \tag{4.4}$$

where the relationship between k and t is

$$t = t(k) = \sum_{i=0}^{k} \beta_i. \tag{4.5}$$

Heuristically, (4.4) can be derived from (4.1) by the assumption that β_k is so small that we can ignore the variance of w_k compared to the variance of x_k for several iterations of (4.1). Thus, if we average (4.1) for K iterations, where K is a large number, we can assume that w_k is a constant and $\langle xx^T \rangle \approx R_x$, $\langle \Delta w \rangle \approx dw$, and $\beta \approx dt$, so (4.3) is transformed into (4.4). Also $t = \int dt \approx \sum \beta_i$, which yields the correspondence (4.5) between the time indices of the ODE and the original stochastic recursive equation.

Let us study (4.4) in more detail, and let us expand the vector $w(t)$ into a linear combination of the orthonormal basis $e_1, e_2, \ldots, e_n$, of eigenvectors of R_x:

$$w(t) = \sum_{i=1}^{n} \alpha_i(t)e_i. \tag{4.6}$$

We obtain

$$\sum_{i=1}^{n} \frac{d\alpha_i(t)}{dt} e_i = \sum_{i=1}^{n} \alpha_i(t)R_x e_i,$$

$$\frac{d\alpha_i(t)}{dt} = \lambda_i \alpha_i(t), \qquad i = 1, 2, \ldots, n. \tag{4.7}$$

The solution is obviously

$$\alpha_i(t) = \alpha_i(0)e^{\lambda_i t}$$

and $\lambda_i > 0$, for all i (since R_x is positive definite), so (4.7) is unstable for all i. Notice, however, that among all the coefficients α_i, α_1 grows fastest since it is associated with the largest eigenvalue λ_1. Thus, regardless of the initial conditions, from some point $t = T$ onward the first component will dominate in $w(t)$, and this dominance will only increase in time, albeit along with the increase in the norm of $w(t)$. Indeed, the projection of the unit vector $u(t) = w(t)/\|w(t)\|$ on the nonprincipal component subspace $\mathcal{L}_{\text{npc}} = \text{span}(e_2, \ldots, e_n)$ tends to zero:

$$\left\| \begin{bmatrix} e_2^T \\ \vdots \\ e_n^T \end{bmatrix} u(t) \right\|^2 = \frac{\sum_{i=2}^{n}(e_i^T w(t))^2}{\|w(t)\|^2} = \frac{\sum_{i=2}^{n} \alpha_i(t)^2}{\sum_{i=1}^{n} \alpha_i(t)^2}$$

$$= \frac{\sum_{i=2}^{n}(\alpha_i(0)/\alpha_1(0))e^{(\lambda_i - \lambda_1)t}}{1 + \sum_{i=2}^{n}(\alpha_i(0)/\alpha_1(0))e^{(\lambda_i - \lambda_1)t}}$$

$$\xrightarrow{t \to \infty} 0.$$

At the same time we have

$$\|w(t)\|^2 \xrightarrow{t \to \infty} \infty,$$

so the vector $w(t)$ tends to the principal component subspace but with ever-increasing magnitude. Thus, we can characterize (4.1) as an *unstable principal component analyzer* for the neuron's input signal.[1]

Equation (4.4) is a gradient ascent law,

$$\frac{dw}{dt} = \frac{\partial J}{\partial w},$$

on the output variance

$$J = E\{(w^T x)^2\} = w^T R_x w.$$

The energy function J is unbounded and w is unconstrained, so (4.4) naturally leads to $w \to \infty$.

An important attribute of Hebb's theory is locality.

Definition 4.1. A neural network learning rule will be called *local* if the equation updating the synaptic weight w_{ab} connecting neuron a with neuron b can be written in such a way as to involve only the activation values of a and b, and the value w_{ab}.

Indeed, the simple Hebbian law (4.1) is local since the synaptic strengths are modified using only information available at the point of synapse, i.e., the neuron activation y and the input value x_i (presumably being the activation of some other neuron). Locality is a very important property that will be referred to often in the following sections. It is also a necessary condition if a model wants to claim biological plausibility. Although it may be sometimes mathematically convenient to ignore locality, it is biologically unjustified to assume that a synapse gets modified taking into account the electrical activity of distant axons or dendrites.

The Hebbian rule has not been used in the above simple form. However, more sophisticated learning schemes have been proposed that modify the connections between neurons according to the locality principle. Such rules include the delta rule [41], the error back-propagation rule (or generalized delta rule) [42], stochastic learning rules (Boltzmann machines) [43], competitive learning rules [44], etc.

---

[1] A quicker, but less insightful, way to prove the instability of the simple Hebbian rule is to observe that the norm of w_k is increasing (if $w_0 \neq 0$):

$$\|w_{k+1}\|^2 = w_{k+1}^T w_{k+1} = w_k^T (I - x_k x_k^T)(I - x_k x_k^T) w_k$$
$$= \|w_k\|^2 + 2(w_k^T x_k)^2 + \|x_k\|^2 (w_k^T x_k)^2 \geq \|w_k\|^2,$$

and, in fact, $\|w_{k+1}\|^2 > \|w_k\|^2$ infinitely many times.

4.2   DERIVATIVES OF THE HEBBIAN RULE

From the above analysis it comes as no surprise that extensions of the Hebbian rule are at the heart of most neural net approaches proposed recently for solving the standard PC problem [12–14, 16–19, 45, 46] As we'll see in Section 4.5 another approach is the use of two-layer networks with linear units but with reduced number of hidden neurons.

4.2.1   Oja's Rule for a Single Principal Component

The simple Hebbian rule (4.1) results in w_k getting increasingly closer to the principal direction e_1, although the magnitude of w_k keeps increasing. If we could somehow keep the magnitude in check we could extract a vector proportional to e_1 without numerical instability. The *normalized Hebbian rule* [16, 20] does exactly that by a simple scaling:

$$\tilde{w}_{k+1} = w_k + \beta_k(y_k x_k), \tag{4.8}$$

$$w_{k+1} = \frac{\tilde{w}_{k+1}}{\|\tilde{w}_{k+1}\|} . \tag{4.9}$$

The normalization at each step, of course, prevents instability, and it is a common feature in many standard eigenvalue-related algorithms, such as the power iteration method (see Chapter 3). Since scaling does not affect the ratio of the coefficients α_i/α_j (refer to (4.6)), it is still expected that α_1 will dominate, and because w_k is kept normalized we shall avoid the instability. In fact we'll have $w_k \to e_1$.

The brute-force normalization of the Hebbian rule works but is less elegant than the learning rule proposed by Oja and Karhunen in 1982 [16, 20]. They proposed a linear single-unit network (see Fig. 4.1) that extracts just the first principal component adaptively from its input vector stochastic process $\{x_k\} \in \mathbb{R}^n$. The output value

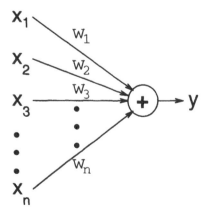

Figure 4.1. Oja's simplified neuron model.

$y \in \mathbb{R}$ is linearly related to the synaptic weights which form the vector $w \in \mathbb{R}^n$:

$$y = w^T x. \tag{4.10}$$

The proposed adaptation rule (referred to as *Oja's rule*) is

$$w_{k+1} = w_k + \beta_k(y_k x_k - y_k^2 w_k). \tag{4.11}$$

It is a linearized version of the normalized Hebbian rule, the Hebbian part being the input-output product $y_k x_k$, while the normalization part corresponding to the term $-y_k^2 w_k$. This can be established through a *linearization* procedure [16]: from (4.8) and (4.9) we obtain

$$\|\tilde{w}_{k+1}\|^2 = \tilde{w}_{k+1}^T \tilde{w}_{k+1} = 1 + 2\beta_k y_k^2 + \mathcal{O}(\beta_k^2),$$
$$w_{k+1} = \tilde{w}_{k+1}(1 + 2\beta_k y_k^2 + \mathcal{O}(\beta_k^2))^{-1/2}.$$

Approximating the inverse square root by a first-order Taylor expansion and ignoring β^2 terms, we get

$$w_{k+1} = \tilde{w}_{k+1}(1 - \beta_k y_k^2).$$

Substituting the right-hand side of (4.8) for $\tilde{w}_{k+1}$ we have

$$w_{k+1} = w_k + \beta_k(y_k x_k - y_k^2 w_k) - \beta_k^2 y_k^3 x_k.$$

Finally, ignoring the β_k^2 term we get the original Oja rule.

The following assumptions are used in the main theorem regarding the convergence of (4.11):

A.1 The input sequence $\{x_k\}$, is at least wide-sense stationary with autocorrelation matrix R_x, whose eigenvalues are positive, arranged in descending order, and the largest eigenvalue has multiplicity 1: $\lambda_1 > \lambda_2 \geq \ldots \geq \lambda_n > 0$. Let us denote the corresponding normalized eigenvectors (choose arbitrarily the sign) by $e_1, e_2, \ldots, e_n$.

A.2 The step-size parameter sequence β_k is such that

$$\beta_k \to 0 \quad \text{as } k \to \infty, \qquad \text{and} \qquad \sum_{k=0}^{\infty} \beta_k = \infty.$$

This assumption will be useful for showing the asymptotic convergence of the algorithm. Later we'll discuss the case where it doesn't hold.

Theorem 4.1. [16] Let Assumptions A.1 and A.2 hold, and further assume that $w_0^T e_1 \neq 0$. Then w_k of (4.11) converges to either e_1 or $-e_1$, with probability 1, as $k \to \infty$.

Proof. This theorem was analyzed in [47] and a sketch of the proof was also provided in [16]. We shall use results from stochastic approximation theory (see Appendix A), according to which the stochastic recursive equation (4.11) corresponds to the deterministic differential equation

$$\frac{dw(t)}{dt} = R_x w(t) - [w(t)^T R_x w(t)] w(t). \tag{4.12}$$

Let us write $w(t)$ as a linear combination of the basis vectors $e_1, e_2, \ldots, e_n$

$$w(t) = \sum_{i=1}^{n} \alpha_i(t) e_i$$

so that (4.12) becomes

$$\sum_{i=1}^{n} \frac{d\alpha_i(t)}{dt} e_i = \sum_{i=1}^{n} \alpha_i(t) \left[R_x e_i - \left(\sum_{j=1}^{n} \alpha_j(t)^2 e_j^T R_x e_j \right) e_i \right],$$

$$\frac{d\alpha_i(t)}{dt} = [\lambda_i - \sigma(t)] \alpha_i(t), \qquad i = 1, 2, \ldots, n. \tag{4.13}$$

where

$$\sigma(t) = w(t)^T R_x w(t) = \sum_{j=1}^{n} \lambda_j \alpha_j(t)^2.$$

From the assumption $a_1(0) \neq 0$, Eq. (4.13) implies $a_1(t) = a_1(0) e^{\lambda_1 t - \int \sigma dt} \neq 0$ for all t. Therefore the coefficient ratios $\alpha_i(t)/\alpha_1(t)$, $i = 2, \ldots, n$, are well defined and we have

$$\frac{d}{dt}\left(\frac{\alpha_i}{\alpha_1}\right) = \frac{d\alpha_i/dt}{\alpha_1} - \frac{\alpha_i \, d\alpha_1/dt}{\alpha_1^2} \tag{4.14}$$

$$= [\lambda_i - \sigma]\frac{\alpha_i}{\alpha_1} - [\lambda_1 - \sigma]\frac{\alpha_i}{\alpha_1} \tag{4.15}$$

$$= [\lambda_i - \lambda_1]\frac{\alpha_i}{\alpha_1}. \tag{4.16}$$

so $\lim_{t \to \infty}(\alpha_i/\alpha_1) \to 0$, since $[\lambda_i - \lambda_1] < 0$,
    Also

$$\frac{d(\|w\|^2)}{dt} = 2w^T \frac{dw}{dt} = 2w^T R_x w(1 - \|w\|^2). \tag{4.17}$$

Thus for any vector w,

$$0 \neq \|w\|^2 < 1 \Rightarrow \frac{d(\|w\|^2)}{dt} > 0, \tag{4.18}$$

$$\|w\|^2 = 1 \Rightarrow \frac{d(\|w\|^2)}{dt} = 0, \tag{4.19}$$

$$\|w\|^2 > 1 \Rightarrow \frac{d(\|w\|^2)}{dt} < 0. \tag{4.20}$$

Equation (4.17) has no other fixed points except for $\|w\| = 0$ and $\|w\| = 1$. With the assumption $w(0) \neq 0$, Eqs. (4.18) through (4.20) imply

$$\lim_{t \to \infty} \|w(t)\|^2 = 1.$$

Hence, $\alpha_1(t) \to 1$ and $a_i(t) \to 0$, $i = 2, \ldots, n$.   ∎

It is worth noting that even if R_x is positive semidefinite, as long as $\lambda_1 > 0$ with multiplicity 1, the theorem still holds. The only part that could be affected is that the strict inequalities (4.18) and (4.20) would become $\geq$ or $\leq$, respectively, because $w(t)^T R_x w(t) \geq 0$. However, equality is not possible because $a_1(t) > 0$ for all t, so $w(t)^T R_x w(t) = \sum_{i=1}^{n} \lambda_1 \alpha_1^2(t) > 0$.

Clearly, any fixed point $w \neq 0$ of (4.12) must be an eigenvector of R_x. The norm of such a point would be determined from the equation $0 = \lambda_i \|w\| e_i - (\lambda_i \|w\|^2) \|w\| e_i$, so $\|w\| = 1$. Conversely, $w = 0$ and all unit-length eigenvectors of R_x are fixed points of (4.12).

From the proof of Theorem 4.1 it becomes clear that the choice of $\sigma(t)$ in the stabilizing term $-\sigma(t) w(t)$ is not important, as far as the dynamics of the ratios $\alpha_i(t)/\alpha_1(t)$ are concerned, since σ cancels in (4.16). Yet σ is very important in terms of stability. Oja chooses $\sigma(t) = w(t)^T R_x w(t)$, which leads to $\|w(t)\| \to 1$. The simple Hebbian rule (without normalization) has $\sigma(t) = 0$, which leads to $\|w(t)\| \to \infty$.

On that, we can show the following

Theorem 4.2. Consider the ODE

$$\frac{dw}{dt} = R_x w - (w^T B w) w, \tag{4.21}$$

where R_x is positive semidefinite with largest eigenvalue $\lambda_1 > 0$ of multiplicity 1, and B is positive definite. Let e_1 be the normalized principal eigenvector of R_x, and assume $e_1^T w(0) \neq 0$. Then $\lim_{t \to \infty} w(t) = \pm \alpha_1^* e_1$, where $\alpha_1^* = \sqrt{\lambda_1 / e_1^T B e_1}$.

Proof. We follow the proof of Theorem 4.1 with some modifications. Positive semi-definiteness of R_x is not a problem as discussed above. Now $\sigma = w^T B w$, but still $\alpha_i(t)/\alpha_1(t) \to 0$ as $t \to \infty$. Thus, for every $\varepsilon > 0$ there is a time T such that

$|\alpha_i(t)/\alpha_1(t)| < \varepsilon$, for all $t \geq T$. So

$$\sigma(t) = \alpha_1(t)^2[e_1^T B e_1] + \sum_{i \neq 1} \alpha_1(t)\alpha_i(t)[e_1^T B e_i] + \sum_{i,j \neq 1} \alpha_i(t)\alpha_j(t)[e_i^T B e_j],$$

$$\alpha_1(t)^2[e_1^T B e_1] - \varepsilon M_1 - \varepsilon^2 M_2 \leq \sigma(t) \leq \alpha_1(t)^2[e_1^T B e_1] + \varepsilon M_1 + \varepsilon^2 M_2$$

for all $t \geq T$, where $M_1 = \sum_{i \neq 1} |e_1^T B e_i|$ and $M_2 = \sum_{i,j \neq 1} |e_i^T B e_j|$.
Equation (4.13) yields

$$\frac{d(\alpha_1^2)}{dt} = 2\alpha_1 \frac{d\alpha_1}{dt} = 2[\lambda_1 - \sigma]\alpha_1^2,$$

$$[\lambda_1 - (e_1^T B e_1 + \varepsilon M_1 + \varepsilon^2 M_2)\alpha_1^2]\alpha_1^2$$

$$\leq \frac{d(\alpha_1^2)}{dt} \leq [\lambda_1 - (e_1^T B e_1 - \varepsilon M_1 - \varepsilon^2 M_2)\alpha_1^2]\alpha_1^2,$$

$$\alpha_1^2 < \frac{\lambda_1}{e_1^T B e_1 + \varepsilon M_1 + \varepsilon^2 M_2} \Rightarrow \frac{d(\alpha_1^2)}{dt} > 0,$$

$$\alpha_1^2 > \frac{\lambda_1}{e_1^T B e_1 - \varepsilon M_1 - \varepsilon^2 M_2} \Rightarrow \frac{d(\alpha_1^2)}{dt} < 0,$$

so

$$\frac{\lambda_1}{e_1^T B e_1 + \varepsilon M_1 + \varepsilon^2 M_2} \leq \lim_{t \to \infty} a_1(t)^2 \leq \frac{\lambda_1}{e_1^T B e_1 - \varepsilon M_1 - \varepsilon^2 M_2}.$$

Since ε can be arbitrarily small we have $\lim_{t \to \infty} \alpha_1(t)^2 = \lambda_1/e_1^T B e_1$. ∎

Yuille et al. [48], have suggested a rule like (4.21) with $\sigma = \|w(t)\|^2 = w^T w$ ($B = I$), which leads to $w \to \pm\sqrt{\lambda_1}e_1$. The advantage of Oja's rule over Yuille's rule is that it updates the synaptic weights using only information local to the synapse, namely, the membrane potential y of the receiving neuron and the signal x_i from the transmitting neuron. In contrast, Yuille's rule involves the norm $\|w\|^2 = w_1^2 + \cdots + w_n^2$, which uses global synaptic weight information.

The drawback of rules like (4.21), in general, is that they cannot be trivially extended to extract more than one component. By just replicating Oja's network for example, each of the neurons will simply extract independently the first component. It is clear that some kind of interaction between the units is necessary if many orthogonal components are to be extracted.

4.2.2 The Generalized Hebbian Algorithm (GHA)

Sanger [46] proposed the *Generalized Hebbian Algorithm* (GHA), a multi-component method equal to Oja's rule for the first component, but also capable of extracting the rest of the eigenvectors in unit length. The model has m output neurons $y_1, \ldots, y_m$ and n inputs $x_1, \ldots, x_n$. There are only feedforward connections between input and output and the output is a linear function of the input

$$y_i = w_i^T x. \tag{4.22}$$

The updating equations for neuron i ($i = 1, \ldots, m$) are

$$\Delta w_{ij,k} = \beta_k \left(y_{ik} x_{jk} - y_{ik} \sum_{l \leq i} y_{lk} w_{lj,k} \right), \tag{4.23}$$

where $w_i = [w_{i1} \quad w_{i2} \quad \cdots \quad w_{in}]^T$.

The model extracts the first m principal normalized eigenvectors of R_x under the slightly modified Assumption A.1′ and Assumption A.2.

A.1′ Same as A.1, except that the m largest eigenvalues are distinct: $\lambda_1 > \cdots > \lambda_m \geq \lambda_{m+1} \geq \cdots \geq \lambda_n > 0$.

Consider the ODE associated with (4.23):

$$\frac{dw_i}{dt} = R_x w_i - \sum_{j<i} w_j w_j^T R_x w_i - w_i^T R_x w_i w_i, \qquad i = 1, \ldots, m, \tag{4.24}$$

We need to show that $\lim_{t \to \infty} w_1 = \pm e_1$, $\lim_{t \to \infty} w_2 = \pm e_2$, ..., $\lim_{t \to \infty} w_m = \pm e_m$. The proof is by induction (following [14]).

The first unit is adapted with Oja's law. Therefore, $w_{1k} \to \pm e_1$ as $k \to \infty$.

Assume that the first $m - 1$ units have extracted the first $m - 1$ normalized eigenvectors; i.e., $w_i = \pm e_i$, $i = 1, \ldots, m - 1$. Equation (4.24) becomes

$$\frac{dw_m}{dt} = \left(I - \sum_{j<m} e_j e_j^T \right) R_x w_m - (w_m^T R_x w_m) w_m$$

$$= \bar{R}_x w_m - \sigma w_m, \tag{4.25}$$

where $\bar{R}_x = \left(I - \sum_{j<m} e_m e_m^T \right) R_x$ and $\sigma = w_m^T R_x w_m$ is a positive-definite function of w_m. Notice that $\bar{R}_x$ is the result of m-times deflation of R_x (see Section 2.2.8). Therefore, the eigenvalues of $\bar{R}_x$ are $[0, \ldots, 0, \lambda_m, \lambda_{m+1}, \ldots, \lambda_n]$. According to the analysis in Section 4.2.1, w_m will converge to some vector $\mu e_m \neq 0$ parallel to the mth eigendirection. The factor μ is easy to establish from the equilibrium condition of (4.24):

$$0 = \mu \bar{R}_x e_m - (\mu^2 e_m^T R_x e_m) \mu e_m,$$

$$0 = \lambda_m - \mu^2 \lambda_m,$$

$$\mu = \pm 1,$$

so $\|w_m\| = 1$ and $w_m \to \pm e_m$, as $t \to \infty$.

Of course, the units are not trained one after the other but in parallel. The first unit is independent of the others, it follows Oja's single unit rule, and thus it will converge extracting the first component. The second unit will start converging no later than the first unit converges, the third unit will start converging no later than the first and second units converge, etc. The induction argument for the mth unit applies posterior to the convergence of the $m - 1$ units. This is not very rigorous since convergence does not happen at a finite time but asymptotically as $t \to \infty$. Still we believe that the inductive argument is educational because it explicates the role of deflation in the extraction of multiple components. We'll see that this role is more than coincidental and deflation is intimately related to the problem.

Using a more rigorous approach, Hornik and Kuan [49] have shown that the only asymptotically stable equilibria of GHA are the points $W = [w_1, \ldots, w_m]^T = [\pm e_1, \ldots, \pm e_m]^T$ while all other equilibria are unstable.

Equation (4.23) is a nonlocal updating rule since the synaptic weight w_{ij} between input i and neuron j is updated using the activation values y_l of other neurons $l = 0, \ldots, i - 1$. This has been a criticism for the biological plausibility of GHA [17].

Sanger [14] responded to this criticism by regrouping the terms in (4.23):

$$\Delta w_{ij,k} = \beta_k \left(y_{ik} \left[x_{jk} - \sum_{l<i} y_{lk} w_{lj,k} \right] - y_{ik}^2 w_{ij,k} \right). \tag{4.26}$$

He claimed that this regrouping is a local implementation of GHA and is equivalent to Oja's single-unit rule on the modified input

$$x^{(i)} = x - \sum_{l<i} y_l w_l$$

since we can now write

$$\Delta w_{ij,k} = \beta_k (y_{ik} x_{jk}^{(i)} - y_{ik}^2 w_{ij,k}). \tag{4.27}$$

Unfortunately this claim is confusing, and the source of this confusion is the lack of definition for the y_i's. Notice that if

$$y_i = w_i^T x$$

as in (4.22) in the original GHA, then the algorithm is still nonlocal for exactly the same reasons as explained above. It is also not equivalent to Oja's rule because for that to be the case we should have $y_i = w_i^T x^{(i)}$.

If, on the other hand, we do have

$$y_i = w_i^T x^{(i)},$$

then the algorithm is local and equivalent to Oja's rule on the modified input $x^{(i)}$, but it is not the original GHA any more!

In the following we shall assume that the second case holds, and we shall ignore the noninteresting first case. The new rule will be referred to as the local GHA, keeping in mind that it is a modified version of the original GHA. The network implementation of this local GHA rule is shown in Figure 4.2.

Notice that the correlation matrix $R_{x^{(i)}}$ of $x^{(i)}$ is given by

$$R_{x^{(i)}} = \left(I - \sum_{l<i} w_l w_l^T \right) R_x \left(I - \sum_{l<i} w_l w_l^T \right) \tag{4.28}$$

Again using induction we assume that the weights prior to w_m have converged to $\pm e_1, \ldots, \pm e_{m-1}$, so the matrix $R_{x^{(m)}}$ is the m-fold deflation of R_x with eigenvalues $[0, \ldots, 0, \lambda_m, \ldots, \lambda_n]$ and principal eigenvector e_m. So w_m will converge to $\pm e_m$, thus establishing the validity of the induction step. The induction basis is again the argument that for $m = 1$ the algorithm (4.27) is simply Oja's rule with input $= x$, so $w_1 \to \pm e_1$.

4.2.3 Földiák's Rule

Another extension of Oja's model to the multicomponent extraction problem was carried out by Földiák [17]. The proposed model has m output neurons with feedforward connections from input to output and full connectivity of the output neurons (Fig. 4.3). The output activations are

$$y_i = w_i^T x - \sum_{j \neq i} c_{ij} y_j. \tag{4.29}$$

Clearly, if we let $y = [y_1 \quad \cdots \quad y_m]^T$, $W = [w_1 \quad \cdots \quad w_m]^T$, and

$$C = \begin{bmatrix} 0 & c_{12} & \cdots & \cdots & c_{1m} \\ c_{21} & 0 & c_{23} & \cdots & c_{2m} \\ \vdots & & \ddots & & \vdots \\ c_{m-1,1} & \cdots & c_{m-1,m-2} & 0 & c_{m-1,m} \\ c_{m1} & \cdots & \cdots & c_{m,m-1} & 0 \end{bmatrix},$$

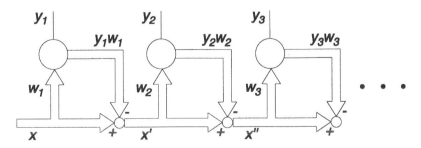

Figure 4.2. The network model implementing the local GHA rule.

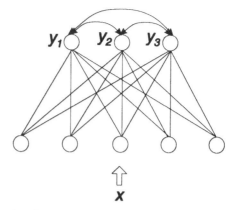

Figure 4.3. Földiák's network has full connectivity among different output neurons. There are no self-loops.

then

$$y = (I + C)^{-1}Wx \equiv Fx.$$

The matrix $F \in \mathbb{R}^{m \times n}$ is the total transfer function from input to output.

The learning rule for the feedforward weights is equal to Oja's law, while the lateral weights are trained with a simple Hebbian inhibition law

$$\Delta w_{ij,k} = \beta_k(y_{ik}x_{jk} - y_{ik}^2 w_{ij,k}), \tag{4.30}$$

$$\Delta c_{ij,k} = \beta_k y_{ik} y_{jk} \qquad (i \neq j). \tag{4.31}$$

The system "learns" the same subspace spanned by the m principal components. In other words, the span of the vectors $w_1, \ldots, w_m$ tends to the span$(e_1, \ldots, e_m)$, although the final vectors are not the components themselves.

The symmetric lateral coupling of the output units proposed by Földiák has the disadvantage of introducing feedback, so in order to compute y one has to perform matrix inversion $(I + C)^{-1}$. This destroys the appealing property of performing only local computations. The recursive computation of y through the equation $y_{i+1} = Cy_i + Wx$ is not really an alternative: in order for this iteration to be stable, C must have all eigenvalues less than 1, a condition not guaranteed by the algorithm [49]. Later we shall see how all these problems can be amended with the use of lateral asymmetric connection network [18, 50].

4.2.4 The Subspace Rule for Multiple Components

This rule was first mentioned by Karhunen and Oja [20] as a stochastic KL technique without expanding it any further. It was later proposed by Baldi [51] as a simplification of the back-propagation algorithm for a two-layer autoassociative network, and analyzed by Oja [45] as a multicomponent extension of the single-unit learning rule (4.11).

Let $W = [w_1 \quad \cdots \quad w_m]^T \in \mathbb{R}^{n \times m}$, $m < n$, be the feedforward weights from input $x \in \mathbb{R}^n$ to output $y \in \mathbb{R}^m$ (Fig. 4.4):

$$y = Wx. \tag{4.32}$$

The learning rule is

$$\Delta W_k = \beta_k(y_k x_k^T - y_k y_k^T W_k), \tag{4.33}$$

which leads to the ODE

$$\frac{dW}{dt} = WR_x - (WR_x W^T)W. \tag{4.34}$$

The first term in (4.34) corresponds to the partial derivative $\partial J_1 / \partial W$ of the output variance

$$J_1 = \frac{1}{2} \text{tr}(WR_x W^T) = \frac{1}{2} \sum_{i=1}^{m} E\{(w_i^T x)^2\}.$$

Hence, the first term is a gradient ascent term pushing the system into maximizing the variance, while the second term $-(WR_x W^T)W$ is a stabilization term to avoid "explosion" of the weights.

Clearly the single-unit Oja rule (4.11) is a special case of (4.33) for $m = 1$. The fixed points of (4.34) satisfy the condition

$$WR_x = WR_x W^T W. \tag{4.35}$$

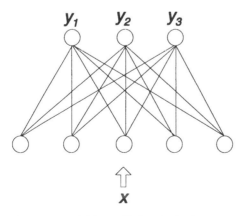

Figure 4.4. The subspace model for multiple principal component extraction.

If rank(W) = m there are m independent rows in the matrix WR_x which are eigenvectors of $W^T W$ associated with eigenvalue 1. Thus the $W^T W$ has $\lambda_1 = 1$ with multiplicity m. Since rank($W^T W$) = m all other eigenvalues must be zero; namely $\lambda_2 = 0$ with multiplicity $n - m$. So $W^T W$ is a projection matrix.

We'll show next that W will eventually span the same subspace as the first m principal eigenvectors. To that end, let us define the partition of the eigenvector matrix $E = [E_1 \mid E_2] = [e_1 \quad \cdots \quad e_m \mid e_{m+1} \quad \cdots \quad e_n]$, $E_1 \in \mathbb{R}^{n \times m}$, $E_2 \in \mathbb{R}^{n \times (n-m)}$, and let us decompose W into the unique sum

$$W = A_1 E_1^T + A_2 E_2^T,$$

where $A_1 \in \mathbb{R}^{m \times m}$, $A_2 \in \mathbb{R}^{m \times (n-m)}$. Postmultiplying (4.34) with E_1 and E_2 we obtain

$$\frac{dA_1}{dt} = A_1 \Lambda_1 - \Sigma A_1, \tag{4.36}$$

$$\frac{dA_2}{dt} = A_2 \Lambda_2 - \Sigma A_2, \tag{4.37}$$

with $\Lambda_1 = \text{diag}[\lambda_1, \ldots, \lambda_m]$, $\Lambda_2 = \text{diag}[\lambda_{m+1}, \ldots, \lambda_n]$, and $\Sigma = WR_x W^T$.

As with the proof of the single-unit rule we proceed to examine the time evolution of the "ratio" $Q(t) = A_1(t)^{-1} A_2(t)$. Assuming $A_1(0)$ = nonsingular (4.36) implies $A_1(t)$ = nonsingular for all t the term $A_1^{-1} A_2$ is well-defined. As shown in Appendix B, $d(A_1^{-1})/dt = -A_1^{-1}(dA_1/dt)A_1^{-1}$, so

$$\begin{aligned}
\frac{dQ}{dt} &= A_1^{-1} \frac{dA_2}{dt} - A_1^{-1} \frac{dA_1}{dt} A_1^{-1} A_2 \\
&= A_1^{-1} A_2 \Lambda_2 - \Lambda_1 A_1^{-1} A_2 \\
&= Q \Lambda_2 - \Lambda_1 Q. \tag{4.38}
\end{aligned}$$

The solution is

$$Q(t) = e^{-\Lambda_1 t} Q(0) e^{\Lambda_2 t}, \tag{4.39}$$

$$q_{ij}(t) = e^{(\lambda_{m+j} - \lambda_i)t} q_{ij}(0). \tag{4.40}$$

Since $\lambda_{m+j} < \lambda_i$ for all $i = 1, \ldots, m$, $j = 1, \ldots, n - m$, we conclude that $Q(t) \to 0$, as $t \to \infty$. So $W \to A_1(\infty) E_1^T$ for some nonsingular matrix $A_1(\infty)$, and span(W^T) = span(E_1).

A different proof has been recently provided in [52].

Like Földiák's model the subspace method does not extract the exact components but finds the subspace spanned by them. Unlike Földiák's model, however, there is no feedback involved and the computation of the output from the input is straightforward.

Is the subspace rule local? Let us take a closer look at (4.33): expanding this equation for the weight w_{ij} connecting input x_j with output y_i we obtain

$$\Delta w_{ij} = \beta \left(y_i x_j - y_i \sum_{l=0}^{m} y_l w_{lj} \right).$$

The subspace rule is not local because it involves more than the values y_i, x_j, and w_{ij}.

4.2.5 Rubner's Model

Rubner and Tavan [19] and Rubner and Schulten [13] proposed a single-layer model with a lateral network among the output units (Fig. 4.5). Unlike Földiák's model, Rubner et al. suggested that the lateral network is not symmetrically connected, but that the units are hierarchically (asymmetrically) organized: unit 1 drives all other units, unit 2 drives all other units except 1, etc. In general, unit i drives all other units except $1, \ldots, i - 1$.

The output vector $y = [y_1, \ldots, y_m]^T$ is given by the formula

$$y = Wx - Cy, \tag{4.41}$$

$$C = \begin{bmatrix} 0 & \cdots & & \cdots & 0 \\ c_{21} & 0 & \cdots & \cdots & 0 \\ \vdots & & \ddots & & \vdots \\ c_{m-1,1} & \cdots & c_{m-1,m-2} & 0 & 0 \\ c_{m,1} & \cdots & \cdots & c_{m,m-1} & 0 \end{bmatrix}. \tag{4.42}$$

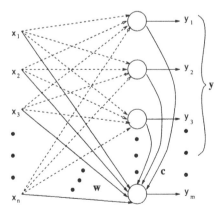

Figure 4.5. Rubner and Tavan proposed a single-layer model with hierarchical lateral connections among the output units. Unit 1 feeds units 2 through n, unit 2 feeds units 3 through n, etc. The feedforward weights are trained using the brute-force normalized Hebbian rule, while the lateral weights are trained using a simple Hebbian rule with a minus sign (called the anti-Hebbian rule).

The feedforward weights $W = [w_1 \quad \cdots \quad w_m]^T$, are trained with the normalized Hebbian rule

$$\tilde{w}_{ij,k} = w_{ij,k} + \beta y_{ik} x_{jk}, \tag{4.43}$$

$$w_{i,k+1} = \frac{\tilde{w}_{ik}}{\|\tilde{w}_{ik}\|}, \tag{4.44}$$

while the lateral weights are trained with the *anti-Hebbian rule*

$$\Delta c_{ij,k} = \beta y_{ik} y_{jk}, \qquad i > j. \tag{4.45}$$

It was shown that the network converges to the first normalized principal eigenvectors $w_i \rightarrow \pm e_i$, $i = 1, \ldots, m$. However, the learning rule is not local in each synapse since the computation of $\|w\|$ requires the sum of the squared weights in all the synapses of the neuron. If we replace the brute-force normalized Hebbian rule (4.43), (4.44) by the linearized version of Oja—namely, if we define

$$\Delta w_{ij,k} = \beta_k (y_{ik} x_{jk} - y_{ik}^2 w_{ij,k}) \tag{4.46}$$

—then the algorithm becomes local.

The introduction of the hierarchical lateral connection network and the use of the Hebbian rule for the lateral weights (the anti-Hebbian rule) are two important contributions of the model. Not only does the network extract the exact eigenvectors (unlike the subspace rule or Földiák's rule), but it also turns out that such a lateral connection network can be useful in many situations involving orthogonalization of weights, as we shall see later.

4.2.6 The APEX Model

Kung and Diamantaras [18] proposed another multiple principal component model called APEX (Adaptive Principal component EXtraction), employing the same lateral connection topology as Rubner's model but using Oja's single-unit rule to train both lateral and feedforward weights (Fig. 4.6):

$$y = Wx - Cy, \tag{4.47}$$

$$C = \begin{bmatrix} 0 & \cdots & \cdots & \cdots & 0 \\ c_{21} & 0 & \cdots & \cdots & 0 \\ \vdots & & \ddots & & \vdots \\ c_{m-1,1} & \cdots & c_{m-1,m-2} & 0 & 0 \\ c_{m,1} & \cdots & \cdots & c_{m,m-1} & 0 \end{bmatrix},$$

$$\Delta w_{ij,k} = \beta_k (y_{ik} x_{jk} - y_{ik}^2 w_{ij,k}), \tag{4.48}$$

$$\Delta c_{ij,k} = \beta_k (y_{ik} y_{jk} - y_{ik}^2 c_{ij,k}), \qquad i > j. \tag{4.49}$$

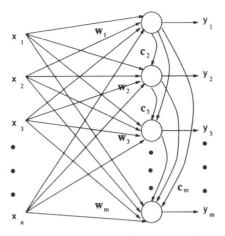

Figure 4.6. The structure of the APEX network.

Inspecting Eqs. (4.48) and (4.49) we observe that the APEX rule is local. Equation (4.48) constitutes the Hebbian part of the algorithm and works toward maximizing the correlation between input and output, since Wx contributes with a positive sign in y. On the other hand, Eq. (4.49) is the anti-Hebbian part of the algorithm, which works towards minimizing the correlation between input and output due to the negative sign of $-Cy$ in y. We also call (4.49) the *orthogonalization rule*, and as we'll see later it is closely related to the Gram-Schmidt orthogonalization procedure.

Theorem 4.3 [50, 53]. Consider the algorithm defined in Eqs. (4.48) and (4.49) subject to the conditions A.1′, A.2, and let $W = [w_1 \quad \cdots \quad w_m]^T$. Then with probability 1, $w_{ik} \to \pm e_i$ and $c_{ij,k} \to 0$, $i = 1, \ldots, m$, $j = 1, \ldots, i - 1$, as $k \to \infty$.

Proof. As with GHA, the proof will be done by induction.

The first unit is trained with Oja's rule (there are no lateral weights affecting it), so $w_{1k} \to \pm e_1$, as $k \to \infty$.

Assume that the first $m - 1$ units have extracted the first $m - 1$ components and the lateral weights to these units have vanished; i.e., $w_i = \pm e_i$, $c_{ij} = 0$, $i = 1, \ldots, m - 1$, $j = 1, \ldots, i - 1$. Then

$$y_m = w_m^T x - \sum_{j<m} c_{mj} y_j = q_m^T x, \tag{4.50}$$

$$q_m \equiv w_m - \sum_{j<m} c_{mj} e_j. \tag{4.51}$$

The associated ODEs for (4.48),(4.49) are as follows:

$$\frac{dw_m(t)}{dt} = R_x w_m(t) - \sum_{j<m} R_x e_j c_{mj}(t) - \sigma(t) w_m(t)$$

$$= R_x w_m(t) - \sum_{j<m} \lambda_j e_j c_{mj}(t) - \sigma(t) w_m(t), \tag{4.52}$$

$$\frac{dc_{mi}(t)}{dt} = e_i^T R_x w_m(t) - \sum_{j<m} e_i^T R_x e_j c_{mj}(t) - \sigma(t)c_{mi}(t)$$

$$= \lambda_i e_i^T w_m(t) - \lambda_i c_{mi}(t) - \sigma(t)c_{mi}(t), \qquad i < m, \tag{4.53}$$

where

$$\sigma(t) \equiv q_m(t)^T R_x q_m(t). \tag{4.54}$$

Let us expand

$$w_m(t) = \sum_{i=1}^{n} \alpha_i(t)e_i$$

to obtain from (4.52) and (4.53)

$$\begin{bmatrix} \dfrac{d\alpha_i(t)}{dt} \\[2mm] \dfrac{dc_{mi}(t)}{dt} \end{bmatrix} = \begin{bmatrix} \lambda_i - \sigma(t) & -\lambda_i \\ \lambda_i & -\lambda_i - \sigma(t) \end{bmatrix} \begin{bmatrix} \alpha_i(t) \\ c_{mi}(t) \end{bmatrix},$$

$$i = 1, \dots, m - 1 \tag{4.55}$$

$$\frac{d\alpha_i(t)}{dt} = \left[\lambda_i - \sigma(t)\right]\alpha_i(t), \qquad i = m, \dots, n. \tag{4.56}$$

Equation (4.55) has a double eigenvalue at $-\sigma(t) = -q_m(t)^T R_x q_m(t) \le 0$. We will show that $q(t) \ne 0$ for all t. Thus $-\sigma(t) < 0$ and the globally asymptotically stable solution of (4.55) is 0. Indeed, $q(t) = 0$ implies $w_m(t) = \sum_{i<m} \alpha_i e_i$, so $w_m(t) \in \text{span}(e_1, \dots, e_{m-1})$. However, from the assumption $w_m(0)^T e_m = \alpha_m(0) \ne 0$, (4.56) implies $a_m(t) = a_m(0)e^{\lambda_m t - \int \sigma\, dt} \ne 0$ for all t, so $w_m(t) \notin \text{span}(e_1, \dots, e_{m-1})$. Therefore

$$\alpha_i(t) \to 0 \quad \text{and} \quad c_{mi}(t) \to 0, \qquad i < m \tag{4.57}$$

as $t \to \infty$.

Multiplying (4.53) from the left by e_i, and subtracting from (4.52) for all $i < m$, we obtain

$$\frac{dq_m}{dt} = \left(I - \sum_{j<m} e_j e_j^T\right) R_x q_m - (q_m^T R_x q_m)q_m \tag{4.58}$$

Equation (4.58) is of the same type as (4.21), so

$$q_m(t) = w_m(t) - \sum_{j<m} c_{mj}(t)e_j \to \pm e_m,$$

$$(4.57) \Rightarrow w(t) \to \pm e_m, \qquad \text{as } t \to \infty. \qquad \blacksquare \tag{4.59}$$

The variance of the ith output neuron ($i = 1, 2, \ldots, m,$) tends to the ith principal eigenvalue λ_i, since

$$E\{(w_{ik}^T x_k)^2\} \rightarrow e_i^T R_x e_i = \lambda_i.$$

As with Sanger's model, the neurons do not converge in finite time, so it is not quite rigorous to assume that units $1, \ldots, m - 1$ have converged before unit m does. Still this inductive argument has tutorial value since it exposes in a simple way the structure of the algorithm without getting lost in details. For the interested reader a more rigorous proof is provided in [54].

Learning Rate   As we discussed in the proof of Theorem 4.3, the decay rate for $c_{mi}(t)$ as well as $\alpha_i(t)$, $i = 1, \ldots, m - 1$, is $-\sigma(t)$. Given that the discrete-time parameters approach the continuous-time ones with the relationship between the two time indices defined in (4.5), we can approximate the decay rate for the discrete-time parameters:

$$\frac{c_{mi,k} - c_{mi,k-1}}{t(k) - t(k-1)} = -\sigma(t(k))c_{mi,k-1},$$

Since $t(k) - t(k-1) = \beta_k$,

$$c_{mi,k} = [1 - \beta_k \sigma_k]c_{mi,k-1}, \tag{4.60}$$

where $\sigma_k = \sigma(t(k)) = E\{y_k^2\}$. Similarly,

$$\alpha_{ik} = [1 - \beta_k \sigma_k]\alpha_{i,k-1}, \qquad i = 1, \ldots, m - 1, \tag{4.61}$$

$$\alpha_{ik} = [1 - \beta_k(\sigma_k - \lambda_i)]\alpha_{i,k-1}, \qquad i = m, \ldots, n. \tag{4.62}$$

From (4.62) we can also derive the rate of decay of the component ratio:

$$r_i = \alpha_i / \alpha_m, \qquad i = m + 1, \ldots, n,$$

$$r_{ik} = \frac{1 - \beta_k(\sigma_k - \lambda_i)}{1 - \beta_k(\sigma_k - \lambda_m)} r_{i,k-1}. \tag{4.63}$$

The decay rate for component i is maximized if we set $\beta_k = 1/(\sigma_k - \lambda_i)$, $i = m + 1, \ldots, n$. Although λ_i is unknown we have $\lambda_i > 0$ for all i, so a seemingly conservative value for the step-size parameter is

$$\beta_k = \frac{1}{\sigma_k}. \tag{4.64}$$

We shall see that this is the optimum least-squares value.

The Learning Rate and Recursive Least Squares (RLS)   Principal component analysis is a mean squares optimization problem. So naturally, we expect that there be a close relationship between recursive PCA learning models and the well-known RLS algorithm [55], which is the recursive solution to the least-squares optimization problem

$$\text{minimize } J_{LS}(w) = \sum_{k=1}^{M} \|y_k - w^T x_k\|^2 \tag{4.65}$$

Establishing such a relationship will not only be educational but useful for speeding up the neural net algorithm. The requirement of stochastic approximation methods in general is to use very small values of β so that the iterative equation may approximate an associated differential equation. As a result, small values of β lead to slow convergence. On the contrary, least-squares methods determine the optimal recursive formula, including the best step-size parameter, for updating the solution from iteration k to $k + 1$.

In PCA the cost to be minimized for the mth component is

$$\text{minimize } J_m(w) = E\{\|x - ww^T (I - W^T W)x\|^2\}, \tag{4.66}$$

where $W = [e_1 \quad \cdots \quad e_{m-1}]^T$ is a fixed matrix of the principal $m - 1$ components. Indeed,

$$\begin{aligned} J_m(w) &= \text{tr}(R_x) - 2\,\text{tr}(ww^T \tilde{R}_x) + \text{tr}(ww^T \tilde{R}_x ww^T) \\ &= \|\tilde{R}_x^{1/2} - ww^T \tilde{R}_x^{1/2}\|_F^2 + \text{tr}(R_x - \tilde{R}_x), \end{aligned} \tag{4.67}$$

where

$$\begin{aligned} \tilde{R}_x &= (I - W^T W)R_x = (I - W^T W)R_x(I - W^T W) \\ &= \sum_{i=m}^{n} e_i \lambda_i e_i^T \end{aligned} \tag{4.68}$$

is the m-times deflated matrix R_x. From the PCA Theorem 3.1 it follows that the optimal w is $\pm e_m$, since e_m is the principal eigenvector of $\tilde{R}_x$.

In order to relate the above mean square cost J_m with least squares we first transform it into a nonstochastic formulation, replacing the expectation by (weighted) average

$$\tilde{J}_m(w, N) = \frac{1}{N+1} \sum_{k=0}^{N} \gamma^{N-k} \|x_k - wy_k\|^2, \tag{4.69}$$

$$y = w^T x - w^T W^T W x,$$

where $0 < \gamma \leq 1$ is a forgetting factor chosen by the user. We shall define

$$c \equiv Ww \tag{4.70}$$

to obtain

$$y = w^T x - c^T W x, \tag{4.71}$$

which is the input-output mapping for the mth neuron in the APEX model.

$\tilde{J}_m(w, N)$ can be minimized iteratively using the RLS algorithm, which yields the following updating equations:

$$w_{k+1} = w_k + \varepsilon_k(x_k - w_k y_k), \tag{4.72}$$

$$\varepsilon_k = \left[\sum_{i=0}^{k} \gamma^{k-i} y_i^2\right]^{-1} y_k. \tag{4.73}$$

Letting

$$\beta_k = \frac{1}{\sum_{i=0}^{k} \gamma^{k-i} y_i^2} \tag{4.74}$$

the RLS algorithm becomes

$$\Delta w_k = \beta_k(y_k x_k - y_k^2 w_k), \tag{4.75}$$

which is the same as the APEX equation (4.48). The only difference is that now we have a specific choice (4.74) for β_k, which is optimal in the sense of the criterion $\tilde{J}_m(w, N)$. This optimal choice of the step-size parameter has a profound impact in the convergence speed of the algorithm, as will be discussed in Section 4.4. Clearly β can also be calculated iteratively by

$$\beta_k = \frac{\beta_{k-1}}{\gamma + y_k^2 \beta_{k-1}}. \tag{4.76}$$

The value of the forgetting factor γ induces an effective time window of size $M = 1/(1 - \gamma)$ in the averaging equation (4.69). For example, with $\gamma = 0.99$ the number of previous values y_k which are used for averaging is effectively 100. Therefore γ should be chosen to be closer to 1 if a larger time window is to be used for the averaging, and further from 1 when past values are less important.

Often we can use a hard-limiting window of size M instead of an effective one induced by γ by setting

$$\beta_k = \frac{M}{\sum_{i=k-M+1}^{k} y_i^2}. \tag{4.77}$$

This formula is more natural in the case where the number of samples is M. Hence, the algorithm uses the same data again and again in a loop (each iteration of the loop is called a *sweep*). This situation may occur, for example, in classification applications where the number of samples is limited and stored in a computer database, the size of which is known a priori. Formula (4.77) for β is very similar to what was originally proposed for APEX [18].

In another publication [56] the authors propose to track the value $1/\sigma_k = 1/\sum_{k-M+1}^{k} y_l^2$ by following a gradient descent on the error surface $J = 1/2[1 - \beta_k \sigma_k]^2$. However, neither of these methods are as general as our current treatment since they are not applicable when M is not defined, while they fail to establish the relationship between β and the least-squares optimality criterion (4.69).

We can proceed further to establish the complete relationship between APEX and RLS by showing that the updating equation for c can also be derived from recursive least-squares optimization. Indeed, premultiplying (4.75) by w and using (4.70), we obtain

$$\Delta c_k = \beta_k(y_k W x_k - c_k y_k^2), \tag{4.78}$$

which is the same as (4.49) if we define $[y_{1k} \quad \cdots \quad y_{m-1,k}] = W x_k$.

4.2.7 Other Rules

In addition to all the adaptive algorithms described above, there is a plethora of alternative techniques that perform PCA either with single-unit or multiple-unit networks [20, 57–67]. This is the result of the fast-growing interest, during the last decade, in principal component analysis in connection with neural network learning, Hebbian dynamics, biological organization of the visual cortex, multilayer perceptrons, etc. Some of these rules are briefly described below.

The earlier models of Krasulina [57] and Owsley [58] did not attempt connections with neural network theory. The corresponding stochastic approximations methods were seen from a signal processing or system-theoretical point of view. Krasulina's algorithm

$$\Delta w_k = \beta_k \left(x_k x_k^T w_k - \frac{w^T x_k x_k^T w_k}{\|w_k\|^2} w_k \right) \tag{4.79}$$

extracts the principal component of the sequence $\{x_k\}$. Observe that this algorithm is very similar to Oja's single unit rule (4.11) if we substitute y for $w^T x$. The difference lies in the normalizing division with $\|w\|^2$.

Owsley's method, on the other hand, achieves multiple component extraction

$$\tilde{w}_{ik} = \left(I - \sum_{l<i} w_{lk} w_{lk}^T \right) (I + \beta_k x_k x_k^T) w_{i,k-1}, \tag{4.80}$$

$$w_{ik} = \frac{\tilde{w}_{ik}}{\|\tilde{w}_{ik}\|}. \tag{4.81}$$

The first factor $(I - \sum_{l<i} w_{lk} w_{lk}^T)$ clearly attempts Gram-Schmidt deflation so that the ith component is dominant, while the second factor $(I + \beta_k x_k x_k^T)$ rotates w_i toward the direction of x_k.

More recently, Leen [59] proposed two models for extracting multiple principal components. The first uses the cost function

$$J = -\frac{1}{2} \sum_{i=1}^m E\{y_i^2\} + \frac{b}{2} \sum_{\substack{i,j \\ i \neq j}} E\{y_i y_j\}$$

$$= -\frac{1}{2} \sum_{i=1}^m w_i^T R_x w_i + \frac{b}{2} \sum_{\substack{i,j \\ i \neq j}} (w_i^T R_x w_j)^2, \tag{4.82}$$

where b is a coupling constant expressing the relative importance between variance maximization (first term) and orthogonality (second term).

If gradient descent is applied directly to J then the weights will grow without bound. To avoid this situation Leen adds a balance term similar to the normalization term in Oja's single component rule (4.12):

$$\frac{dw_i}{dt} = -\nabla_{w_i} J - (w_i^T R_x w_i) w_i$$

$$= R_x w_i - b \sum_{j \neq i} (w_i^T R_x w_j) R_x w_j - (w_i^T R_x w_i) w_i. \tag{4.83}$$

The discrete version of (4.83) is

$$\Delta w_{ik} = \beta_k \left[y_{ik} x_k - b \sum_{j \neq i} E\{y_{ik} y_{jk}\} y_{jk} x_k - y_{ik}^2 w_{ik} \right]. \tag{4.84}$$

Notice that (4.84) contains an expectation term $E\{y_{ik} y_{jk}\}$; therefore it is not a proper iteration rule. To estimate this expectation term an additional variable η_{ij} is introduced:

$$\Delta \eta_{ij,k} = h \beta_k (b y_{ik} y_{jk} - \eta_{ij,k}), \qquad i \neq j. \tag{4.85}$$

The parameter h is introduced to underline the fact that the learning rates of (4.84) and (4.85) need not be the same. The associated ODE is

$$\frac{d\eta_{ij}}{dt} = bE\{y_i y_j\} - \eta_{ij},$$

so the equilibrium (if it exists) is $\eta_{ij} = bE\{y_i y_j\}$. Substituting $\eta_{ij,k}$ for $bE\{y_{ik} y_{jk}\}$ in (4.84) we obtain

$$\Delta w_{ik} = \beta_k \left[y_{ik} x_k - \sum_{j \neq i} \eta_{ij,k} y_{jk} x_k - y_{ik}^2 w_{ik} \right]. \tag{4.86}$$

Equations (4.85) and (4.86) constitute the first learning rule proposed by Leen. He actually showed that the equilibrium $w_i = \pm e_i$, $\eta_{ij} = 0$, is asymptotically stable provided

$$h > \max_{i,j} \left\{ (\lambda_i - \lambda_j)^2 (\lambda_i + \lambda_j)/(\lambda_i^2 - \lambda_j^2) \right\},$$

$$b > \max_{i,j} \left\{ 1/(\lambda_i + \lambda_j) \right\}.$$

The second model proposed by Leen resembles Földiák's network:

$$y_i = w_i^T x + \sum_{j \neq i} c_{ij} y_j;$$

$$y = (I - C)^{-1} W x,$$

$$\Delta w_{ik} = \beta_k (y_{ik} x_k - y_{ik}^2 w_i), \tag{4.87}$$

$$\Delta c_{ij,k} = \beta_k (h c_{ij,k} - b y_i y_j), \qquad i \neq j. \tag{4.88}$$

The stability condition for this rule is

$$h > 0,$$

$$b > \max_{ij} \left\{ h/(\lambda_i + \lambda_j) + (\lambda_i - \lambda_j)^2/(\lambda_i^2 + \lambda_j^2) \right\}.$$

Chauvin [60] proposed to use gradient descent adaptation on the cost function

$$J = -a \sum_k y_k^2 + b \left(1 - \sum_{i=1}^n w_i^2 \right)$$

to achieve maximization of the output variance under the constraint of weight normalization. This cost function applies to a single linear unit $y = w^T x$, yielding the rule

$$\Delta w_k = \beta_k \left[a y_k x_k + b \left(1 - \sum_{l=1}^n w_{lk}^2 \right) w_k \right]. \tag{4.89}$$

This is a single-unit rule, and the constants a, b are chosen by the user as the relative importance between variance maximization and weight constraint.

The subspace method has been modified by Oja so that the true PCA eigenvectors are extracted. Remember that the original subspace method extracts the subspace of the components but not the components themselves. The modified rule [65]

$$\Delta w_{ik} = \beta_k y_{ik} \left[x_k - \epsilon_i \sum_{l=1}^{m} y_{lk} w_{lk} \right],$$ (4.90)

where $y_i = w_i^T x$, contains the scalar constants $\epsilon_1, \ldots, \epsilon_m$. If $\epsilon_1 = \cdots = \epsilon_m = 1$ then we go back to the original subspace rule. However, if $\epsilon_m > \epsilon_{m-1} > \cdots > \epsilon_1 > 0$ then (4.90) is called the *weighted subspace algorithm*, and it has been shown to extract the exact principal eigenvector of $\{x_k\}$.

White [66] introduced the *competitive Hebbian rule*

$$\Delta w_{ij,k} = \beta_k y_{ik} x_{jk} \left[1 - 4 \sum_{l \neq i} y_{lk}^2 \right]$$ (4.91)

under some constraint of the form $\sum_j |w_{ij}| \leq L_1 = $ constant, or $\sum_j w_{ij}^2 \leq L_2 = $ constant, where, unlike other models, some nonlinearity is involved in y:

$$y_i = f \left(\sum_j w_{ij} x_j \right).$$

White shows, through simulation, that the model extracts different orthogonal components of the input sequence, but not the principal components, in general.

Most algorithms in this section are not local in the sense required from neural models if they want to claim biological plausibility. We have to mention, however, that some of these models were not intended to claim any relationship to biological neural networks. It is in retrospect that we find such algorithms to resemble some later proposed neural models. This section certainly does not exhaust the wide literature of stochastic PCA algorithms, but it attempts to give a summary of some important models which, due to lack of space, were not fully analyzed and expanded. It also makes it apparent that there is a growing interest in this area with a multitude of related models appearing in the literature, especially in recent years.

Minor Component Analysis   The opposite of principal component analysis is *minor component analysis (MCA)*, where one seeks to find these directions that minimize the projection variance. These directions are the eigendirections corresponding to the minimum eigenvalues. The applications of minor component analysis arise in total-least squares and eigenvalue-based spectral estimation methods (e.g., Pisarenko's method). Both topics are discussed in more detail in most advanced signal processing textbooks, such as [68, 69]. We shall not further elaborate on these topics here. The interested reader may refer to the above publications and references therein.

Xu et al. [70] have proposed a straightforward modification of Oja's single-unit rule to obtain the minor component of the input sequence. A change of sign compared to (4.11) leads to the minor component rule

$$\Delta w_k = -\beta_k(y_k x_k - y_k^2 w_k). \tag{4.92}$$

It is shown that if the smallest eigenvalue λ_n has multiplicity 1 then $w(t) \to \eta(t)e_n$ as $t \to \infty$, where $w(t)$ is the solution of the associated ODE and $\eta(t)$ is a scalar function. This simple change of sign does not produce as an elegant result in the minor component case as with the principal component case. In other words, rule (4.92) does not extract the normalized minor component.

Oja modified the rule into [65]

$$\Delta w_{ij,k} = \beta_k[-y_{ik}x_{jk} + (y_{ik}^2 + 1 - \|w_i\|^2)w_{ij,k} - \epsilon \sum_{l>i} y_{lk}y_{ik}w_{lk}],$$

$$i = n, n-1, \ldots, n-m+1, \tag{4.93}$$

corresponding to the ODE

$$\frac{dw_i}{dt} = -R_x w_i + (w_i^T R_x w_i)w_i - \epsilon \sum_{l>i} w_l^T R_x w_i + (1 - \|w_i\|^2)w_i,$$

$$i = n, n-1, \ldots, n-m+1. \tag{4.94}$$

Although this rule is nonlocal it achieves the desired result and extracts multiple minor components for appropriate choice of ϵ.

Theorem 4.4 [65]. Consider the ODE (4.94). Assume that the eigenvalues of R_x obey the condition $\lambda_1 > \lambda_2 > \cdots > \lambda_n > 0$, and $\epsilon > \lambda_{n-m+1}/\lambda_n - 1$. If $w_i(0)^T e_i \neq 0$ then $w_i(t) \to \pm e_i$, as $t \to \infty$, for $i = n, n-1, \ldots, n-m+1$.

4.3   UNIFICATION OF HEBBIAN PCA RULES

All principal component rules discussed so far are special cases of the following general formulation

Unit Activation

$$y = [y_1, \ldots, y_m]^T = Wx - sCy \quad \text{(output)}, \tag{4.95}$$

$$x = [x_1, \ldots, x_n]^T \quad \text{(input)}$$

for $s = 0$ or 1.

Learning Rule

$$\Delta W_k = \beta_k[y_k x_k^T - F(y_k y_k^T)W_k] \quad \text{(feedforward)}, \quad (4.96)$$

$$\Delta C_k = \beta_k[G(y_k y_k^T) - H(y_k y_k^T)C_k] \quad \text{(lateral)} \quad (4.97)$$

for some functions $F(\cdot)$, $G(\cdot)$, $H(\cdot)$.

Indeed, Table 4.1 summarizes these rules as special cases of the general formula. Hornik and Kuan [49] treat the general case of PCA models resulting from Eqs. (4.95) through (4.97), under the assumption $H(X) = 0$. They call the cases in which $C = \text{OffDiag}(C)$, $G(X) = \text{OffDiag}(X)$ algorithms "in symmetric mode," whereas the cases in which $C = \text{LowTr}(C)$, $G(X) = \text{LowTr}(X)$ they call algorithms in "asymmetric mode." Földiák's model is symmetric by this definition, while, for instance, Rubner's model and APEX are asymmetric algorithms. For either kind of algorithms we have $s = 1$ and, from (4.95),

$$y = Q(C)Wx, \quad Q(C) = (I + C)^{-1}. \quad (4.98)$$

Table 4.1. PCA Rules Derived as Special Cases of (4.95)–(4.97).[a]

	Oja's Single-Unit Rule	
$s = 0,$	$C = 0,$	$F(x) = x,$
	$G(x) = 0,$	$H(x) = 0$
	Subspace Method	
$s = 0,$	$C = 0,$	$F(X) = X,$
	$G(X) = 0,$	$H(X) = 0$
	GHA	
$s = 0,$	$C = 0,$	$F(X) = \text{LowTr}(X) + \text{Diag}(X),$
	$G(X) = 0,$	$H(X) = 0$
	Földiák's Model	
$s = 1,$	$C = \text{OffDiag}(C),$	$F(X) = \text{Diag}(X),$
	$G(X) = \text{OffDiag}(X),$	$H(X) = 0$
	Linearized Rubner Model	
$s = 1,$	$C = \text{LowTr}(C),$	$F(X) = \text{Diag}(X),$
	$G(X) = \text{LowTr}(X),$	$H(X) = 0$
	APEX Model	
$s = 1,$	$C = \text{LowTr}(C),$	$F(X) = \text{Diag}(X),$
	$G(X) = \text{LowTr}(X),$	$H(X) = \text{Diag}(X)$

[a] LowTr(X) and UpperTr(X) are the low- and upper-triangular parts of the matrix X (not including the diagonal); Diag(X) and OffDiag(X) are the diagonal and off-diagonal parts of the matrix X.

Since for these algorithms $C_k \neq 0$ in general, we have

$$Q(C_k) \neq I.$$

For algorithms in asymmetric mode the same authors find the following result.

Theorem 4.5 [49]. For asymmetric algorithms the only asymptotically stable equilibria are the points

$$W = [\pm e_1, \dots, \pm e_m]^T, \qquad C = 0,$$

and all other equilibria are unstable.

For symmetric algorithms the same applies when we compute y_k before the next x_{k+1} enters. If we want to avoid inversion of matrices, which are biologically rather implausible, and if $C = \text{OffDiag}(C) \neq 0$ (e.g., Földiák's algorithm), the computation of y_k takes infinite steps through the iterative procedure

$$y_k^{(p)} = W_k x_k - C_k y_k^{(p-1)}, \qquad p = 1, 2, \dots, \tag{4.99}$$

which may, in addition, be unstable if one eigenvalue of C_k is outside the unit circle. Földiák's algorithm unfortunately does not guarantee that this will not happen. Note that for asymmetric algorithms, since $C_k = \text{LowTr}(C_k)$ for all k, the inversion takes a finite number of steps because

$$(I + C)^{-1} = I - C + \cdots + (-1)^{m-1} C^{m-1}$$

and there is no risk for instability. The finite sum doesn't have to be explicitly computed. Since there is no feedback in the lateral connections we can compute $y_{1k}, \dots, y_{mk}$ sequentially: $y_{1k} = w_{1k}^T x_k$, $y_{2k} = w_{2k}^T x_k \pm c_{21,k} y_{1k}, \dots, y_{mk} = w_{mk}^T x_k \pm \sum_{i=1}^{m-1} c_{mi,k} y_{ik}$.

An alternative approach for symmetric methods is to use a finite number of steps from the recursion (4.99). For example, after p steps we obtain

$$y_k \approx y_k^{(p)} = (-1)^p C_k^p y_k^{(0)} + (I - C_k + \cdots + (-1)^{p-1} C_k^{p-1}) W_k x_k.$$

If we set $y_k^{(0)} = y_{k-1}$ we get the recursive input-output law

$$y_k = C_k^p y_{k-1} + (I - C_k + \cdots + (-1)^{p-1} C_k^{p-1}) W_k x_k \tag{4.100}$$

instead of (4.95). Hornik and Kuan showed, however, that for such algorithms all equilibria are unstable.

In conclusion, hierarchical decorrelation using asymmetric lateral weights $C = \text{LowTr}(C)$ (e.g., the APEX rule) should be preferred in terms of performance over the slower and less biologically plausible symmetric decorrelation methods such as Földiák's rule. As pointed out in [49], it is not difficult to explain biologically why symmetric, competitive rules lack in performance compared to asymmetric, hierarchical rules. The desired result is for each unit to maximize the variance, but in such a way that it is orthogonal with all components higher than it. The hierarchical network structure imposes this constraint by its own topology. In symmetric models, on the other hand, units are allowed to compete equally for variance and no order is forced explicitly by the structure of the network.

4.4 COMPUTATIONAL ISSUES

4.4.1 Neural Nets versus Batch Methods

The solution of the PCA problem is related to the eigenvalue decomposition of a matrix R_x, which happens to be the average of the outer product xx^T of the input sequence. Therefore, one way to compute the principal components of x is to use the eigenvalue techniques described in Section 3.4 after we have somehow estimated R_x. We shall refer to such PCA methods as "batch methods" because the data x are collected and processed in a batch. The comparison between neural PCA models and batch PCA methods is not straightforward because they approach the problem using different assumptions. They are also applicable for different situations.

Batch methods are used to process finite sets of data. Because of storage considerations batch methods are preferred when relatively few data are to be processed relatively few times. In contrast, consider the problem of PC analysis of a sequence $\{x_k \in \mathbb{R}^n\}$ where $n = 1000$. In such very high dimensional cases the batch techniques often become computationally prohibitive. R_x would be a 1000×1000 array, and the accumulation of orthogonal transformations (in any eigenvalue technique) for the computation of the eigenvectors would require consecutive multiplications of many 1000×1000 arrays. Even if we ignore the memory problem for storing such huge arrays (which are not necessarily sparse), the computational requirement is still extremely high.

Adaptive methods, on the other hand, are preferred when arbitrarily long or infinite sets of data are to be processed. Such methods require less memory for data storage, since intermediate matrices like R_x are not explicitly formed. In addition, adaptive methods with constant step-size parameters, or step-size parameters that do not tend to 0 as $k \rightarrow \infty$, can track gradual changes in the optimal solution rather inexpensively compared to batch methods. On the negative side, if the autocorrelation matrix is known, adaptive methods tend to consume a lot of iterations in order to produce as accurate results as produced by batch methods. In such cases neural nets have a disadvantage. However, one can easily argue that if R_x is known there is no need to use adaptive techniques to begin with. The interest for adaptive techniques arises precisely when R_x is not known.

Batch and neural methods cannot be compared in the case of infinite data series. In the case of finite data, simulation evidence supports the proposition that QR is faster for reasonable data dimension n and for the same accuracy requirement if the desired number of components is comparable to n. On the other hand, using the QR method for computing the eigenvalues every time a new pattern arrives would incur too many floating-point operations (flops) per pattern. This puts the QR method at a disadvantage compared to neural models.

Another point of comparison between batch and adaptive PCA techniques is their hardware implementation. When high performance is required, special architectures must be designed for the parallel or analog implementation of these algorithms. The issues involved in such a comparison is the cost of the implementation, the parallelizability of the algorithms, the speedup gained by the best parallel implementation, etc. Such issues will be considered in detail in Chapter 8.

4.4.2 Comparison between Neural Models

In this section we shall compare the main neural algorithms presented in detail in the previous sections, namely Oja's single-unit rule, the two versions of GHA, Földiák's model, the subspace model, Rubner's model, and APEX. The models will be compared in terms of locality, capability for incremental or concurrent extraction of the components, flexibility in adding more components, whether exact components are extracted or not, etc.

According to Definition 4.1, among the rules in question, the ones which are not local are Földiák's model, the subspace model, and the first version of GHA (4.23). The second GHA version (4.27) is local, and the same is true for Oja's single-unit rule, Rubner's rule, and APEX.

Oja's single-unit rule is the only one not capable of extracting multiple components. Among the other rules, some extract the exact components (Rubner's model, APEX, and both versions of GHA), and others extract the principal component subspace (the subspace model and Földiák's model). Models that extract the precise components are flexible in adding more units to extract more components because they do not need to retrain units that have already learned the higher components.

Rubner's model and APEX are very similar except for the lateral connection rule, which is a simple Hebbian in the first case and a normalized Hebbian (i.e., Oja's rule) in the second case. The second approach brings about the relationship to the RLS algorithm and determines a specific value for the optimal step-size constant. Sanger's local GHA algorithm is also related to APEX. In GHA the updating rule for the vector w_i is

$$\Delta w_{ik} = \beta_k (y_{ik} x^{(i)} - y_i^2 w_{ik}),$$

where

$$x^{(i)} = x - \sum_{l<i} y_l w_l,$$

$$y_i = w_i^T x - \sum_{l<i} y_l w_i^T w_l$$

For APEX the rule is similar

$$\Delta w_{ik} = \beta_k(y_{ik}x - y_i^2 w_{ik}),$$

$$y_i = w_i^T x - \sum_{l<i} c_{il} y_l.$$

If we associate c_{il} with $w_i^T w_l$ the rules become almost the same except that local GHA uses the modified input $x^{(i)}$ while APEX uses x.

Table 4.2 summarizes the properties of the above PCA neural models.

4.4.3 Simulation Experiments

Using simulation we compared five multiple-component PCA models, namely GHA, APEX, Rubner's, Földiák's, and subspace models. We tested them on the same data set using the same initial weight matrix W. For those models that have lateral weights we initialized C to zero.

The data were created using a uniform random generator and an iterative noise coloring scheme. Precisely, we created 512 random patterns of dimension $n = 16$, where each element in each pattern vector was an independent random number uniformly distributed between -1 and 1. Subsequently the data were colored using the iterative scheme

$$x_k \leftarrow x_k + \frac{x_{k-1}}{2}, \qquad k = 1, 2, \ldots.$$

The aggregate correlation matrix $R_x = \frac{1}{512} \sum_k x_k x_k^T$ had eigenvalue distribution

$$\sigma(R_x) = \{0.7318052, 0.6921095, 0.6043660, 0.5692448,$$

$$0.5516361, 0.4882809, 0.4559472, 0.4265897,$$

$$0.4111828, 0.3711804, 0.3635896, 0.3359240,$$

$$0.3229920, 0.2928984, 0.2494060, 0.2405963\}.$$

Table 4.2. Properties of the Major PCA Neural Models

	Local	Exact Comp.	Single/ Multiple Comp.	Flexible Model Growth
Oja's single unit	Yes	Yes	Single	N/A
Földiák's model	No	No	Multiple	No
Subspace model	No	No	Multiple	No
GHA version 1	No	Yes	Multiple	No
GHA version 2	Yes	Yes	Multiple	Yes
Rubner's model	Yes	Yes	Multiple	Yes
APEX model	Yes	Yes	Multiple	Yes

As a measure of the algorithms' performance we use the average square error

$$J = \sum_k \|x_k - W^+ W x_k\|^2.$$

This is minimized if W spans the principal component subspace. We tested the algorithms using four components, so the minimum error is

$$J_{\min} = \sum_{i=5}^{16} \lambda_i = 4.5102234.$$

Figures 4.7a, b, and c show typical runs of the five algorithms for different step-size constants $\beta = 0.005$, 0.01, and 0.02. The APEX model uses the adaptive step size determined from iterative equation (4.76) with $\gamma = 0.99$. Each unit in APEX has its own β adapted according to its own output square value y^2. Especially in APEX the externally supplied value of β is only used for initialization. In all other models the value of β is kept constant throughout the run.

We observe that the performance of the APEX model is almost independent of the initial value of β. Clearly this is explained by assuming that the optimal value of β is attained within few hundred iterations (since $M = 1/(1 - \gamma) = 100$). In the other four models the value of β has a major impact: if it is too small (Fig. 4.7a) the APEX model is markedly faster; as the value of β becomes larger (Fig. 4.7b, c) the gap between the convergence speed of APEX and the other four models narrows and finally vanishes, but then the steady-state error becomes larger compared to APEX. This readily demonstrates the trade-off between convergence speed and final error, and also justifies the claim that the APEX step-size constant is optimal.

Observe finally that the performances of GHA, Rubner's model, Földiák's model, and the subspace model are almost identical independent of the choice of β.

4.5   LINEAR MULTILAYER NETWORKS AND PCA

Single-layer networks with or without lateral connections, such as the ones described above, are not the only structures that have been shown to extract the principal components of their input signal. Consider a two-layer neural network such as the one shown in Figure 4.8. If this network is trained with an output target d equal to the input x, then we say that it operates in *autoassociative mode*. The network then tries to implement the identity mapping: it must reconstruct x at the output layer.

Let us assume now that the number of units p in the hidden layer is less than the number of units $n = \dim(x)$ in the input and output layers. The hidden layer is a bottleneck which forces the network to represent (i.e., to code) the input with fewer parameters than n, i.e., to perform compression on x. Based on the hidden-layer representation the input is to be optimally reconstructed at the output layer. In such

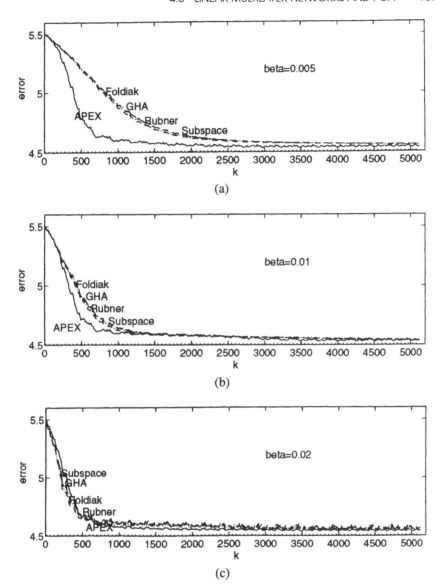

Figure 4.7. Performance comparison of GHA, APEX, Rubner's model, Földiák's model, and the subspace model. APEX uses an adaptive step-size parameter determined by (4.76) with $\gamma = 0.99$; all other models use a constant step size. Three experiments are shown for different values of the step-size parameter (for APEX this is the initial value): (a) $\beta = 0.005$, (b) $\beta = 0.01$, (c) $\beta = 0.02$. The error in the vertical axis is the least-squares error, while the dotted horizontal line in each plot shows the minimum error.

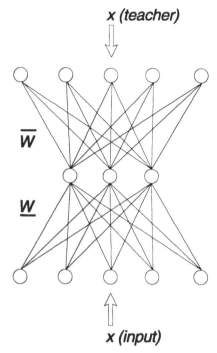

Figure 4.8. A linear two-layer network performs PCA when operating in autoassociative mode (target = input) and the hidden layer contains fewer units than the input (and output) layer. The network forces itself to reproduce the input as accurately as possible, in the least-squares sense, using only a few representation nodes, i.e., the hidden units. The weights will tend to a combination of the principal eigenvectors so they will span the same subspace.

a setting the identity mapping from input to output is in general not achievable. For example, assume that the units' activation function is $f(x) = x$ and for simplicity assume that thresholds θ are not present. The output is then a linear function of the input

$$y = \overline{W}\underline{W}^T x, \tag{4.101}$$

where $\overline{W} = [\overline{w}_{ij}] \in \mathbb{R}^{n \times p}, \underline{W}^T = [\underline{w}_{ij}] \in \mathbb{R}^{p \times n}$ are the weights of the upper and lower layer respectively. Since the input-output mapping $W = \overline{W}\underline{W}^T$ is the product of two matrices with rank less than p, we have rank$(W) \leq p$ as well, so $W \neq I$ and $y \neq x$ in general. The quality of the match between y and x is measured by a cost function such as the mean square error

$$J = \frac{1}{2N} \sum_{k=1}^{N} \|x_k - y_k\|^2. \tag{4.102}$$

In the stochastic context the sum is replaced by expectation

$$J = \frac{1}{2}E\{\|x - y\|^2\}. \tag{4.103}$$

This is the square error function used for PCA/SVD.

It is interesting to study the properties of two-layer networks with bottleneck hidden layer and ask ourselves what are the features extracted by the hidden layer of such a network, whether there are any differences in the optimal solution from PCA/SVD, or whether the two techniques are somehow related. It turns out that there is indeed a close relationship between PCA/SVD and networks of this type, as will be shown below.

The following analysis is based on the work of Bourlard and Kamp [71]. They studied both linear and nonlinear hidden-layer networks and found that the optimal weights can be determined via SVD analysis. The operations in a two-layer network can be described by the equations

$$y = \overline{W}a + \overline{\theta}, \tag{4.104}$$

$$a = f(\underline{W}^T x + \underline{\theta}), \tag{4.105}$$

where $a \in \mathbb{R}^p$ is the activation vector of the hidden layer, $\overline{\theta}$ and $\underline{\theta}$ are the bias vectors of the upper and lower layer units, and f is a nonlinear activation function such as (1.2) operating on all the elements of the vector argument $(\underline{W}^T x + \underline{\theta})$. Using (4.104) the square error cost becomes

$$J = \frac{1}{2N} \sum_{k=1}^{N} \|x_k - \overline{W}a_k - \overline{\theta}\|^2. \tag{4.106}$$

Setting

$$\frac{\partial J}{\partial \overline{\theta}} = -\frac{1}{N} \sum_{k=1}^{N} (x_k - \overline{W}a_k - \overline{\theta}) = 0,$$

we obtain the optimal $\overline{\theta}$

$$\overline{\theta} = \frac{1}{N} \sum_{k=1}^{N} (x_k - \overline{W}a_k) = \langle x \rangle - \overline{W}\langle a \rangle, \tag{4.107}$$

which substituted into the cost function yields

$$J = \frac{1}{2N} \sum_{k=1}^{N} \|x_k' - \overline{W}a_k'\|^2 = \frac{1}{2N}\|X' - \overline{W}A'\|_F^2, \tag{4.108}$$

where $x_k' = x_k - \langle x \rangle$, $a_k' = a_k - \langle a \rangle$, $X' = [x_1', \dots, x_N']$, and $A' = [a_1', \dots, a_N']$.

Observe that rank($\overline{W}A'$) $\leq p$ because rank($\overline{W}$) $\leq p$. Therefore the minimizer of (4.108), if we allow the freedom to choose both $\overline{W}$ and A', is the best rank-p approximation of X' (Section 3.2):

$$\overline{W}A' = U_p \Sigma_p V_p^T, \tag{4.109}$$

where $U\Sigma V^T$ is the SVD of X' and Σ_p, U_p, V_p are the partial matrices containing the p largest singular values and their corresponding singular vectors. Thus optimality is obtained for

$$\overline{W} = U_p M \tag{4.110}$$

and

$$A' = M^{-1}\Sigma_p V_p^T \tag{4.111}$$

for some nonsingular matrix M. The question, however, is whether the optimal matrix A' is achievable for some choice of $\underline{W}$, $\underline{\theta}$. If not, we have to redo our analysis, taking into account the achievable values of A' only. Luckily, this does not have be done. We shall show next that the "total optimum" is achievable under either choice of the activation function f: (a) $f(x) = bx + c$, or (b) $f(x) =$ nonlinear.
  (a) If $f(x) = bx + c$ then

$$a'_k = b\underline{W}^T x_k - b\underline{\theta} + c - \langle b\underline{W}^T x - b\underline{\theta} + c \rangle = \underline{W}^T x'_k,$$

$$A' = b\underline{W}^T X',$$

so one solution is[2]

$$\underline{W} = \frac{1}{b}U_p M^{-T}, \qquad A' = b\underline{W}^T X' = M^{-1}U_p^T X' = M^{-1}\Sigma_p V_p^T.$$

The hidden unit biases $\underline{\theta}$ do not enter the equation so they are free to assume any value without affecting the optimality of the solution.
  (b) If $f(x)$ is nonlinear it is still reasonable to use, for small x, a first-order approximation

$$f(x) \approx bx + c,$$

where $b = df/dx(0)$ and $c = f(0)$. For example, the sigmoid function (1.2) can be approximated by $\frac{1}{4}x + \frac{1}{2}$ for small x. Under this approximation the problem is reduced to case (a)

$$\underline{W} = \frac{1}{b}U_p M^{-T}, \qquad A' = b\underline{W}^T X' \tag{4.112}$$

---

[2]There are more solutions to the equation but this is enough to show that A' is achievable.

(θ again is arbitrary). In order for the approximation to hold we must make sure that A' is small. However, this is not difficult to accomplish since we have freedom to choose both $\underline{\theta}$ and M. If, for example, we set $\underline{\theta} = 0$, then $A' = M^{-1}\Sigma_p V_p^T$ can become arbitrarily small by setting M as large as needed.

The conclusion of the above analysis is that for the autoassociation problem in a two-layer network with a bottleneck hidden layer and a linear output layer, usage of either linear or nonlinear activation function in the hidden layer results in the same error. This is the error of the best rank-p approximation of the data matrix X'. Not only does nonlinearity not improve the final estimate, it also introduces local minima in the error surface, so that optimization algorithms (e.g., back-propagation) risk getting trapped in suboptimal solutions. Therefore, the usefulness of nonlinearity is objectionable in this setting.

The same conclusion essentially holds for networks with more than two layers where the output layer is linear and the next-to-last layer is reduced. Again the matrix $(\overline{W}A')$ has rank $p < n$ and the optimal solution $U_p \Sigma_p V_p^T$ is still achievable for the linear case. Therefore, the nonlinear case cannot perform any better than the linear case.

The upper layer weights $\overline{W}$ span the same subspace as the p most important left-singular-vectors of X', which are equal to the p principal eigenvectors of $\frac{1}{N}X'X'^T$. We have $\lim_{N\to\infty} \frac{1}{N}X'X'^T = E\{(x - \langle x\rangle)(x - \langle x\rangle)^T\} = R_{x'}$, so span$(\overline{W})$ tends to the principal eigenspace of $R_{x'}$.

Baldi and Hornik [72] first studied the generalized problem of hetero-association (*teacher ≠ input*) on multilayer linear networks with hidden layer bottleneck. This problem is discussed in detail in Section 6.1.

4.5.1 Non-PCA Hebbian Rules

There is more than one way to extend the Hebbian law to produce simple feature-extracting networks. We saw earlier that one way is to use linear networks with some normalized learning rule, which leads to PCA and thus to feature extraction.

Another approach, which leads to feature extraction without relation to PCA, was proposed in 1988 by Linsker [12]. He studied a multilayer self-adaptive network with feedforward connections (Fig. 4.9). Each layer is a two-dimensional assembly of neurons, and each neuron receives input from an overlying neighborhood of cells in the previous layer. Linsker studies only linear units with activation function of the form

$$y = \sum_{i=1}^{n} w_i x_i + \theta. \tag{4.113}$$

Although using nonlinear activation functions, such as sigmoids, is closer to reality, Linsker observes remarkable organization properties in this network even with the linear activation function. He then argues that the mathematical analysis of the linear case gives insight to the nonlinear case as well.

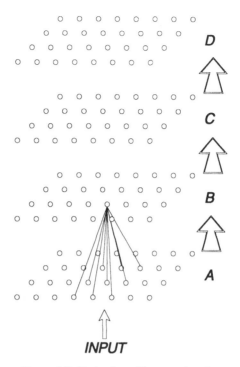

Figure 4.9. Linsker's multilayer network.

The learning rule adopted by Linsker for unit m in layer l is

$$\Delta w_i = ayx_i + by + cx_i + d, \qquad (4.114)$$

where the parameters a, b, c, d, as well as the threshold θ, are arbitrary constants with $a > 0$. The Hebbian influence again lies in the term ayx_i, which is proportional to the correlation between the unit activation y and the input x_i. All the learning parameters a, b, c, d are assumed small enough to ensure that the w values change slowly from the presentation of one pattern to the next. Furthermore, to prevent instability during training the weights are constrained to lie between two extreme values c_-, c_+. The input at layer A is an image, typically some random array of numbers with stationary statistics such as white Gaussian noise.

Taking the average on both sides of (4.114) we obtain the associated ODE

$$\frac{dw}{dt} = R_x w + k_1 + k_2 \left[\sum_{i=1}^{n} w_i \right] v, \qquad (4.115)$$

where $v = [1 \quad 1 \quad \cdots \quad 1]^T$, $w = [w_1, \ldots, w_n]^T$, $x = [x_1, \ldots, x_n]^T$, $R_x = E\{xx^T\}$, and k_1, k_2, are two constants whose values depend on the values of a, b, c, and d. If the input at layer l is white Gaussian noise with power σ^2, then $R_x = \sigma^2 I$.

Equation (4.115) is the gradient descent law

$$\frac{dw}{dt} = -\frac{\partial E}{\partial w}$$

for the energy function

$$E = -w^T R_x w - \frac{1}{2}\left(k_1 + k_2 \sum_i w_i\right)^2 . \tag{4.116}$$

Therefore, Linsker's rule maximizes the output variance under the soft constraint $\sum_i w_i = -k_1/k_2$ and, of course, under the clipping constraint $c_- \leq w_i \leq c_+$ for all i. The equilibrium is not achieved at a point with $dw/dt = 0$ (because then (4.115) would require v to be an eigenvector of R_x, which is not true in general) but rather at a point where all the weights, except one, have reached their saturation values; i.e., $w_i = c_+$ and $dw_i/dt \geq 0$, or $w_i = c_-$ and $dw_i/dt \leq 0$ [73]. For detailed analysis of this and other related learning rules see [74].

Interestingly, Linsker observed that a series of feature-analyzing types of units emerge as one layer converges after the other. First the units in layer B, for some selection of learning parameters, saturate to c_+. Thus the activation of the units in layer B is the average of their corresponding local neighborhoods in layer A. Then in layer C *center-surround* cells emerge; i.e., cells that respond maximally to input in the form of bright spots surrounded by dark background or dark spots surrounded by white background. In layer D units organize to respond maximally to bands of brightness surrounded by dark background (or dark bands in white background) in certain orientations. Such cells are called *orientation selective*.

Such cell organization has a striking similarity to biological neural structures found in the mammalian visual cortex. It is known that the same feature analyzers such as center-surround cells and orientation-selective cells exist in the visual cortex of mammals [4]. It is not claimed, of course, that actual biological organization is done using exactly the same equations or learning rules, but it was suggested that a Hebb-type adaptation process in a multilayer network may be a natural explanation for the existence of such feature-analyzing cells.

4.6 APPLICATION EXAMPLES

Example 4.1 (Vowel Recognition). Principal component neural models have been used to code phonemes by Leen et al. [75] as a preprocessing stage for vowel recognition. The 12 vowel classes to be discriminated were /iy/ (b*ea*t), /ih/ (b*i*t), /eh/ (b*e*t), /ae/ (b*a*t), /ix/ (ros*e*s), /ax/ (th*e*), /ah/ (b*u*tt), /uw/ (b*oo*t), /uh/ (b*oo*k), /ao/ (b*ou*ght), /aa/ (c*o*t), /er/ (b*i*rd). The data were drawn from the DARPA-TIMIT phonetic database.

The GHA model was applied for extracting the principal components of the input data vector which contained the first 64 DFT coefficients covering the range from 0 to 4 kHz of a 10-msec slice from the center of each vowel. Training was performed on 342 examples of each vowel (total 4104 vectors), while the test data consisted of 137 examples of each vowel (total 1644 vectors).

The compression network was followed by a two-layer feedforward net trained using conjugate gradient descent. This network is responsible for performing the actual classification. The input layer of the classification network consists of the output nodes of the GHA model. The number varies from 5 to 30. The number of hidden nodes also varies from 8 to 32.

The results of their experiments show that if we use 10 principal components we achieve similar performance as if we had used all the principal components. The performance when using all the 64 DFT coefficients without compression is also similar. The misclassification error ranges between 40% and 48.2%, which may seem poor but it is comparable to human performance, which only comes up to 50%. This is simply a very difficult classification task.

As the authors remark, using only 10 components without compromising classification accuracy not only reduces the size of the classification network (six times) but also makes training of this network faster. The training time is observed to be roughly linear to the number of input units in the classification network.

Example 4.2 (Signal Detection). Consider the problem of deciding between the two alternative hypotheses:

$$H_0 : x_k = n_k,$$
$$H_1 : x_k = s_k + n_k = A \cos(\omega k + \xi \theta_k + \phi) + n_k.$$

The scalar observation process x_k, is either just white Gaussian noise n_k or noise plus a harmonic with frequency ω, amplitude A, and nonconstant phase $\xi \theta_k + \phi$. The stochastic process θ_k is a unit Brownian motion[3] and ϕ is an independent random initial phase uniformly distributed in $[0, 2\pi]$. The constant ξ is called the *bandwidth* of the phase drift. Without loss of generality we can assume that n_k has unit variance.

The above model is suitable for the detection problem of weak underwater acoustic signals which require relatively long observation intervals. Although the signal might be nominally harmonic, during such long intervals the phase of the signal cannot be assumed constant [76]. Another example where this problem formulation arises is in optical communications, where θ_k models the laser phase noise [77].

The optimal Neyman-Pearson (N-P) detector [78] compares the likelihood ratio

$$L(x) = \frac{\text{Prob}(x \mid H_1)}{\text{Prob}(x \mid H_0)} \tag{4.117}$$

with a threshold τ which is determined by the desired level of false alarm probability. In general, the optimal N-P detector for these hypotheses is difficult to compute analytically.

---

[3] θ_k is a zero-mean Gaussian process with autocorrelation function $E\{\theta_k \theta_m\} = \min\{k, m\}$.

Given an observation sequence of length N which satisfies the condition $\omega N \gg 2\pi$, we can approximate the optimal N-P detector as follows [50, 79]:

$$L(x) = K\Lambda(x) \underset{<}{\overset{>}{\gtrless}} \tau, \tag{4.118}$$

$$\Lambda(x) = 1 + \sum_{n=2,4,6,8,\ldots} \frac{A^n}{n!} \left[\sum_{k_1,\ldots,k_n=1}^{N} \prod_{i=1}^{n} x_{k_i} G_n(k_1,\ldots,k_n) \right], \tag{4.119}$$

where K is a scalar constant and

$$G_n(k_1,\ldots,k_n) = E_\theta E_\phi \left\{ \prod_{i=1}^{n} \cos(\omega k_i + \xi \theta_{k_i} + \phi) \right\}.$$

The term corresponding to G_2 (4.119) can be written as

$$\frac{A^2}{2} \sum_{k,m} x_k G_2 x_m = \frac{A^2}{4} \sum_{k,m} x_k \cos\big(\omega(k-m)\big) \exp\big(-\xi|k-m|\big) x_m$$

$$= \frac{A^2}{4} x^T R_s x, \tag{4.120}$$

where R_s is the autocorrelation matrix of s_k with entries

$$r_{ij} = \cos\big(\omega(i-j)\big)\exp\big(-\xi|i-j|\big).$$

It can be shown [80] that (4.120) is the optimal second-order test statistic for this problem.

Still, the test function (4.120) is very computationally costly for long observation sequences. Various alternative techniques have been proposed in the literature [76, 81].

In [50, 79] we proposed to use principal component neural networks for attacking the problem. The idea is to project the observation on the space spanned by its first two principal eigenvectors. The projection, of course, results in the two principal components of x. For $\xi = 0$ the first two components contain all the energy of the signal s, the principal eigenfunctions are cos and sin, and the resulting detector called the quadrature detector is optimal. For $\xi > 0$ there is no optimality claim, but most of the energy of the signal is still contained in the first two components. The proposed test statistic is

$$\tilde{\Lambda}_m = \sum_{i=0}^{m-1} (y_{1,k}^2 + y_{2,k}^2)\big|_{k=Ni/m}, \tag{4.121}$$

where $y_{1,k}$ and $y_{2,k}$ are the principal components of x estimated by the first two output neurons of an APEX network.

The constant m was introduced for the sake of comparing the performance of the above statistic with the mth-order noncoherent detector (proposed in [77] and used in [76])

$$\Lambda_m(x) = \sum_{i=0}^{m-1} \left[\left(\sum_{k=(Ni/m)+1}^{N(i+1)/m} \cos(\omega k)x_k \right)^2 + \left(\sum_{k=(Ni/m)+1}^{N(i+1)/m} \sin(\omega k)x_k \right)^2 \right]. \quad (4.122)$$

The mth order noncoherent detector is almost as good as the optimal quadratic detector and is computationally inexpensive, unlike the quadratic detector.

We wanted to determine how much better is the eigenspace projection compared to the projection to the space spanned by cos, sin. Figure 4.10 shows the simulation comparison between $\tilde{\Lambda}_m$ and Λ_m using artificially created data, with $\xi = 10$ and corresponding $m = 5$. The probability of false alarm was set at 0.001 and the appropriate threshold was determined by 10,000 simulation experiments for each detector. Using this threshold we then computed, again via simulation, the miss probability for the two detectors. We plot the result in Figure 4.10 versus the signal-to-noise ratio defined as

$$SNR = 10 \log_{10} \left(N \frac{E\{s_k^2\}}{E\{n_k^2\}} \right).$$

We see that the APEX detector clearly outperforms the mth-order noncoherent detector by 0.5 to 1 dB in the range of SNR between -15 dB and -10 dB.

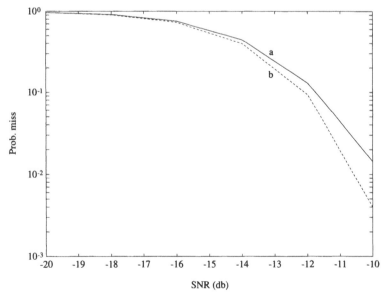

Figure 4.10. Probability of miss comparison between (a) the mth order noncoherent detector and (b) the eigenvalue-based detector.

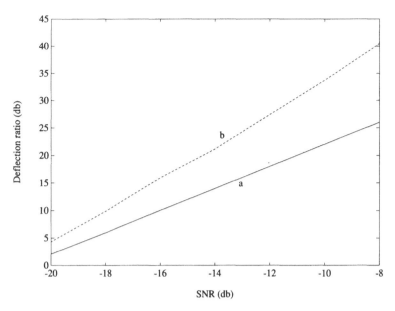

Figure 4.11. Deflection ratio comparison between (a) the *m*th order noncoherent detector and (b) the eigenvalue based detector.

The deflection ratio

$$H = \frac{(E_1\{\Lambda\} - E_0\{\Lambda\})^2}{\mathrm{var}_0\{\Lambda\}}$$

of a test statistic Λ is another useful comparison criterion. E_1 and E_0 denote means with respect to the two hypotheses. The larger the value of H the better is the separation of the means and the better is the performance of the detector. The comparison of the two detectors under this criterion is depicted in Figure 4.11. We see that the eigenvector-based method significantly outperforms the *m*th-order noncoherent detector, which is consistent with the results of Figure 4.10.

Example 4.3 (Moving Picture Compression). Most digital image processing applications such as HDTV, videoconferencing, CD-ROM image database, etc., use data compression techniques to handle the large amounts of image related data. The MPEG standard [82] is an ISO recommended protocol for coding moving picture sequences. Briefly, MPEG is described next.

The normalized color signals R, G, B are transformed into luminance and chrominance components, $Y = 0.299R + 0.587G + 0.114B$, $C_R = R - Y$, $C_B = B - Y$, which are quantized and digitally represented by numbers in the range 0 to 255. Coding separately the luminance and chrominance signals results in lower bit rate due to the lower bandwidth of the chrominance components [83]. The luminance and chrominance components are coded in a very similar way except that the chrominance components are subsampled. Without loss of generality we'll focus here in the luminance component only. The frames in an image sequence are of three types:

1. *I-frames (Intraframes):* coded using 2-D DCT on blocks of size 8×8 pixels. They have the worst compression rate compared to the other two frame types.

2. *P-frames (Prediction frames):* predicted using motion compensation with reference to the previous I- or P-frame, and prediction error coded using DCT. Their compression rate is better than I-frames.

3. *B-frames (Bidirectionally predicted frames):* same as P-frames except that for their prediction we use both the previous and the following I- or P-frame. They have the best compression rate among the three frame types.

A typical frame sequence is:

Frame type:	I	B	B	P	B	B	P	B	B	I
Frame no.:	1	2	3	4	5	6	7	8	9	10

The encoder reorders the sequence

Frame type:	I	P	B	B	P	B	B	I	B	B
Frame no.:	1	4	2	3	7	5	6	10	8	9

Thus, for example, frames B-2 and B-3 succeed frames I-1 and P-4, which are used for predicting B-2 and B-3. After B-2 and B-3 have been estimated at the decoder the sequence is rearranged to its original order for displaying purposes.

Compression is achieved through the quantization of the DCT coefficients. More bits are allocated to the most important components (the low-frequency ones) using small quantization steps, while fewer bits and coarse quantization are used for high-frequency components. The quantization steps for each coefficient in an I-frame are q times the elements of the *intraquantization matrix* (Table 4.3). The same adjustable *quantization coefficient q*, is used to compute the quantization step for each AC DCT coefficient(i, j) by multiplying by $m_{i,j}$. For an AC coefficient c_{ij} the

Table 4.3. The Intraquantization Matrix

$$
M = \begin{bmatrix}
8 & 16 & 19 & 22 & 26 & 27 & 29 & 34 \\
16 & 16 & 22 & 24 & 27 & 29 & 34 & 37 \\
19 & 22 & 26 & 27 & 29 & 34 & 34 & 38 \\
22 & 22 & 26 & 27 & 29 & 34 & 37 & 40 \\
22 & 26 & 27 & 29 & 32 & 35 & 40 & 48 \\
26 & 27 & 29 & 32 & 35 & 40 & 48 & 58 \\
26 & 27 & 29 & 34 & 38 & 46 & 56 & 69 \\
27 & 29 & 35 & 38 & 46 & 56 & 69 & 83
\end{bmatrix}
$$

(a)

(b)

Figure 4.12. Samples from the sequences used in our simulation: (a) table-tennis sequence; (b) football sequence.

corresponding quantized value is

$$c_{ij}^{(q)} = \frac{8c_{ij}}{qm_{ij}} \tag{4.123}$$

rounded to the nearest integer toward zero. With $q > 1$ the granularity of the quantizers is reduced and, therefore, so is the number of bits required to code them. Notice that quantization is a lossy coding process; i.e., it incurs a certain amount of error. The DC is the only coefficient that has a quantization step size independent of q and always equal to 8. The DC coefficient is coded differentially[4] with (4.123), while the value of q is fixed at 1.

---

[4]Instead of coding the coefficient itself we code the difference of it with respect to the DC coefficient of the previous block.

Diamantaras and Kung [84] demonstrate the application of PCA neural network compression for I-frames in MPEG sequences. Traditionally, the major disadvantage of PCA compression is the image dependence of the transform basis. Not only does one have to compute the eigenvectors but one also needs to transmit them to the decoder. This, of course, implies additional bit rate. However, if the decoder can estimate the eigenvectors by using a similar picture as reference, then the estimation error can be significantly reduced compared to the DCT transform.

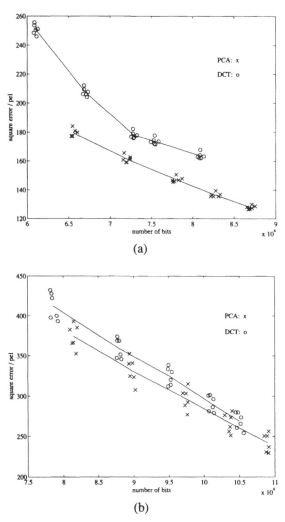

Figure 4.13. Performance comparison between methods 1 and 2 in terms of compression error vs. bit rate, using quantized components with $q' = 5$: (a) table tennis sequence; (b) football sequence.

Based on this idea the authors compared the following two compression methods.

Method 1. The I-frame is divided into 8×8 blocks which are coded using 2-D DCT in accordance to MPEG.

Method 2. First, the I-frame is divided into four equal parts. The blocks in each part are independently transformed by an eigenvector estimate obtained from the corresponding part of the previous P-frame of the purely MPEG coded sequence. In order to avoid estimating the components from scratch for every new I-frame the APEX model was run using as initial conditions the component estimates for the previous I-frame.

The standard table-tennis and football MPEG test sequences were used in the simulations (see Fig. 4.12).

For both methods the intraquantization matrix M of MPEG was used with the quantization coefficient $q^l = 5$. The coding is also the same used in MPEG (run-level coding). A plot of the error versus the bit rate for the two methods is depicted in Figure 4.13. We show the mean curve for each method and a scatterplot of each individual experiment (we ran the methods on six different I-frames). There is a clear advantage to the PCA method on the average: for the same bit rate we have 10–20% error savings in the tennis sequence and 2–5% savings in the football sequence.

A similar approach has been reported recently regarding the PCA coding of I-frames in stereo MPEG sequences [85].

5

CHANNEL NOISE AND HIDDEN UNITS*

PCA is the linear deterministic coding of a high-dimensional random vector $x \in \mathbb{R}^n$ by a lower-dimensional representation $y = \underline{W}x \in \mathbb{R}^m$, $m < n$. This representation minimizes the reconstruction error $E\|x - \overline{W}y\|^2$ over all choices of $\underline{W}, \overline{W}$. In this chapter we investigate the situation where the compressed representation y is not a perfectly deterministic function of x.

For example, let

$$y = \underline{W}x + e, \tag{5.1}$$

$$\hat{x} = \overline{W}y = \overline{W}(\underline{W}x + e), \tag{5.2}$$

where $x, \hat{x} \in \mathbb{R}^n$, $y, e \in \mathbb{R}^m$, and e is an additive (possibly colored) noise term.

In the two-layer neural network paradigm this model corresponds to the situation where the hidden units are unreliable (stochastic) processing elements (Fig. 5.1a). This assumption is closer to reality than the deterministic assumption, according to experimental results in neurobiology [86, Chapter 20]. In a data communications setting (Fig. 5.1b) y is the coded signal received through a noisy channel, x is the message to be transmitted, and the reconstructed message $\hat{x}$ is desired to be as close as possible to x.

The random vector e may be due to an intrinsic unreliability of the network units, or it may be an external noise affecting the transmission of the signals. We assume that x and e are uncorrelated, namely $E\{xe^T\} = 0$, and e is zero mean. Obviously this is not the only possible noise model but probably the simplest one. This situation was first studied in [35, 87] and [88].

*This chapter is, for the most part, the result of joint work with K. Hornik.

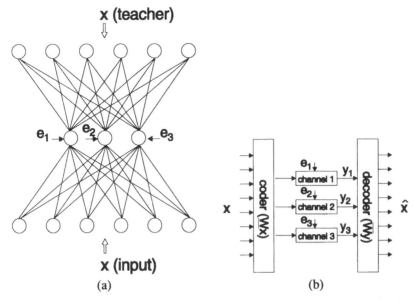

Figure 5.1. Noisy PCA: (a) neural network pradigm: bottleneck linear network with unreliable hidden units learning the identity map; (b) communications paradigm: multiple channels with noise and high-dimensional message.

Let

$$R_x = E\{xx^T\} = U_x\Lambda_x U_x^T, \qquad \Lambda_x = \mathrm{diag}[\lambda_{x,1}, \ldots, \lambda_{x,n}], \qquad (5.3)$$

$$R_e = E\{ee^T\} = U_e\Lambda_e U_e^T, \qquad \Lambda_e = \mathrm{diag}[\lambda_{e,1}, \ldots, \lambda_{e,m}], \qquad (5.4)$$

be the eigenvalue decompositions of the positive-definite matrices R_x and R_e. Assume that the eigenvalues for both matrices are arranged in decreasing order, so, for example, $u_{x,1}$ is the principal eigenvector of R_x and $u_{e,m}$ is the least principal eigenvector of R_e.

Like regular PCA we want to minimize the mean square error

$$J = E\|x - \hat{x}\|^2$$
$$= \mathrm{tr}\left\{(I - \overline{W}\underline{W})R_x(I - \underline{W}^T\overline{W}^T)\right\} + \mathrm{tr}\{\overline{W}R_e\overline{W}^T\}, \qquad (5.5)$$

but this error now contains a noise term $\overline{W}R_e\underline{W}$. We refer to this problem as *noisy principal component analysis* (NPCA).

The noisy principal component vector y contains a signal term y_s and a noise term y_n:

$$y = \overline{W}\underline{W}x + \overline{W}e = y_s + y_n.$$

If there is no constraint on the size of the matrices $\underline{W}$ and $\overline{W}$, then one could make $\underline{W}$ as large as possible in order to increase the signal-to-noise ratio:

$$SNR = \frac{E\|y_s\|^2}{E\|y_n\|^2} = \frac{E\|\overline{W}\underline{W}x\|^2}{E\|\overline{W}e\|^2}.$$

Making $\overline{W}$ as small as possible would at the same time balance the effects of $\underline{W}$ on x (for the sake of reconstruction) and minimize the effects of e.

Precisely, if a pair of matrices $\underline{W}$ and $\overline{W}$ achieves an error J_1, then the pair $c\underline{W}$, $c^{-1}\overline{W}$, for any $c > 1$, achieves error $J_2 < J_1$. Therefore, minimization leads to $\underline{W} \to \infty$ and $\overline{W} \to 0$. Thus the problem is not bounded.

In order to obtain a meaningful solution we need to introduce some constraints that would either restrict the size of $\underline{W}$ from above or the size of $\overline{W}$ from below. We may, for example, impose a soft constraint on $\underline{W}$ by adding a regularization term $\mathrm{tr}(\underline{W}M\underline{W}^T)$ in the cost function, for some symmetric positive-definite M. Hard constraints can also be imposed by explicitly requiring $\underline{W}$ or $\overline{W}$ to belong to a suitable compact set.

In the following we'll investigate various such hard or soft constraints on both $\underline{W}$ and $\overline{W}$. First, observe that if either $\underline{W}$ or $\overline{W}$ is fixed it is straightforward to find the optimal solution. Computing the derivatives of J with respect to $\underline{W}$ and $\overline{W}$ we obtain

$$D_{\overline{W}}J = 2(\overline{W}\underline{W}R_x\underline{W}^T - R_x\underline{W}^T + \overline{W}R_e), \tag{5.6}$$

$$D_{\underline{W}}J = 2(\overline{W}^T\overline{W}\underline{W}R_x - \overline{W}^TR_x). \tag{5.7}$$

There are two simple cases.

1. $\underline{W}$ *is given:* The optimal $\overline{W}$ is computed from (5.6) setting $D_{\overline{W}}J = 0$:

$$\overline{W}_{\mathrm{opt}} = R_x\underline{W}^T[\underline{W}R_x\underline{W}^T + R_e]^{-1} \tag{5.8}$$

(the matrix $[\underline{W}R_x\underline{W}^T + R_e]$ is invertible since both R_x and R_e are positive definite). This solution can be obtained alternatively from the observation that given $\underline{W}$, $\overline{W}$ is the regression matrix from y to x: $\overline{W}_{\mathrm{opt}} = E\{xy^T\}\left[E\{yy^T\}\right]^{-1}$, which yields the same expression as (5.8).

2. $\overline{W}$ *is given:* The optimal $\underline{W}$ is computed from (5.7) setting $D_{\underline{W}}J = 0$

$$\underline{W}_{\mathrm{opt}} = \overline{W}^{+}. \tag{5.9}$$

Equations (5.8) and (5.9) are, in general, not consistent with each other; i.e.,

$$\underline{W}_{\mathrm{opt}}(\overline{W}_{\mathrm{opt}}(\underline{W})) \neq \underline{W},$$

$$\overline{W}_{\mathrm{opt}}(\underline{W}_{\mathrm{opt}}(\overline{W})) \neq \overline{W},$$

implying that, in general, there is no (finite) critical point. Of course, in the special case where $R_e = 0$, the two equations are indeed consistent, and the solution is the standard PCA solution given by Theorem 3.1.

CONSTRAINT: $\underline{W} = \overline{W}^T$

Forcing $\underline{W}$ and $\overline{W}$ to have the same size invalidates the previous argument regarding the unboundedness of the solution. Now the SNR must be compromised at a finite value since we cannot increase the signal term y_s without also increasing the noise term y_n. In this case the cost becomes

$$J = \text{tr}\left\{(I - W^T W)R_x(I - W^T W)\right\} + \text{tr}\{W^T R_e W\}. \tag{5.10}$$

Taking the derivative with respect to W we obtain the following first-order condition:

$$D_W J = 2WR_x(W^T W - I) + 2W(W^T W - I)R_x + 2R_e W = 0. \tag{5.11}$$

We'll find that the solution W_{opt} of (5.11) is a combination of eigenvectors from both R_x and R_e and the rank of W_{opt} is diminishing as the noise power increases.

Theorem 5.1. Assume $\lambda_{e,1} > \cdots > \lambda_{e,m} > 0$ and $\lambda_{x,1} > \cdots > \lambda_{x,n} > 0$. Then

$$J(W_{\text{opt}}) = \min_W J(W) = \sum_{i=1}^{n} \lambda_{x,i} - 2\sum_{i=1}^{m} \gamma_i^4 \lambda_{x,i}, \tag{5.12}$$

where

$$W_{\text{opt}} = \sum_{i=1}^{m} \gamma_i u_{e,\pi(i)} u_{x,i}^T, \tag{5.13}$$

$$\gamma_i^2 = \begin{cases} 1 - \frac{1}{2}\lambda_{e,\pi(i)}/\lambda_{x,i} & \text{if } \lambda_{e,\pi(i)} < 2\lambda_{x,i}, \\ 0 & \text{otherwise,} \end{cases} \tag{5.14}$$

and π is some permutation of the indices $\langle 1, 2, \ldots, m\rangle$.

Proof. See the appendix at the end of the chapter.   ∎

The rank of the solution $r = \text{rank}(W_{\text{opt}})$ equals the number of nonzero γ_i's in the sum (5.14). Since $\gamma_i \neq 0$ iff $\lambda_{e,\pi(i)} < 2\lambda_{x,i}$, it becomes obvious that if the noise eigenvalues increase relative to the signal eigenvalues the rank of the solution decreases. In fact, if $\lambda_{e,m} \geq 2\lambda_{x,1}$ then $\gamma_i = 0$ for all i, and thus $W = 0$. On the other extreme, if $\lambda_{e,1} < 2\lambda_{x,m}$ then $\text{rank}(W) = m$. Between these two extremes we can formulate the following condition:

$$\lambda_{e,m} \geq 2\lambda_{x,p+1} \Rightarrow \text{rank}(W) \leq p,$$

since only the eigenvalues $\lambda_{x,1}, \ldots, \lambda_{x,p}$ have a chance to produce a nonzero γ_i.

Corollary 5.1. If $2\lambda_{x,1} > \lambda_{e,m} \geq 2\lambda_{x,2}$ then

$$W_{\text{opt}} = \gamma u_{e,m} u_{x,1}^T,$$

where $\gamma^2 = 1 - \lambda_{e,m}/2\lambda_{x,1}$.

The phenomenon of rank reduction when the noise power gets high relative to the signal power will arise often in other cases of our analysis as well. It seems that as the noise becomes too high, *orthogonality* between the columns (or rows) of the solution turns into *correlation*.

If we interpret the solution matrix as the weights of a neural network then we can claim that *competition* between neurons turns into *cooperation*. Indeed, when the noise is zero then the units compete for variance (assuming that every unit corresponds to a principal component): the first unit gets the maximum variance, the second unit gets most of the variance left over by the first, and so on. In contrast, as the noise relative to the signal gets higher and higher, the span of the units' weights becomes smaller and smaller. As the weight vectors tend more and more toward the same direction, so units turn more and more into the same component. For the particular constraint in this section in the limit as the noise gets too high the units turn to zero. For other constraints however, the rank never reaches zero.

5.1 OPTIMIZATION UNDER HARD CONSTRAINTS

5.1.1 Constraints on $\underline{W}$

Substituting $\overline{W}_{\text{opt}}(\underline{W})$ of (5.8) for $\overline{W}$ in the error (5.5) we obtain

$$J(\underline{W}) = \text{tr}\{R_x - R_x\underline{W}^T(\underline{W}R_x\underline{W}^T + R_e)^{-1}\underline{W}R_x\}$$
$$= \text{tr}\left\{(R_x^{-1} + \underline{W}^T R_e^{-1}\underline{W})^{-1}\right\}, \tag{5.15}$$

where in the last step we made use of the matrix inversion lemma 2.2. Any minimization problem with constraints on $\underline{W}$ should minimize (5.15) under these constraints.

The following lemmata will be very useful in the subsequent analysis.

Lemma 5.1 [88]. Let $\lambda_1 \geq \cdots \geq \lambda_n$ and $\mu_1 \geq \cdots \geq \mu_n$ be two nonincreasing sequences in $\mathbb{R}$. If π denotes any permutation of $\{1, \ldots, n\}$ then

$$\min_{\pi}\left\{\sum_{i=1}^{n}\lambda_i\mu_{\pi(i)}\right\} = \sum_{i=1}^{n}\lambda_i\mu_{n-i+1}, \tag{5.16}$$

$$\max_{\pi}\left\{\sum_{i=1}^{n}\lambda_i\mu_{\pi(i)}\right\} = \sum_{i=1}^{n}\lambda_i\mu_i, \tag{5.17}$$

$$\min_{\pi} \left\{ \sum_{i=1}^{n} (\lambda_i + \mu_{\pi(i)})^{-1} \right\} = \sum_{i=1}^{n} (\lambda_i + \mu_{n-i+1})^{-1}, \tag{5.18}$$

$$\max_{\pi} \left\{ \sum_{i=1}^{n} (\lambda_i + \mu_{\pi(i)})^{-1} \right\} = \sum_{i=1}^{n} (\lambda_i + \mu_i)^{-1}. \tag{5.19}$$

Proof. Each of the above statements can be easily proved by assuming accordingly that $\mu_{\pi(k)} > \mu_{\pi(l)}$ (or $\mu_{\pi(k)} < \mu_{\pi(l)}$) for some $k < l$ and deriving a contradiction. ∎

Lemma 5.2 [88]. Let $M, N \in \mathbb{R}^{n \times n}$ be two symmetric matrices with eigenvalues $\lambda_{M,i}$ and $\lambda_{N,i}$ arranged in nonincreasing order. Let U_M, U_N be any orthogonal eigenvector matrices of M and N corresponding to the above ordering of the eigenvalues. Then

$$\min_{X:\text{orthogonal}} \text{tr}(MX^T NX) = \sum_{i=1}^{n} \lambda_{M,i} \lambda_{N,n-i+1}, \tag{5.20}$$

$$\text{optimum: } X_{\min} = U_N \begin{bmatrix} 0 & \cdots & \pm 1 \\ \vdots & & \vdots \\ \pm 1 & \cdots & 0 \end{bmatrix} U_M^T, \tag{5.21}$$

$$\max_{X:\text{orthogonal}} \text{tr}(MX^T NX) = \sum_{i=1}^{n} \lambda_{M,i} \lambda_{N,i}, \tag{5.22}$$

$$\text{optimum: } X_{\max} = U_N \begin{bmatrix} \pm 1 & \cdots & 0 \\ \vdots & & \vdots \\ 0 & \cdots & \pm 1 \end{bmatrix} U_M^T. \tag{5.23}$$

Proof. See the appendix at the end of the chapter. ∎

Many of the constraints to be discussed later involve sets of matrices that are invariant under multiplication with orthogonal matrices. We therefore provide the following

Definition 5.1. A compact set $\mathcal{A}$ will be called *orthogonally right-invariant* if for any orthogonal matrix Y, $A \in \mathcal{A}$ implies $AY \in \mathcal{A}$.

Lemma 5.3 [88]. Let $\mathcal{A}$ be orthogonally right-invariant. Then the minimizer of $J(\underline{W})$ under the constraint $\underline{W} \in \mathcal{A}$ is of the form

$$\underline{W} = R_e^{1/2} X D S_r U_x^T,$$

where $X \in \mathbb{R}^{p \times p}$ is orthogonal, $D \in \mathbb{R}^{p \times p}$ is diagonal, and $S_r \in \mathbb{R}^{p \times n}$ is a row selection matrix. This is equivalent to the statement

$$U_x^T \underline{W}^T R_e^{-1} \underline{W} U_x = D^2 = \text{diagonal}.$$

Proof. See the appendix at the end of the chapter. ∎

Constraining the Rows of $\underline{W}$ to Be Orthonormal This is an interesting constraint to study since the optimal PCA solution has orthonormal rows. Clearly, the constraint set $\mathcal{A}_o = \{\underline{W} : \underline{W}\,\underline{W}^T = I\}$ is orthogonally right-invariant. The following result can be shown

Theorem 5.2 [88]. The minimum of $J(\underline{W})$ under the constraint $\underline{W}\,\underline{W}^T = I$ is

$$\min_{\underline{W}:\underline{W}\,\underline{W}^T=I} J(\underline{W}) = \sum_{i=1}^{m} (\lambda_{x,i}^{-1} + \lambda_{e,m-i+1}^{-1})^{-1} + \sum_{i=m+1}^{n} \lambda_{x,i},$$

and it is attained for

$$\underline{W} = \sum_{i=1}^{m} u_{e,m-i+1} u_{x,i}^T.$$

Proof. Since $\mathcal{A}_o$ is orthogonally right-invariant by Lemma 5.3, the minimizer has the form $\underline{W} = R_e^{1/2} X D S_r U_x^T$, so

$$\underline{W}\,\underline{W}^T = R_e^{1/2} X D^2 X^T R_e^{1/2} = I,$$

$$X D^2 X^T = R_e^{-1},$$

so without loss of generality $D^2 = \text{diag}[\mu_{e,1}, \ldots, \mu_{e,m}]$ where $\mu_{e,1} \geq \cdots \geq \mu_{e,m}$ are the eigenvalues of R_e^{-1}. Defining $\mu_{x,1}, \ldots, \mu_{x,n}$ to be the eigenvalues of R_x^{-1} in nonincreasing order as well, the cost to be minimized becomes

$$J = \text{tr}\{\Lambda_x^{-1} + S_r^T D^2 S_r\} = \sum_{i=1}^{n} (\mu_{x,i} + \mu_{e,\pi(i)})^{-1},$$

where π is some permutation of $\{1, 2, \ldots, n\}$ and $\mu_{e,m+1} = \cdots = \mu_{e,n} = 0$. By Lemma 5.1 this is mimimized by choosing $\pi(1) = m, \ldots, \pi(m) = 1$ and the theorem follows. ∎

Constraint on the Frobenius Norm of $\underline{W}$ Originally Hornik (1992) [49] dealt with this constraint using the asymptotic noise power assumption $\|R_e\|_F \to \infty$. He found that under the constraint $\underline{W} \in \mathcal{A} = \{\text{tr}(\underline{W}\,\underline{W}^T) \leq s^2\}$ the optimum is

$$\underline{W} = s u_{e,m} u_{x,1}^T;$$

that is, the rank of $\underline{W}$ is 1. It appears that as the noise power gets too large extracting the first principal component is better than full PCA. This is similar to the result of Theorem 5.1. Still, for zero noise power ($R_e = 0$) the full PCA solution is optimal. Let us define the noisy principal directions $\underline{w}_i = su_{e,mi}u_{x,1}$, and the noisy principal components $y_i = \underline{w}_i^T x$, and let us compute the cross-correlations

$$E\{y_iy_j\} = s^2u_{e,mi}u_{e,mj}(u_{x,1}^T R_x u_{x,1}) = s^2u_{e,mi}u_{e,mj}\lambda_{x,1}.$$

So for very large noise power, $E\{y_iy_j\} \neq 0$ even for $i \neq j$ (unless of course $u_{x,1i} = 0$ or $u_{x,1j} = 0$, in which case y_i or y_j are identically zero). For very large noise the units *cooperate* and the noisy principal components are projections of x on the same principal subspace $u_{x,1}$ with just different scaling. Without noise, recalling from standard PCA, the principal directions are orthogonal and $E\{y_iy_j\} = 0$ for $i \neq j$, namely the units *compete* for variance. There must be a critical point in the noise power where competition turns into cooperation. Diamantaras and Hornik (1993) [88] showed that in fact the solution loses rank gradually as the noise power increases, and were able to determine the analytical solution under the Frobenius norm constraint:

Theorem 5.3 [88]. The minimizer of $J(\underline{W})$ under the constraint $\|\underline{W}\|_F^2 \le s^2$ is

$$\underline{W} = \sum_{i=1}^{r} \gamma_i u_{e,m-i+1}u_{x,i}^T,$$

where

$$\gamma_i^2 = \lambda_{e,m-i+1}^{1/2} \frac{s^2 + \sum_{k=1}^{r} \lambda_{e,m-k+1}\lambda_{x,k}^{-1}}{\sum_{k=1}^{r} \lambda_{e,m-k+1}^{1/2}} - \lambda_{e,m-i+1}\lambda_{x,i}^{-1}, \tag{5.24}$$

$$r = \max\left\{ k : \sum_{i=1}^{k-1} \lambda_{e,m-i+1}^{1/2}\left(\frac{\lambda_{e,m-k+1}^{1/2}}{\lambda_{x,k}} - \frac{\lambda_{e,m-i+1}^{1/2}}{\lambda_{x,i}} \right) < s^2 \right\}. \tag{5.25}$$

Proof. See the chapter appendix. ∎

From (5.25) it becomes clear that the rank r decreases as the noise eigenvalues increase. In the limit $\lambda_{e,m-i+1} \to \infty$ the rank-1 solution $\gamma_1 u_{e,m}u_{x,1}^T$ of the asymptotic problem is optimal, where $\gamma_1^2 = ((s^2 - \lambda_{x,1}^{-1}\lambda_{e,m})/\lambda_{e,m}^{1/2})\lambda_{e,m}^{1/2} - \lambda_{e,m}\lambda_{x,1}^{-1} = s^2$.

Constraining $\underline{w}_i$ to Have Unit Length The Frobenius constraint is a global one because it involves the total sum of squares $\underline{w}_{ij}^2$ over all synaptic weights in the lower layer. From the biological point of view locality is a desired property, so the Frobenius norm is not a good candidate. The localized version would be to constrain the rows of $\underline{W}$ to have say, unit length (or less than unit length). The row

$\underline{w}_i^T$ comprises the weights $\underline{w}_{ij}$, $j = 1, \ldots, n$, which are local to the ith unit in the hidden layer.

The constraint set

$$\mathcal{A}_r = \left\{ \underline{W} = \begin{bmatrix} \underline{w}_1^T \\ \vdots \\ \underline{w}_m^T \end{bmatrix} : \|\underline{w}_i^T\|^2 \leq 1, \ i = 1, \ldots, m \right\}$$

is again orthogonally right-invariant but now the solution is not known.

5.1.2 Constraints on $\overline{W}$

From (5.9) $\underline{W}_{\text{opt}} = \overline{W}^+$, so for given $\overline{W}$ the cost (5.5) becomes

$$J(\overline{W}) = \text{tr}\left\{ (I - \overline{W}\,\overline{W}^+)R_x(I - \overline{W}\,\overline{W}^+)^T \right\} + \text{tr}\{\overline{W}R_e\overline{W}^T\}. \tag{5.26}$$

Let $\overline{U}\,\overline{\Sigma}\,\overline{V}^T$ be the SVD of $\overline{W}$, where $\overline{U} \in \mathbb{R}^{n \times n}$, $V \in \mathbb{R}^{m \times m}$ are orthogonal, and $\overline{\Sigma} \in \mathbb{R}^{n \times m}$ is pseudodiagonal with diagonal entries the singular values $\overline{\sigma}_1 \geq \cdots \geq \overline{\sigma}_m > 0$ of $\overline{W}$. Using SVD notation we have $\overline{W}^+ = \overline{V}\,\overline{\Sigma}^+\overline{U}^T$ and $J(\overline{W})$ becomes

$$J(\overline{W}) = \text{tr}\left\{ (I - \overline{\Sigma}\,\overline{\Sigma}^+)\overline{U}^T R_x \overline{U}(I - \overline{\Sigma}\,\overline{\Sigma}^+)^T \right\} + \text{tr}\{\overline{\Sigma}\,\overline{V}^T R_e \overline{V}\,\overline{\Sigma}^T\}.$$

Theorem 5.4. Let $s_1 \geq \cdots \geq s_m > 0$ and consider the constraint set $\mathcal{A}_{\overline{\sigma}} = \{\overline{W} : \overline{\sigma}_i \geq s_i, \ i = 1, \ldots, m\}$. Then

$$\min_{\overline{W} \in \mathcal{A}_{\overline{\sigma}}} J(\overline{W}) = \sum_{i=m+1}^{n} \lambda_{x,i} + \sum_{i=1}^{m} s_i^2 \lambda_{e,m-i+1}, \tag{5.27}$$

and the minimum is attained for

$$\overline{W} = \sum_{i=1}^{m} s_i u_{x,i} u_{e,m-i+1}^T. \tag{5.28}$$

Proof.

$$J(\overline{W}) = \text{tr}\{\Lambda_1 \overline{U}^T R_x \overline{U}^T\} + \text{tr}\{\Lambda_2 \overline{V}^T R_e \overline{V}\},$$

where

$$\Lambda_1 = (I - \overline{\Sigma}\,\overline{\Sigma}^+)^T(I - \overline{\Sigma}\,\overline{\Sigma}^+) = \text{diag}[\underbrace{0 \ldots, 0}_{m}, \underbrace{1, \ldots, 1}_{n-m}],$$

and $\Lambda_2 = \overline{\Sigma}^T \overline{\Sigma}$. If we fix $\overline{\Sigma}$ the first and second terms in $J(\overline{W})$ can be minimized independently with respect to $\overline{U}$ and $\overline{V}$, and from Lemma 5.2 we obtain

$$\overline{U} = [u_{x,1}, \ldots, u_{x,n}], \quad \overline{V} = [u_{e,m}, \ldots, u_{e,1}],$$

yielding error

$$J(\overline{W}) = \sum_{i=m+1}^{n} \lambda_{x,i} + \sum_{i=1}^{m} \overline{\sigma}_i^2 \lambda_{e,m-1+1}.$$

Since $\overline{\sigma}_i^2 \geq s_i^2$, the theorem follows. ∎

Corollary 5.2. We have

$$\inf_{\overline{W}:\|\overline{W}\|_F^2 \geq s^2} J(\overline{W}) = \sum_{i=m+1}^{n} \lambda_{x,i} + s^2 \lambda_{e,m}.$$

No matrix $\overline{W}$ attains the infimum.

Proof. Since $\|\overline{W}\|_F^2 = \sum_{i=1}^{m} \overline{\sigma}_i^2 \geq s^2$, we have

$$\inf_{\overline{W}:\|\overline{W}\|_F^2 \geq s^2} J(\overline{W}) = \inf_{\sum_{i=1}^{m} s_i^2 = s^2} \inf_{\overline{\sigma}_i^2 \geq s_i^2} J(\overline{W})$$

$$= \inf_{\sum_{i=1}^{m} s_i^2 = s^2} \left[\sum_{i=m+1}^{n} \lambda_{x,i} + \sum_{i=1}^{m} s_i^2 \lambda_{e,m-i+1} \right]$$

$$= \sum_{i=m+1}^{n} \lambda_{x,i} + s^2 \lambda_{e,m}.$$

This infimum cannot be achieved, however, because the first term $\sum_{i=m+1}^{n} \lambda_{x,i}$ requires that $\text{rank}(\underline{W}) = m$, while the second term $s^2 \lambda_{e,m}$ requires that $\overline{\sigma}_1 = s, \overline{\sigma}_2 = 0, \ldots, \overline{\sigma}_m = 0$. Hence $\text{rank}(\overline{W}) = 1$. ∎

Still, it is possible to come arbitrarily close to the infimum by choosing

$$\overline{\Sigma} = \text{diag}[s, \varepsilon, \ldots, \varepsilon] \in \mathbb{R}^{n \times m}, \quad \overline{W}(\varepsilon) = [u_{x,1}, \ldots, u_{x,n}] \overline{\Sigma} [u_{e,m}, \ldots, u_{e,1}]^T$$

by letting ε go to, but not reach, 0. Indeed for any $\varepsilon > 0$ we obtain error

$$J(\overline{W}(\varepsilon)) = \sum_{i=m+1}^{n} \lambda_{x,i} + s^2 \lambda_{e,m} + \varepsilon^2 \sum_{i=2}^{m} \lambda_{e,m-i+1},$$

while $\|\overline{W}(\varepsilon)\|_F^2 = s^2 + (m-1)\varepsilon^2 > s^2$. If, however, $\varepsilon = 0$ the error increases abruptly to $J(\overline{W}(0)) = \sum_{i=2}^{n} \lambda_{x,i} + s^2 \lambda_{e,m}$.

5.2 OPTIMIZATION UNDER SOFT CONSTRAINTS

We shall investigate two soft-constraint alternatives concerning the lower-layer weights. Clearly, similar soft constraints can be formulated for the upper-layer weights as well.

5.2.1 Case (a)

The first case we study is to add the regularization term $\mu E\|y\|^2$, where μ is a fixed, positive scalar:

$$J_a(\mu) = E\|x - \overline{W}y\|^2 + \mu E\|y\|^2$$
$$= J + \mu \operatorname{tr}\{WR_x\underline{W}^T\} + \mu \operatorname{tr}\{R_e\}. \tag{5.29}$$

This would penalize large variances of y which, for fixed noise power, are results of large $\underline{W}$.

Notice that the cost (5.29) is essentially the same as (5.5) with the addition of the term $\mu \operatorname{tr}\{WR_x\underline{W}^T\}$ (clearly, the constant term $\mu \operatorname{tr}\{R_e\}$ is unimportant). The partial derivatives of $J_a(\mu)$ w.r.t. $\underline{W}$ and $\overline{W}$ are

$$D_{\underline{W}}J_a(\mu) = 2(\overline{W}^T\overline{W}\underline{W}R_x - \overline{W}^TR_x + \mu\underline{W}R_x), \tag{5.30}$$
$$D_{\overline{W}}J_a(\mu) = 2(\overline{W}\underline{W}R_x\underline{W}^T - R_x\underline{W}^T + \overline{W}R_e). \tag{5.31}$$

The usual

$$D_{\underline{W}}J_a(\mu) = 0 \qquad \text{and} \qquad D_{\overline{W}}J_a(\mu) = 0$$

now yields

$$\underline{W}^T(\overline{W}^T\overline{W} + \mu) = \overline{W}, \tag{5.32}$$
$$(WR_x\underline{W}^T + R_e)\overline{W}^T = \underline{W}R_x. \tag{5.33}$$

Theorem 5.5. The minimum of J_a is

$$\min J_a = \sum_{i=r+1}^{n} \lambda_{x,i} + 2\sqrt{\mu} \sum_{i=1}^{r} \sqrt{\lambda_{x,i}\lambda_{e,m-i+1}} + \mu \sum_{i=r+1}^{m} \lambda_{e,m-i+1},$$

where

$$r = \max\left[\{0\} \cup \{i = 1, \ldots, m : \mu < \gamma_i\}\right],$$
$$\gamma_i = \frac{\lambda_{x,i}}{\lambda_{e,m-i+1}}.$$

The minimum is attained for

$$\underline{W} = \sum_{i=1}^{m} \underline{\sigma}_i u_{e,m-i+1} u_{x,i}^T, \qquad \overline{W} = \sum_{i=1}^{m} \overline{\sigma}_i u_{x,i} u_{e,m-i+1}^T,$$

$$\underline{\sigma}_i^2 = \begin{cases} 1/\sqrt{\gamma_i \mu} - 1/\gamma_i & \text{if } \mu < \gamma_i, \\ 0 & \text{otherwise,} \end{cases}$$

$$\overline{\sigma}_i^2 = \begin{cases} \sqrt{\gamma_i \mu} - \mu & \text{if } \mu < \gamma_i, \\ 0 & \text{otherwise.} \end{cases}$$

Proof. See chapter appendix.   ∎

The variance of the optimal hidden units' representation is

$$E\|y\|^2 = \text{tr}\{\underline{W}R_x\underline{W}^T\} + \text{tr}\{R_e\} = \sum_{i=1}^{m} \underline{\sigma}_i^2 \lambda_{x,i} + \sum_{i=1}^{m} \lambda_{e,i}$$

$$= 1/\sqrt{\mu} \sum_{i=1}^{r} \sqrt{\lambda_{e,m-i+1}\lambda_{x,i}} + \sum_{i=r+1}^{m} \lambda_{e,m-i+1}. \tag{5.34}$$

Similarly, the reconstruction error is

$$J = J_a(\mu) - \mu E\|y\|^2 = \sum_{i=r+1}^{n} \lambda_{x,i} + \sqrt{\mu} \sum_{i=1}^{r} \sqrt{\lambda_{xi}\lambda_{e,m-i+1}}. \tag{5.35}$$

5.2.2   Case (b)

The soft version of the Frobenius constraint on $\underline{W}$ will have the form

$$J_b(\mu) = J + \mu\|\underline{W}\|_F^2, \tag{5.36}$$

Now

$$D_{\underline{W}}J_b(\mu) = 2\left(\overline{W}^T\overline{W}\underline{W}R_x - \overline{W}^T R_x + \mu\underline{W}\right), \tag{5.37}$$

$$D_{\overline{W}}J_b(\mu) = 2\left(\overline{W}\underline{W}R_x\underline{W}^T - R_x\underline{W}^T + \overline{W}R_e\right), \tag{5.38}$$

from which we get that any critical point should satisfy

$$R_x\underline{W}^T\overline{W}^T\overline{W} + \mu\underline{W}^T = R_x\overline{W}, \tag{5.39}$$

$$(\underline{W}R_x\underline{W}^T + R_e)\overline{W}^T = \underline{W}R_x. \tag{5.40}$$

Theorem 5.6. The minimum of J_b is

$$\min J_b = \sum_{i=r+1}^{n} \lambda_{x,i} + 2 \sum_{i=1}^{r} \sqrt{\mu \lambda_{e,m-i+1}} - \mu \sum_{i=1}^{r} \frac{\lambda_{e,m-i+1}}{\lambda_{x,i}},$$

where r is defined as in Theorem 5.5.

The minimum is attained for

$$\underline{W} = \sum_{i=1}^{m} \underline{\sigma}_i u_{e,m-i+1} u_{x,i}^T, \qquad \overline{W} = \sum_{i=1}^{m} \overline{\sigma}_i u_{x,i} u_{e,m-i+1}^T,$$

$$\underline{\sigma}_i^2 = \begin{cases} \sqrt{\lambda_{x,i}/\gamma_i \mu} - 1/\gamma_i) & \text{if } \mu < \gamma_i, \\ 0 & \text{otherwise,} \end{cases}$$

$$\overline{\sigma}_i^2 = \begin{cases} \sqrt{\gamma_i \mu/\lambda_{xi}} - \mu/\lambda_{x,i} & \text{if } \mu < \gamma_i, \\ 0 & \text{otherwise.} \end{cases}$$

Proof. See chapter appendix. ∎

5.3 INFORMATION-THEORETICAL CONNECTIONS

We have often found a close relationship between information maximization (in the Gaussian setting) and PCA. We expect similar connections for the noisy PCA case as well. Indeed, the following theorem taken from [34] (Theorem 7.5.1) bears strong analogies to noisy PCA.

Theorem 5.7 (Parallel Additive Gaussian Noise Channels). Consider a set of n memoryless channels $y_1, \ldots, y_n$, with additive zero-mean Gaussian noise $e_1, \ldots, e_n$:

$$y_i = x_i + e_i.$$

We denote the noise variances by $\lambda_{e,i} = E\{e_i^2\}$, $i = 1, \ldots, n$, and we define the input and output vectors $x = [x_1, \ldots, x_n]$, $y = [y_1, \ldots, y_n]$. If the energy of the input messages is constrained so that

$$\sum_{i=1}^{n} E\|x_i\|^2 \leq \mathcal{E},$$

then the mutual information $I(x, y)$ is maximized by choosing the inputs to be statistically independent, zero-mean Gaussian random variables with variance $E\|x_i\|^2 = \lambda_{x,i}$, where

$$\lambda_{x,i} = \begin{cases} B - \lambda_{e,i} & \text{if } \lambda_{e,i} < B, \\ 0 & \text{if } \lambda_{e,i} \geq B, \end{cases}$$

and B is chosen so that $\sum_{i=1}^{n} \lambda_{x,i} = \mathcal{E}$.

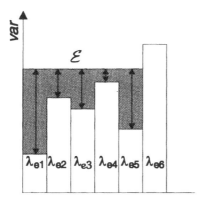

Figure 5.2. The optimal energy distribution of the parallel noisy channels resembles a vessel with bottom shaped according to the noise variances filled with water of quantity $\mathcal{E}$.

The interpretation of the solution is shown in Figure 5.2. The system puts most of its energy to the least noisy channels and progressively less energy to the more noisy channels. This is analogous to the noisy PCA situation where the least principal noise component pairs with the most principal signal component, and vice versa. The situation in the information-theoretical setting resembles a container filled with water (and justifiably it is called the *water-filling analogy*) where the bottom of the container is shaped according to the sizes of the noise variances $\lambda_{e,i}$ and the quantity of the water is $\mathcal{E}$.

It is even more interesting to observe that as the noise variances $\lambda_{e,i}$ become larger compared to $\mathcal{E}$ more and more channels are left without signal. In the limit, as $\lambda_{e,i} \rightarrow \infty$ and assuming that the noise variances are not equal, then all the signal is concentrated in only one channel, the one with smallest noise. Again there is a striking similarity with noisy PCA where increasing the noise variance results in rank loss and asymptotically leads to a rank-1 solution.

Linsker (1989) [89] had observed similar phenomena when optimizing noisy networks under his information-theoretical criterion called INFOMAX. He also mentions the resemblance of his solution with the water-filling analogy.

5.4 NEURAL NETWORKS AND NOISY PCA

It is interesting to observe that most of the PCA neural network models described in Chapter 4 fail in the noisy PCA case. The basic Oja rule

$$\Delta w_k = \beta_k (y_k x_k - y_k^2 w_k)$$

leads, under the noisy setting $y = w^T x + e$, to the ODE

$$\frac{dw}{dt} = R_x w - [(w^T R_x w)I + R_e]w \tag{5.41}$$

$$= (R_x - R_e)w - (w^T R_x w)w. \tag{5.42}$$

The critical points of (5.42) are the zero vector and the eigenvectors of the matrix $R_x - R_e$. If the noise power, however, is so high that $R_x - R_e$ becomes negative definite,[1] then the only equilibrium is $w = 0$, since the nonnegative $w^T R_x w$ could not be the eigenvalue of $R_x - R_e$.

Hornik [49] demonstrated that in the simple case $R_e = \lambda I$, $\lambda > \lambda_{x,1}$, the only attractor (in fact the global attractor) is zero. Even in the general case for R_e, if $R_x - R_e$ is negative definite, we obtain, from (5.42),

$$\frac{d(\|w\|^2)}{dt} = 2\big(w^T R_x w - w^T R_e w - (w^T R_x w)\|w\|^2\big) \leq 0$$

(with equality only if $w = 0$), so $\|w\|^2 \to 0$. So Oja's rule ceases to learn anything interesting as the noise power gets too large.

As many PCA learning rules (Sanger's rule, APEX, etc.) are based on Oja's single-unit rule, they are also deemed inappropriate for the NPCA problem.

Even in the least-squares learning rules such as back-propagation, some constraint (hard or soft, for $\overline{W}$ or for $\underline{W}$) must be incorporated to avoid the degeneracy $\overline{W} \to 0$, $\underline{W} \to \infty$. Such rules must, in addition, be local in order to have biological plausibility. Such rules are still to be developed.

APPENDIX

Proof of Theorem 5.1

Define $Q \equiv U_e^T W$, so (5.11) yields

$$QR_x(I - Q^T Q) + Q(I - Q^T Q)R_x = \Lambda_e Q. \tag{5.43}$$

Letting $A \equiv R_x(I - Q^T Q) + (I - Q^T Q)R_x$, we have $QA = \Lambda_e Q$. Thus the rows of Q are eigenvectors of A. Since A has distinct eigenvalues (the same as R_e) Q must have the following form: $Q = \Gamma S U_a^T$, where $U_a \in \mathbb{R}^{n \times n}$ is the orthogonal eigenvector matrix of A, $S \in \mathbb{R}^{m \times n}$ is a row selection matrix, and $\Gamma \in \mathbb{R}^{m \times m}$ is a diagonal matrix whose diagonal elements we shall denote by $\gamma_1, \ldots, \gamma_m$.

Postmultiplying (5.43) by Q^T we obtain

$$(2I - \Gamma^2)QR_x Q^T - QR_x Q^T \Gamma^2 = \Lambda_e \Gamma^2$$

---

[1]For example, if $\lambda_{e,m} > \lambda_{x,1}$, then $w^T R_x w - w^T R_e w \leq \lambda_{x,1}\|w\|^2 - \lambda_{e,m}\|w\|^2 < 0$, for all $w \neq 0$.

or

$$(2I - \Gamma^2)B - B\Gamma^2 = \Lambda_e\Gamma^2, \tag{5.44}$$

where we have set $B = [b_{ij}] = QR_xQ^T$. Equation (5.44) implies

$$(2 - 2\gamma_i^2)b_{ii} = \lambda_{e,i}\gamma_i^2, \tag{5.45}$$

$$(2 - \gamma_i^2 - \gamma_j^2)b_{ij} = 0, \qquad i \neq j, \tag{5.46}$$

Since B is positive definite we have $b_{ii} > 0$, so the first condition implies $\gamma_i^2 < 1$ for all i. Subsequently the second condition implies $b_{ij} = 0$ for all $i \neq j$. So B is a diagonal matrix and

$$Q = \Gamma SU_x^T, \qquad W = U_e\Gamma SU_x^T. \tag{5.47}$$

Plugging (5.47) into (5.10) we get

$$\begin{aligned} J &= \text{tr}\{R_x\} - 2\,\text{tr}\{S^T\Gamma^2S\Lambda_x\} + \text{tr}\{\Gamma^2S\Lambda_xS^T\Gamma^2\} + \text{tr}\{\Lambda_e\Gamma^2\} \\ &= \sum_{i=1}^{n}\lambda_{x,i} - 2\sum_{i=1}^{m}\gamma_i^2\lambda_{x,s(i)} + \sum_{i=1}^{m}\gamma_i^4\lambda_{x,s(i)} + \sum_{i=1}^{m}\gamma_i^2\lambda_{e,i}, \end{aligned} \tag{5.48}$$

where $s(\cdot)$ is a selection function from the indices $\langle 1, \ldots, n \rangle$.

$$\frac{\partial J}{\partial \gamma_i} = 0$$

$$\Rightarrow -4\gamma_i\lambda_{x,s(i)} + 4\gamma_i^3\lambda_{x,s(i)} + 2\gamma_i\lambda_{e,i} = 0,$$

$$\Rightarrow \gamma_i^2 = \begin{cases} 1 - \frac{1}{2}\lambda_{e,i}/\lambda_{x,s(i)} & \text{if } \lambda_{e,i} < 2\lambda_{x,s(i)}, \\ 0 & \text{otherwise,} \end{cases} \tag{5.49}$$

$$J = \sum_{i=1}^{n}\lambda_{x,i} - 2\sum_{i=1}^{m}\gamma_i^4\lambda_{x,s(i)}. \tag{5.50}$$

The ith term in the rightmost sum can be expanded as

$$d_i \equiv \gamma_i^4\lambda_{x,s(i)} = [\lambda_{x,s(i)} - \lambda_{e,i} + \tfrac{1}{4}\lambda_{e,i}^2/\lambda_{x,s(i)}]\,t(\lambda_{e,i}, \lambda_{x,s(i)}),$$

where $t(x, y) = 1$, if $x < 2y$, else $t(x, y) = 0$. It is not difficult to show that d_i increases if $\lambda_{x,s(i)}$ is replaced by a larger number. Therefore, the sum must contain the m largest eigenvalues of R_x. If that was not true there would exist a term $d_{i'}$ such that $s(i') = i_1 > m$, and there would exist some index $i_2 \leq m$ not in the set $\{s(1), \ldots, s(m)\}$. But then we could set $s(i') = i_2$ and increase $d_{i'}$, therefore reducing J, since λ_{x,i_1} is replaced by the larger value λ_{x,i_2}. Thus the index set $\{s(1), s(2), \ldots, s(m)\}$ must be equal to the set $\{1, 2, \ldots, m\}$, and the theorem follows.

∎

Proof of Lemma 5.2

We'll treat only the minimization case here; the maximization case is proved similarly. We have

$$\mathrm{tr}\{MX^T NX\} = \mathrm{tr}\{\Lambda_M U_M^T X^T U_N \Lambda_N U_N^T X U_M\},$$

where $\Lambda_M = \mathrm{diag}[\lambda_{M,1}, \ldots, \lambda_{M,n}]$, $\Lambda_N = \mathrm{diag}[\lambda_{N,1}, \ldots, \lambda_{N,n}]$. Let $\tilde{X} = U_N^T X U_M$. $\tilde{X}$ is clearly orthogonal so the problem is transformed into minimizing, over all orthogonal matrices $\tilde{X}$, the function

$$\mathrm{tr}\{\Lambda_M \tilde{X}^T \Lambda_N \tilde{X}\} = \sum_{i,j} \tilde{x}_{ji}^2 \lambda_{M,i} \lambda_{N,j} = \mathrm{tr}\{\Lambda_M P \Lambda_N\},$$

where the matrix $P = [\tilde{x}_{ji}^2] = \tilde{X} \circ \tilde{X}$ is doubly stochastic. Hence,

$$\min_{\tilde{X}:\text{orthogonal}} \mathrm{tr}\{\Lambda_M \tilde{X}^T \Lambda_N \tilde{X}\} \geq \min_{P:\text{doubly stochastic}} \mathrm{tr}\{\Lambda_M P \Lambda_N\}.$$

According to Birkhoff's theorem 2.7 the set of all doubly stochastic matrices is the convex hull of all the permutation matrices and because the trace function to be minimized is linear in P, both the minimum and maximum are achieved at a vertex of the convex hull. Therefore the optimal P is a permutation matrix and $\tilde{x}_{ij} = \pm p_{ij}$, so $\tilde{X}$ is indeed orthogonal. Thus

$$\min_{\tilde{X}:\text{orthogonal}} \mathrm{tr}\{\Lambda_M \tilde{X}^T \Lambda_N \tilde{X}\} = \sum_{i=1}^{n} \lambda_{M,i} \lambda_{N,\pi(i)}$$

for some permutation π. Now, with the assistance of Lemma 5.1 we can find the optimal π, and the lemma follows immediately. ∎

Proof of Lemma 5.3

Assume that for some $\underline{W} \in \mathcal{A}$,

$$\mathrm{tr}\left\{(R_x^{-1} + \underline{W}^T R_e^{-1} \underline{W})^{-1}\right\} = \mathrm{tr}\left\{(\Lambda_x^{-1} + U_x^T \underline{W}^T R_e^{-1} \underline{W} U_x)^{-1}\right\}$$

is minimal. Multiplying from the right with the orthogonal Givens rotation matrix

$$C_{kl}(\varepsilon) = \begin{array}{c} \\ \\ k \\ \\ l \\ \\ \\ \end{array} \begin{bmatrix} 1 & \cdots & 0 & \cdots & 0 & \cdots & 0 \\ \vdots & \ddots & \vdots & & \vdots & & \vdots \\ 0 & \cdots & \cos(\varepsilon) & \cdots & \sin(\varepsilon) & \cdots & 0 \\ \vdots & & \vdots & \ddots & \vdots & & \vdots \\ 0 & \cdots & -\sin(\varepsilon) & \cdots & \cos(\varepsilon) & \cdots & 0 \\ \vdots & & \vdots & & \vdots & \ddots & \vdots \\ 0 & \cdots & 0 & \cdots & 0 & \cdots & 1 \end{bmatrix},$$

we have $\underline{W}U_xC_{kl}(\varepsilon) \in \mathcal{A}$, by orthogonal right-invariance. $C_{kl}(\cdot)$ has the following properties

$$C_{kl}(0) = I,$$

$$\frac{dC_{kl}(\varepsilon)}{d\varepsilon}\bigg|_{\varepsilon=0} \equiv J_{kl} = \begin{array}{c} \\ \\ k \\ \\ l \\ \\ \\ \end{array} \begin{bmatrix} 0 & \cdots & 0 & \cdots & 0 & \cdots & 0 \\ \vdots & \ddots & \vdots & & \vdots & & \vdots \\ 0 & \cdots & 0 & \cdots & 1 & \cdots & 0 \\ \vdots & & \vdots & \ddots & \vdots & & \vdots \\ 0 & \cdots & -1 & \cdots & 0 & \cdots & 0 \\ \vdots & & \vdots & & \vdots & \ddots & \vdots \\ 0 & \cdots & 0 & \cdots & 0 & \cdots & 1 \end{bmatrix}.$$

Since $\underline{W}$ is optimum in $\mathcal{A}$ we must have (writing $Q = U_x^T \underline{W}^T R_e^{-1} \underline{W} U_x$ to simplify the notation)

$$\begin{aligned} 0 &= \frac{d}{d\varepsilon} \operatorname{tr}\left\{ [\Lambda_x^{-1} + C_{kl}(\varepsilon)^T U_x^T \underline{W}^T R_e^{-1} \underline{W} U_x C_{kl}(\varepsilon)]^{-1} \right\}\bigg|_{\varepsilon=0} \\ &= -\operatorname{tr}\left\{ (\Lambda_x^{-1} + Q)^{-1}(Q J_{kl} + J_{kl}^T Q)(\Lambda_x^{-1} + Q)^{-1} \right\} \\ &= -2\operatorname{tr}\left\{ (\Lambda_x^{-1} + Q)^{-2} Q J_{kl} \right\} \\ &= -2\left\{ [(\Lambda_x^{-1} + Q)^{-2} Q]_{kl} - [(\Lambda_x^{-1} + Q)^{-2} Q]_{lk} \right\}. \end{aligned}$$

for all k, l. Thus $(\Lambda_x^{-1} + Q)^{-2}Q$ is symmetric. The fact that $(\Lambda_x^{-1} + Q)^{-1} - (\Lambda_x^{-1} + Q)^{-2}Q = \Lambda_x^{-1}(\Lambda_x^{-1} + Q)^{-2}$ is also symmetric implies finally that Q is diagonal. ∎

Proof of Theorem 5.3

To start with, observe that the constraint set $\mathcal{A}_F = \{\underline{W} : \operatorname{tr}(\underline{W}\,\underline{W}^T) \le s^2\}$ is orthogonally right-invariant, so by Lemma 5.3

$$\underline{W} = R_e^{1/2} X D S_r U_x^T,$$

where $X \in \mathbb{R}^{m \times m}$ is orthogonal, $D = \operatorname{diag}[d_1, \ldots, d_r, 0, \ldots, 0] \in \mathbb{R}^{m \times m}$, $S_r \in \mathbb{R}^{m \times n}$ is a row selection matrix, and $r = \operatorname{rank}(\underline{W}) \le m$. We have

$$\begin{aligned} J(\underline{W}) &= \operatorname{tr}\left\{ (\Lambda_x^{-1} + U_x^T \underline{W}^T R_e^{-1} \underline{W} U_x)^{-1} \right\} \\ &= \operatorname{tr}\left\{ (\Lambda_x^{-1} + S_r^T D^2 S_r)^{-1} \right\} \\ &= \sum_{i=1}^n (\lambda_{x,i}^{-1} + d_{\pi(i)}^2)^{-1}, \end{aligned}$$

where π is a permutation of $\{1, \ldots, n\}$ and $d_{m+1} = \cdots = d_n = 0$. From Lemma 5.1 the minimum is attained for $\{d_{\pi(i)}\} = [d_1, \ldots, d_r, 0, \ldots, 0]$, assuming that $d_1 \geq d_2 \geq \cdots \geq d_r$, so

$$J = \sum_{i=1}^{r} (\lambda_x^{-1} + d_i^2)^{-1} + \sum_{i=r+1}^{n} \lambda_x.$$

Furthermore, given the optimal D,

$$\text{tr}(\underline{W}\,\underline{W}^T) = \min_{X:\text{orthogonal}} \text{tr}(XD^2X^T R_e) = \sum_{i=1}^{m} d_i^2 \lambda_{e,m-i+1}, \tag{5.51}$$

where the minimum is obtained for

$$X_{\text{opt}} = [u_{e,m}, \ldots, u_{e,1}].$$

Equation (5.51) is true because if $\text{tr}(\underline{W}\,\underline{W}^T) = \text{tr}(XD^2X^T R_e) = c\,\text{tr}(X_{\text{opt}}D^2 X_{\text{opt}}^T R_e)$, for some $c > 1$, then the matrix $\underline{W}' = R_e^{1/2} X_{\text{opt}}(cD)S_r U_x^T$ achieves smaller error J, while $\|\underline{W}'\|_F = \|\underline{W}\|_F$. So we may assume $X = X_{\text{opt}}$. Similarly, $\text{tr}(\underline{W}\,\underline{W}^T) = s^2$ because if $\text{tr}(\underline{W}\,\underline{W}^T) < s^2$ we could scale $\underline{W}$ to reduce the error.

So the problem is transformed to the following:

$$\text{minimize} \quad \sum_{i=1}^{r} (\lambda_{x,i}^{-1} + d_i^2)^{-1},$$

$$\text{under the constraint} \quad \sum_{i=1}^{r} d_i^2 \lambda_{m-i+1} = s^2,$$

which can be solved using the Lagrange multiplier ξ to form a new function

$$J_c = \sum_{i=1}^{r} (\lambda_x^{-1} + d_i^2)^{-1} + \xi \left(s^2 - \sum_{i=1}^{r} d_i^2 \lambda_{m-i+1} \right).$$

Setting $\partial J_c / \partial(d_i^2) = 0$ and $\partial J_c / \partial \xi = 0$ we obtain

$$d_i^2 = (\xi \lambda_{e,m-i+1})^{-1/2} - \lambda_{x,i}^{-1}, \tag{5.52}$$

$$\xi^{1/2} = \frac{\sum_{i=1}^{r} \lambda_{e,m-i+1}^{1/2}}{s^2 + \sum_{i=1}^{r} \lambda_{x,i}^{-1} \lambda_{e,m-i+1}}. \tag{5.53}$$

Since $d_r^2 > 0$ we must have

$$\xi^{-1/2}\lambda_{e,m-r+1}^{-1/2} > \lambda_{x,r}^{-1}$$

$$\Rightarrow s^2 + \sum_{i=1}^{r} \lambda_{x,i}^{-1}\lambda_{e,m-i+1} > \lambda_{x,r}^{-1}\lambda_{e,m-r+1}^{1/2} \sum_{i=1}^{r}(\lambda_{e,m-i+1})^{1/2}$$

$$\Rightarrow s^2 > \sum_{i=1}^{r-1}[\lambda_{x,r}^{-1}\lambda_{e,m-i+1}^{1/2}\lambda_{e,m-r+1}^{1/2} - \lambda_{x,i}^{-1}\lambda_{e,m-i+1}],$$

from which (5.25) follows.

The optimal $\underline{W}$ is

$$\underline{W} = R_e^{1/2}[u_{e,m}, \ldots, u_{e,1}] D [u_{x,1}, \ldots, u_{x,m}]^T$$

$$= \sum_{i=1}^{r} \lambda_{e,m-i+1}^{1/2} d_i u_{e,m-i+1} u_{x,i}^T.$$

Defining $\gamma_i = \lambda_{e,m-i+1}^{1/2} d_i$, (5.25) follows immediately. ∎

Proof of Theorem 5.5

From (5.32) it is easy to show that if the SVD of $\underline{W}$ is UDV^T then the SVD of $\overline{W}$ is $V\overline{D}U^T$ such that $\underline{D}^T = \overline{D}(\overline{D}^T\overline{D} + \mu)^{-1}$; i.e.,

$$\underline{\sigma}_i = \frac{\overline{\sigma}_i}{\overline{\sigma}_i^2 + \mu},$$

where $\underline{\sigma}_i$ and $\overline{\sigma}_i$ are the singular values of $\underline{W}$ and $\overline{W}$. If we replace $\underline{W}$ and $\overline{W}$ by their SVDs in (5.29) after some simple manipulations we get

$$J_a(\mu) = \mathrm{tr}\left\{[(I - \overline{D}\underline{D})^2 + \mu\underline{D}^T\underline{D}]V^T R_x V\right\}$$
$$+ \mathrm{tr}\{\overline{D}^T\overline{D}U^T R_e U\} + \mu\,\mathrm{tr}\{R_e\}. \tag{5.54}$$

Let's assume that the optimal $\underline{D}$ and $\overline{D}$ are given and, without loss of generality, that $\overline{\sigma}_i$ are arranged in decreasing order. The first two terms of (5.54) are decoupled with respect to the involvement of matrices U and V. Therefore, for fixed $\overline{D}$, $\underline{D}$, each term can be minimized separately. Applying Lemma 5.2 on the second right-hand-side term, we obtain $U = [u_{e,m}, \ldots, u_{e,1}]$.

Regarding the first term, observe that the matrix $[(I - \overline{D}\underline{D})^2 + \mu\underline{D}^T\underline{D}]$ is diagonal. The first m entries are not equal to 1 and the rest $n - m$ entries equal to 1.

The first m diagonal entries are

$$\left(1 - \frac{\overline{\sigma}_i^2}{\overline{\sigma}_i^2 + \mu}\right)^2 + \mu \frac{\overline{\sigma}_i^2}{(\overline{\sigma}_i^2 + \mu)^2} = \frac{\mu}{\overline{\sigma}_i^2 + \mu}.$$

Since we assumed $\overline{\sigma}_i$ are in decreasing order, the sequence $\mu/(\overline{\sigma}_i^2 + \mu)$ is in increasing order and always less than 1, so the diagonal entries of $[(I - \overline{D}\underline{D})^2 + \mu\underline{D}^T\underline{D}]$ are arranged in increasing order. Hence Lemma 5.2 again leads to $V = [u_{x,1}, \ldots, u_{x,n}]$.

Then from (5.32), (5.33) we obtain

$$\underline{\sigma}_i = \frac{\overline{\sigma}_i}{\overline{\sigma}_i^2 + \mu}, \tag{5.55}$$

$$\overline{\sigma}_i = \frac{\lambda_{x,i}\underline{\sigma}_i}{\lambda_{x,i}\underline{\sigma}_i^2 + \lambda_{e,m-i+1}} = \frac{\underline{\sigma}_i}{\underline{\sigma}_i^2 + \gamma_i^{-1}} \tag{5.56}$$

where

$$\gamma_i \equiv \frac{\lambda_{x,i}}{\lambda_{e,m-i+1}}, \qquad i = 1, \ldots, m \tag{5.57}$$

One solution is obviously

$$\underline{\sigma}_i = 0, \qquad \overline{\sigma}_i = 0.$$

However, if $\mu < \gamma_i$, then we have the nontrivial solution

$$\underline{\sigma}_i^2 = \sqrt{1/\gamma_i\mu} - 1/\gamma_i, \tag{5.58}$$

$$\overline{\sigma}_i^2 = \sqrt{\gamma_i\mu} - \mu. \tag{5.59}$$

The sequence of eigenvalue ratios γ_i is decreasing, so for a given $\mu > 0$ we can define

$$r = \max\left[\{0\} \cup \{i = 1, \ldots, m : \mu < \gamma_i\}\right].$$

Hence, only the pairs $(\underline{\sigma}_i, \overline{\sigma}_i)$ for $i = 1, \ldots, r$ can accept the nontrivial values. It is interesting to notice that as μ gets larger the rank r of the solution is decreasing similarly to the hard constraint on the Frobenius norm where rank was being lost by increasing the noise power. In the worst case, if $\mu \geq \lambda_{x,1}/\lambda_{e,m}$, we are eliminating all nontrivial solutions, forcing ourselves to the 0 solution. In that case it seems that we prefer to put all our efforts to minimizing the regularization term of $J_a(\mu)$, ignoring all the reconstruction error (i.e., the first term).

If $\underline{\sigma}_i, \overline{\sigma}_i, i = 1,\ldots,r$, assume their nontrivial values (5.58),(5.59), then using (5.54) the error is computed to be

$$
\begin{aligned}
J_a(\mu) &= \sum_{i=1}^{r} \left(\frac{\mu}{\overline{\sigma}_i^2 + \mu} \right) \lambda_{x,i} + \sum_{i=r+1}^{n} \lambda_{x,i} + \sum_{i=1}^{r} \overline{\sigma}_i^2 \lambda_{e,m-i+1} + \mu \operatorname{tr}\{R_e\} \\
&= \sum_{i=1}^{r} \sqrt{\frac{\mu}{\gamma_i}} \lambda_{x,i} + \sum_{i=r+1}^{n} \lambda_{x,i} + \sum_{i=1}^{r} (\sqrt{\gamma_i \mu} - \mu)\lambda_{e,m-i+1} + \mu \sum_{i=1}^{m} \lambda_{e,i} \\
&= \sum_{i=r+1}^{n} \lambda_{x,i} + 2\sqrt{\mu} \sum_{i=1}^{r} \sqrt{\lambda_{x,i} \lambda_{e,m-i+1}} + \mu \sum_{i=1}^{m-r} \lambda_{e,i}.
\end{aligned}
\tag{5.60}
$$

Since $\mu < \gamma_i$, for $i = 1,\ldots,r$, then $\sqrt{\mu \gamma_i}\, \lambda_{e,m-i+1} < \lambda_{x,1}$, so the error is lower than if we had used the trivial values $\underline{\sigma}_i = 0$, $\overline{\sigma}_i = 0$, for $i = 1,\ldots,r$. The use of the trivial values in that case would simply correspond to a nonglobally optimal critical point.   ∎

Proof of Theorem 5.6

Multiplying (5.39) and (5.40) by $\underline{W}$ and $\overline{W}$ from the left and right respectively, we get

$$
\underline{W}R_x \underline{W}^T \overline{W}^T \overline{W} + \mu \underline{W}\,\underline{W}^T = \underline{W}R_x \overline{W},
\tag{5.61}
$$

$$
\underline{W}R_x \underline{W}^T \overline{W}^T \overline{W} + R_e \overline{W}^T \overline{W} = \underline{W}R_x \overline{W}.
\tag{5.62}
$$

Adding (5.61) and (5.62), we obtain

$$
2 \operatorname{tr}\{\underline{W}R_x \underline{W}^T \overline{W}^T \overline{W}\} + \operatorname{tr}\{R_e \overline{W}^T \overline{W}\} + \mu \operatorname{tr}\{\underline{W}\,\underline{W}^T\} = 2 \operatorname{tr}\{\underline{W}R_x \overline{W}\}.
\tag{5.63}
$$

Subtracting (5.62) from (5.61), we obtain

$$
\mu \underline{W}\,\underline{W}^T = R_e \overline{W}^T \overline{W},
\tag{5.64}
$$

from which $\overline{W}^T \overline{W}R_e = \mu \underline{W}\,\underline{W}^T = R_e \overline{W}^T \overline{W}$; i.e., the matrices R_e and $\overline{W}^T \overline{W}$ commute. Since both matrices are symmetric it follows that they share the same eigenvectors. Therefore if $\overline{W} = \overline{U}\,\overline{D}\,V^T$ is the SVD of $\overline{W}$ then V is the eigenvector matrix of R_e (with some permutation of the columns). Without loss of generality, we may assume $V = [u_{e,m},\ldots,u_{e,1}]$.

Also from (5.63) it follows that V is the eigenvalue matrix of $\underline{W}\,\underline{W}^T$; namely, the SVD of $\underline{W}$ must be of the form $VD\,U^T$. Furthermore, if $\underline{W}$ has no zero singular values then the same must be true for $\overline{W}$.

For any critical point the cost is

$$J_b(\mu) = \mathrm{tr}\{R_x\} - 2\,\mathrm{tr}\{\underline{W}R_x\overline{W}\} + \mathrm{tr}\{\underline{W}R_x\underline{W}^T\overline{W}^T\overline{W}\}$$
$$+ \mathrm{tr}\{R_e\overline{W}^T\overline{W}\} + \mu\,\mathrm{tr}\{\underline{W}\,\underline{W}^T\}.$$

From (5.63) we get

$$J_b(\mu) = \mathrm{tr}\{R_x\} - \mathrm{tr}\{\underline{W}R_x\underline{W}^T\overline{W}^T\overline{W}\}$$
$$= \mathrm{tr}\{R_x\} - \mathrm{tr}\{\underline{U}^T R_x\underline{U}\,\underline{D}^T\overline{D}^T\overline{D}\underline{D}\}. \tag{5.65}$$

For fixed $\overline{D}$, $\underline{D}$, minimization of J_b means maximization of $\mathrm{tr}\{\underline{U}^T R_x\underline{U}\Lambda\}$, where $\Lambda = \underline{D}^T\overline{D}^T\overline{D}\underline{D}$. Lemma 5.2 implies that the optimum is achieved for $\underline{U} = U_xP$, P a permutation matrix performing a permutation π on the columns of U_x. Then (5.40) becomes $(\underline{D}\Lambda_x^\pi\underline{D}^T + \Lambda_e')\overline{D}^T = \underline{D}\Lambda_x^\pi(\underline{U}^T\overline{U})$, $\Lambda_x^\pi = \mathrm{diag}[\lambda_{x,\pi(1)},\dots,\lambda_{x,\pi(n)}]$, $\Lambda_e' = \mathrm{diag}[\lambda_{e,m},\dots,\lambda_{e,1}]$, which implies that the first m columns of $\underline{U}$ are equal to the first m columns of $\overline{U}$. Without loss of generality we may assume $\overline{U} = \underline{U}$ since the choice of the last $n - m$ columns is immaterial (it corresponds to the columns of $\underline{D}$ and $\overline{D}^T$). Hence the optimum is attained for

$$\underline{W} = U_e\underline{D}P^T U_x^T, \tag{5.66}$$
$$\overline{W} = U_xP\overline{D}U_e^T. \tag{5.67}$$

Equations (5.39), (5.40) yield

$$\underline{\sigma}_i = \frac{\lambda_{x,\pi(i)}\overline{\sigma}_{m-i+1}}{\lambda_{x,\pi(i)}\overline{\sigma}_i^2 + \mu}, \tag{5.68}$$

$$\overline{\sigma}_i = \frac{\lambda_{x,\pi(i)}\underline{\sigma}_{m-i+1}}{\lambda_{x,\pi(i)}\underline{\sigma}_i^2 + \lambda_{e,i}}. \tag{5.69}$$

The trivial solution is

$$\underline{\sigma}_i = 0, \qquad \overline{\sigma}_i = 0.$$

However, if $\mu < \lambda_{x,\pi(i)}^2/\lambda_{e,m-i+1}$, then we also have the nontrivial solution

$$\underline{\sigma}_i^2 = \sqrt{\frac{\lambda_{e,m-i+1}}{\mu}} - \frac{\lambda_{e,m-i+1}}{\lambda_{x,\pi(i)}}, \tag{5.70}$$

$$\overline{\sigma}_i^2 = \sqrt{\frac{\mu}{\lambda_{e,m-i+1}}} - \frac{\mu}{\lambda_{x,\pi(i)}}. \tag{5.71}$$

The rank of the solution is

$$r = \max_i\left[\{0\} \cup \{i = 1, 2, \dots, m : \mu < \lambda_{x,\pi(i)}^2/\lambda_{e,m-i+1}\}\right].$$

If the nontrivial solution is adopted then the error is

$$
J_b(\mu) = \sum_{i=1}^{n} \lambda_{x,\pi(i)} - \sum_{i=1}^{r} \lambda_{x,\pi(i)} \underline{\sigma}_i^2 \overline{\sigma}_i^2
$$

$$
= \sum_{i=1}^{n} \lambda_{x,\pi(i)} - \sum_{i=1}^{r} \lambda_{x,\pi(i)} \left[1 - \frac{2}{\lambda_{x,\pi(i)}} \sqrt{\mu \lambda_{e,m-i+1}} + \mu \frac{\lambda_{e,m-i+1}}{\lambda_{x,\pi(i)}^2} \right]
$$

$$
= \sum_{i=r+1}^{n} \lambda_{x,\pi(i)} + 2 \sum_{i=1}^{r} \sqrt{\mu \lambda_{e,m-i+1}} - \mu \sum_{i=1}^{r} \frac{\lambda_{e,m-i+1}}{\lambda_{x,\pi(i)}}. \tag{5.72}
$$

Using Lemma 5.1 it follows that all three terms on the right-hand side of (5.72) are minimized by the choice of permutation $\pi = \langle 1, 2, \ldots, n \rangle$.   ∎

6

HETEROASSOCIATIVE MODELS

In this chapter we investigate two generalizations of PCA: Asymmetric PCA and Nonlinear PCA. For either one, the standard PCA is a special case, being symmetric and linear. Asymmetric PCA has itself two variations; linear approximation [90] and cross-correlation [91], to be treated respectively in Sections 6.3 and 6.5. In the literature, the term nonlinear PCA has been used to denote the statistical representation of a random vector with a few nonlinear parameters. This subject will be discussed in Section 6.6.

6.1 ASYMMETRIC PCA

Recall that the PCA optimization criterion for a random vector or stationary process x can be described in two ways:

(a) Maximization of variance

$$J_{PCA}(W) = \text{tr}\{W^T R_x W\}; \tag{6.1}$$

(b) Minimization of error

$$J'_{PCA}(W) = E\|x - WW^T x\|^2, \tag{6.2}$$

both under the constraint $W^T W = I$.

In this section we study heteroassociation, namely, the problem where the target $y \neq x$. We observe in the outset that there are two possible directions to generalize PCA: one according to the variance criterion (6.1) and another via the reconstruction error criterion (6.2). Both generalizations may be called *asymmetric*

146

PCA [90, 92]. Ordinary PCA, which is identical for both costs, will be called, in contrast, *symmetric PCA*.

1. Autoassociative networks (ordinary PCA). Two-layer linear networks with hidden-layer bottleneck perform ordinary PCA when the target y is identical to the input x. Such a network is called autoassociative or self-supervised. Symmetric—i.e., ordinary—PCA optimizes both criteria J_{PCA} and J'_{PCA}. As discussed in Chapter 4, a linear two-layer network with hidden-layer bottleneck performs PCA when trying to learn the identity mapping (autoassociation mode).

2. Heteroassociative networks (APCA). Let the target $y \in \mathbb{R}^m$ be not equal to but correlated with the input $x \in \mathbb{R}^n$ and define $R_x = E\{xx^T\}$, $R_y = \{yy^T\}$, $R_{xy} = R_{yx}^T = E\{xy^T\}$. Asymmetric PCA extends PCA along two directions:

- Linear Approximation APCA[90]. Minimize the reconstruction error cost

$$J'_{APCA}(\overline{W}, \underline{W}) = E\|y - \overline{W}\underline{W}x\|^2, \tag{6.3}$$

$\underline{W} \in \mathbb{R}^{p \times n}$, $\overline{W} \in \mathbb{R}^{m \times p}$, $p < \min\{m, n\}$. The problem is thus to find the best linear components $\theta = [\theta_1, \ldots, \theta_p] = \underline{W}x$ of x so that they may best recover y through a linear reconstruction $\overline{W}\theta$. Scharf [93] calls the problem *reduced-rank Wiener filtering* because it is the search of the optimal linear filter under rank constraint. One can also call the problem reduced-rank linear regression since we try to linearly estimate y from x under the constraint of a reduced-rank mapping.

- Cross-correlation APCA[91]. Maximize the cross-correlation cost

$$J_{APCA}(\overline{W}, \underline{W}) = E\left\{ \text{tr}\left[(\overline{W}^T y)(\underline{W}x) \right] \right\} = \text{tr}(\underline{W}R_{xy}\overline{W}), \tag{6.4}$$

$\underline{W} \in \mathbb{R}^{p \times n}$, $\overline{W} \in \mathbb{R}^{m \times p}$, $p < \min\{m, n\}$, under the constraint $\overline{W}^T \overline{W} = \underline{W}\underline{W}^T = I$;

Before we move on, we discuss the generalized eigenvalue and singular value decompositions, which extend the standard ED, SVD decompositions and bear close relationship to the APCA problem.

6.2 GENERALIZED EIGENVALUES/SVD

We have seen that PCA is very closely related to the symmetric eigenvalue decomposition (SED) and SVD (among other things). Both SED and SVD can be extended in various ways that provide a general framework in which PCA, SED, SVD, etc., are simply special cases. Studying such generalizations not only helps understand deeper the special cases but also gives rise to new applications and new approaches for dealing with old problems.

The standard eigenvalue problem studies the equation

$$(A - \lambda I)x = 0,$$

where $A \in \mathbb{R}^{n \times n}$. The eigenvalue decomposition locates those directions in $\mathbb{R}^n$ where the application of the linear operator A is equivalent to scalar multiplication (simple scaling). These eigendirections are the link between one-dimensional and n-dimensional analysis.

For example, the equation $x_{k+1} = Ax_k$ reduces to $x_{k+1} = \lambda_i x_k$ if $x_0 = e_i$ is any eigenvector of A corresponding to an eigenvalue λ_i. Thus, the matrix is reduced to a scalar, and the reduced equation is very easy to solve: $x_k = \lambda_i^k x_0$.

Even if $x_0 = \sum_i \alpha_{i0} e_i$ the equation can be decomposed into decoupled parts, $\alpha_{i,k+1} = \lambda_i \alpha_{ik}$, which again make the solution straightforward: $x_k = \sum_i \lambda_i^k e_i$.

Not surprisingly, stability and convergence issues even in complex dynamical systems can often be answered by studying the spectrum of an appropriate matrix.

The study of the equation

$$(A - \lambda B)x = 0, \quad A, B \in \mathbb{R}^{n \times n}, \tag{6.5}$$

is commonly referred to as the **generalized eigenvalue problem**. We refer to the family of matrices $\mathcal{P} = \{(A - \lambda B); \lambda \in \mathbb{R}\}$ as the matrix pencil (A, B). We are looking for those directions in $\mathbb{R}^n$ where the application of the linear operator A is proportional to the application of the operator B. A scalar λ that satisfies (6.5) is called a **generalized eigenvalue** of the pencil (A, B), while the corresponding x is called a **generalized eigenvector** of this pencil.

Clearly, if B is nonsingular then

$$(B^{-1}A - \lambda I)x = 0.$$

In this case the generalized eigenvalue problem of the matrix pencil (A, B) is the same as the eigenvalue problem of $B^{-1}A$.

Very often, A, B are symmetric and B is positive definite, such as when A and B are correlation or covariance matrices. Then the following result does not follow from the eigenvalue decomposition of $B^{-1}A$.

Theorem 6.1 (Generalized Spectral Theorem) [36]. Let $A \in \mathbb{R}^{n \times n}$ be symmetric and $B \in \mathbb{R}^{n \times n}$ positive definite. Then there exists a nonsingular $X = [x_1 \cdots x_n] \in \mathbb{R}^{n \times n}$ which simultaneously diagonalizes A and B:

$$X^T AX = \text{diag}[\alpha_1 \quad \cdots \quad \alpha_n], \tag{6.6}$$

$$X^T BX = \text{diag}[\beta_1 \quad \cdots \quad \beta_n], \quad \beta_i > 0. \tag{6.7}$$

Spectral Theorem 2.3 is a special case of Theorem 6.1 for $B = I$:

$$X^T AX = \text{diag}[\alpha_1 \quad \cdots \quad \alpha_n],$$

$$X^T X = \text{diag}[1 \quad \cdots \quad 1] = I.$$

Corollary 6.1. The ratios $\lambda_i = \alpha_i/\beta_i$ are the generalized eigenvalues, while the columns of X are the generalized eigenvectors of the matrix pencil (A, B).

This is obvious since

$$X^T A X = \text{diag}[\lambda_1 \quad \cdots \quad \lambda_n] X^T B X,$$

$$A x_i = \lambda_i B x_i.$$

The generalized eigenvalues are the stationary values of the generalized Rayleigh quotient

$$r_g(x) = \frac{x^T A x}{x^T B x}.$$

Indeed, each stationary point satisfies the condition

$$\frac{\partial r_g(x)}{\partial x} = 2Ax - 2r_g(x)Bx = 0,$$

which implies

$$Ax = r_g(x)Bx,$$

so $(r_g(x), x)$ is a generalized eigenvalue/vector pair.

Much like the spectral theorem for matrices of the form $A^T A$ is the consequence of the SVD theorem, the generalized Spectral Theorem 6.1 results from the deeper generalized SVD (GSVD) theorem.

Theorem 6.2 (Generalized SVD) [36, 94]. For any pair of matrices $A \in \mathbb{R}^{m \times n}$ and $B \in \mathbb{R}^{p \times n}$, there exist three matrices:

$$U \in \mathbb{R}^{m \times m} : \text{orthogonal,}$$

$$V \in \mathbb{R}^{p \times p} : \text{orthogonal,}$$

$$X \in \mathbb{R}^{n \times n} : \text{nonsingular,}$$

such that

$$U^T A X = D_A = \text{diag}[\alpha_1 \quad \cdots \quad \alpha_n], \qquad \alpha_i \geq 0, \tag{6.8}$$

$$V^T B X = D_B = \text{diag}[\beta_1 \quad \cdots \quad \beta_q], \qquad \beta_i \geq 0, \tag{6.9}$$

where $q = \min\{p, n\}$.

6.3 LINEAR APPROXIMATION APCA

The problem of linear approximation APCA was studied originally by Baldi and Hornik [72]. They showed that if R_x is invertible then the solution is of the form

$$\overline{W} = U_0 M, \tag{6.10}$$

$$\underline{W} = M^{-1} U_0^T R_{xy}^T R_x^{-1}, \tag{6.11}$$

where the columns of $U_0 \in \mathbb{R}^{m \times p}$ are the principal eigenvectors of $R_{xy}^T R_x^{-1} R_{xy}$ and $M \in \mathbb{R}^{p \times p}$ is any invertible matrix.

Scharf [93] and Kung and Diamantaras [92] also studied the problem independently to obtain the solution

$$\overline{W} = U_1 M, \tag{6.12}$$

$$\underline{W} = M^{-1} \Sigma_1 U_2^T R_x^{-1/2}, \tag{6.13}$$

where the columns of $U_1 \in \mathbb{R}^{m \times p}$ and $U_2 \in \mathbb{R}^{n \times p}$ are the principal left and right singular vectors of $R_{xy}^T R_x^{-1/2}$, and Σ_1 is a diagonal matrix containing the principal singular values. All the above solutions are equivalent. Indeed, it can be shown that $U_0 = U_1$ and $\Sigma_1 U_2^T R_x^{-1/2} = U_0^T R_{xy}^T R_x^{-1}$.

Diamantaras and Kung [90] unified the two approaches working directly on the data matrices. Consider the reduced-rank linear approximation problem formulated as follows: given N input/target pairs (x_k, y_k) minimize the cost

$$J = \sum_{k=1}^{N} \|y_k - W x_k\|^2 = \|Y - WX\|_F^2, \tag{6.14}$$

$$Y = [y_1, y_2, \ldots, y_N], \qquad X = [x_1, x_2, \ldots, x_N],$$

under the constraint $\mathrm{rank}(W) = p \le \min\{m, n\}$.

Assume that $N \ge n$, and consider the GSVD

$$U^T X^T Q = D_1 \in \mathbb{R}^{N \times n}, \tag{6.15}$$

$$V^T Y X^T Q = D_2 \in \mathbb{R}^{m \times n} \tag{6.16}$$

of the matrix pair (YX^T, X^T). Let $\alpha_1, \ldots, \alpha_n$ and $\gamma_1, \ldots, \gamma_{\min\{m,n\}}$ be the entries in the main diagonal of D_1 and D_2. Then for $r = \mathrm{rank}(X)$ we have

$$\alpha_1, \ldots, \alpha_r > 0, \qquad \alpha_{r+1} = \cdots = \alpha_n = 0$$

and

$$\gamma_1, \ldots, \gamma_s > 0, \qquad \gamma_{s+1} = \cdots = \gamma_{\min\{m,n\}} \ge 0$$

for $s = \mathrm{rank}(YX^T) \le r$.

Let us further assume that the diagonal entries of D_1, D_2 are arranged so that the finite generalized eigenvalues

$$\lambda_i \equiv \frac{\gamma_i}{\alpha_i}, \qquad i = 1, \ldots, \hat{r} \equiv \min\{m, n, r\},$$

are arranged in nonincreasing order $\lambda_1 \geq \lambda_2 \geq \cdots \geq \lambda_s > \lambda_{s+1} = \cdots = \lambda_{\hat{r}} = 0$. Given the above definitions we can write

$$D_1 = \begin{array}{c} r \\ N-r \end{array} \begin{bmatrix} \overset{r}{D_{1r}} & \overset{n-r}{0} \\ 0 & 0 \end{bmatrix}, \tag{6.17}$$

$$D_2 = m \begin{bmatrix} \overset{r}{D_{2r}} & \overset{n-r}{\tilde{D}_2} \end{bmatrix}, \tag{6.18}$$

$$U = N-r \begin{bmatrix} \overset{r}{U_r} & \overset{N-r}{\tilde{U}} \end{bmatrix}, \tag{6.19}$$

where D_{1r} is a diagonal nonsingular $r \times r$ matrix, the matrices D_{2r}, U_r comprise the first r columns of the D_2 and U, while $\tilde{D}_2$, $\tilde{U}$ comprise the remaining columns. Then from (6.15) we obtain

$$X^T Q = U_r [D_{1r} \ 0]. \tag{6.20}$$

Theorem 6.3 [90]. Let $v_1, \ldots, v_m$ and $q_1, \ldots, q_n$ denote the columns of V and Q respectively. If $\text{rank}(W) = p \leq \min\{m, n\}$ then (6.15) is minimized for

$$W^* = V_p \Lambda_p D_{1p}^{-1} (Q_p^T + \Phi^T Q_{n-r}^T), \tag{6.21}$$

where $V_p \equiv [v_1 \ \cdots \ v_p] \in \mathbb{R}^{m \times p}$, $Q_p \equiv [q_1 \ \cdots \ q_p] \in \mathbb{R}^{n \times p}$, $D_{1p} \equiv \text{diag}[\alpha_1, \ldots, \alpha_p] \in \mathbb{R}^{p \times p}$, $\Lambda_p = \text{diag}[\lambda_1, \ldots, \lambda_p] \in \mathbb{R}^{p \times p}$, $Q_{n-r} \equiv [q_{r+1} \ \cdots \ q_n] \in \mathbb{R}^{n \times n-r}$, and Φ is any $(n-r) \times p$ matrix. Furthermore, the minimum error is

$$J_{\min} = \|V^T Y \tilde{U}\|_F^2 + \sum_{i=p+1}^{s} \lambda_i^2. \tag{6.22}$$

The minimum error contains two terms. The first term

$$L = \|V^T Y \tilde{U}\|_F^2$$

is the absolute minimum error achievable regardless of the rank constraint. The second term

$$L_p = \sum_{i=p+1}^{s} \lambda_i^2$$

is the excess error due to the rank constraint.

6.3.1 Unifying Different Results

1. X has full rank. In this case $r = n$, $\Phi = 0$, and XX^T is invertible. From the GSVD of (YX^T, X^T), (6.15), (6.16) we obtain

$$Q^T XX^T Q = D_1^T D_1, \tag{6.23}$$

$$Q^T XY^T YX^T Q = D_2^T D_2, \tag{6.24}$$

$$V^T YX^T (XX^T)^{-1} XY^T V = D_2(D_1^T D_1)^{-1} D_2^T. \tag{6.25}$$

We assume ergodicity, so time averages tend to their corresponding expected values

$$R_x = \lim_{N \to \infty} \frac{1}{N} XX^T, \tag{6.26}$$

$$R_{xy} = \lim_{N \to \infty} \frac{1}{N} XY^T. \tag{6.27}$$

Multiplying both sides of Eqs. (6.23), (6.24), and (6.25) by $1/N$ or $1/N^2$, as appropriate, and taking the limit $N \to \infty$ leads to

$$R_x^{-1} R_{xy} R_{xy}^T Q = Q \Lambda_n^2, \tag{6.28}$$

$$R_{xy}^T R_x^{-1} R_{xy} V = V \Lambda_m^2, \tag{6.29}$$

where

$$\Lambda_n^2 = \lim_{N \to \infty} \frac{1}{N} (D_1^T D_1)^{-1} D_2^T D_2$$

$$= \lim_{N \to \infty} \frac{1}{N} \operatorname{diag}\{\lambda_1^2, \dots, \lambda_s^2, 0, \dots, 0\} \in \mathbb{R}^{n \times n},$$

$$\Lambda_m^2 = D_2 (D_1^T D_1)^{-1} D_2^T$$

$$= \lim_{N \to \infty} \frac{1}{N} \operatorname{diag}\{\lambda_1, \dots, \lambda_s, 0, \dots, 0\} \in \mathbb{R}^{m \times m}.$$

The diagonal matrices Λ_n, Λ_m, have the same nonzero diagonal entries, but they have different sizes. If we let $\tilde{Q} = R_x^{1/2} Q$, then

$$R_x^{-1/2} R_{xy} R_{xy}^T R_x^{-1/2} \tilde{Q} = \tilde{Q} \Lambda_n^2, \tag{6.30}$$

so $\tilde{Q}$ consists of the eigenvectors of $R_x^{-1/2} R_{xy} R_{xy}^T R_x^{-1/2}$, which are also the right singular vectors of $R_{yx} R_x^{-1/2}$. This agrees with the results presented in [92] and [93]. Similarly, V consists of the eigenvectors of $R_{xy}^T R_x^{-1} R_{xy}$, which are at the same time the left singular vectors of $R_{yx} R_x^{-1/2}$, in accordance again with the results published in [72, 92, 93].

2. *Linear Regression / Wiener Filtering.* When X has full rank and W has no rank restriction, (6.21) yields the least-squares solution

$$W^* = VD_2 D_{1n}^{-1} D_{1n}^{-1} Q^T$$
$$= VD_2 Q^{-1}(XX^T)^{-1}$$
$$= YX^T(XX^T)^{-1}. \tag{6.31}$$

Taking the limit $N \to \infty$, W^* tends to the classical linear regression matrix $R_{yx}R_x^{-1}$.

3. *Auto-association:* $Y = X$. In this case $R_{xy} = R_x$ and (6.29), (6.29) imply that the columns Q and V are eigenvectors of R_x (or XX^T before we take the limit). So generalized eigenvectors turn to ordinary eigenvectors and the solution is the expected PCA solution. This is also in agreement with the results of Bourlard and Kamp (see Section 4.5).

6.3.2 Heterosupervised Neural Networks

Consider a two-layer network, with input $x \in \mathbb{R}^n$ and output $z \in \mathbb{R}^m$,

$$a = \underline{W}^T x, \qquad z = \overline{W}a, \tag{6.32}$$

where $\overline{W} \in \mathbb{R}^{m \times p}$, $\underline{W} \in \mathbb{R}^{n \times p}$ are the upper- and lower-layer weights, respectively, and $a \in \mathbb{R}^p$ is the hidden units activation vector. The square error cost

$$J_{\text{NET}} = \sum_{k=1}^N \|y_k - z_k\|^2 = \|Y - \overline{W}\underline{W}^T X\|_F^2. \tag{6.33}$$

In [72], it is shown that under the assumption

$$\lambda_1 > \lambda_2 > \cdots > \lambda_{\hat{r}} > 0 \quad (\text{so } s = \hat{r}) \tag{A}$$

the error function contains no local minima (all critical points are saddle points) provided that XX^T is invertible. In fact, even if XX^T does not have full rank the problem has no local minima [90].

Since rank$(W \equiv \overline{W}\underline{W}) \le p$ the reduced-rank approximation error (6.22) will be a lower bound for the network error (6.33).

Theorem 6.4 [90]. The minimum network cost J_{NET} is given by (6.22), and the general solution of the minimization problem (6.33) is

$$\overline{W}_{\text{opt}} = V_p M, \tag{6.34}$$

$$\underline{W}_{\text{opt}} = (Q_p + Q_{n-r}\Phi)D_{1p}^{-1}\Lambda_p M^{-T}, \tag{6.35}$$

where Φ is any $(n - r) \times p$ matrix. If the input has full rank then $r = n$ and the optimal solution is simplified:

$$\overline{W}_{opt} = V_p M, \tag{6.36}$$

$$\underline{W}_{opt} = Q_p D_{1p}^{-1} \Lambda_p M^{-T} = Q_p \text{ diag} \left\{ \frac{\gamma_1}{\alpha_1^2}, \ldots, \frac{\gamma_p}{\alpha_p^2} \right\} M^{-T}. \tag{6.37}$$

Since there are no local minima (under Assumption (A)) then any gradient descent algorithm for minimizing (6.33) will produce the global minimum solution (6.34), (6.35). For example, the back-propagation learning rule, which for the linear network becomes

$$\overline{W}_{k+1} = \overline{W}_k + \beta_k \left[y_k - \overline{W}_k a_k \right] a_k^T, \tag{6.38}$$

$$\underline{W}_{k+1} = \underline{W}_k + \beta_k x_k \left[\overline{W}_k^T y_k - \overline{W}_k^T \overline{W}_k a_k \right]^T, \tag{6.39}$$

results in $\overline{W}_k \rightarrow \overline{W}_{opt}$ and $\underline{W}_k \rightarrow \underline{W}_{opt}$.

Observe that the involvement of the arbitrary matrix M in the optimal solution leads to span$(\overline{W}_{opt}) = $ span(V_p) and not $\overline{W}_{opt} = V_p$. This means that there is an arbitrary matrix P such that $\overline{W}_{opt} = V_p P$. Clearly neither $\overline{W}$ nor $\underline{W}$ can be uniquely determined, but they multiply up to the optimal solution.

6.3.3 Obtaining the Exact Asymmetric Components Using BP

The discussion in this section is based on [90]. In the following we shall assume for simplicity that X has full rank. A similar discussion can be carried out for the reduced-rank case.

First Component   A linear network with a single hidden unit ($p = 1$, Fig. 6.1a) extracts the first component. According to (6.36), (6.37), the global minimum is achieved for $\overline{w}_{opt} = \mu_1 v_1$, $\underline{w}_{opt} = \mu_1^{-1} (\gamma_1 / \alpha_1^2) q_1$, for some $\mu_1 \neq 0$.

It is interesting to note that in the self-supervised BP network where $X = Y$, $Q = V$, and $\gamma_i = \alpha_i^2$, the upper-layer rule

$$\Delta \overline{w}_k = \beta_k \left[x_k - a_k \overline{w}_k \right] a_k \tag{6.40}$$

looks like Oja's single-unit rule, except that $a = \underline{w}^T x$ rather than $a = \overline{w}^T x$ [14]. If we set $\underline{w}_k = \overline{w}_k = w_k$ for all k, then (6.40) becomes Oja's rule. This may seem arbitrary at first, but let us observe that $\overline{w}$ and $\underline{w}$ tend anyway to the same final vector v_1 (up to a scaling factor).

Multiple Components   For the extraction of multiple components it is intrumental to use an extended notion of deflation.

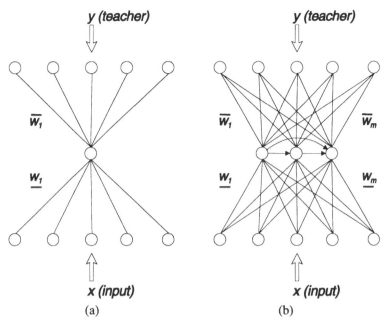

Figure 6.1. (a) The linear BP network with one hidden unit. (b) The proposed model for many hidden units with lateral orthogonalization network.

Definition 6.1. Let UD_1Q^{-1}, VD_2Q^{-1}, be the GSVD of a matrix pair (X^T, YX^T) and let the generalized eigenvalues be $\lambda_1 \geq \lambda_2 \geq \cdots \geq \lambda_f \geq 0$. Then the transformed pairs

$$(X^T, \tilde{Y}X^T) \equiv \left(X^T, \left(Y - \frac{\gamma_1}{\alpha_1^2} v_1 q_1^T X \right) X^T \right), \tag{6.41}$$

$$(X^T, \tilde{Y}X^T) \equiv \left(X^T, (Y - v_1 v_1^T Y) X^T \right), \tag{6.42}$$

$$(X^T, Y\tilde{X}^T) \equiv \left(X^T, Y \left(X - \frac{1}{\alpha_1^2} XX^T q_1 q_1^T X \right) \right), \tag{6.43}$$

where v_1, q_1 are the first columns of V and Q respectively, are called **deflation transformations** of the pair (X^T, YX^T) with respect to GSVD.

Let us, for instance, examine the transformation $YX^T \rightarrow \tilde{Y}X^T$. The GSVD of the pair $(X^T, \tilde{Y}X^T)$ is

$$V^T \tilde{Y} X^T Q = V^T YX^T Q - \frac{\gamma_1}{\alpha_1^2} V^T v_1 q_1^T XX^T Q$$

$$= \text{diag}\{0 \quad \gamma_2 \quad \cdots \quad \gamma_q\} \equiv \hat{D}_2, \tag{6.44}$$

$$U^T X^T Q = D_1, \tag{6.45}$$

so the generalized eigenvalues now are

$$\hat{\lambda}_1 = 0, \quad \hat{\lambda}_2 = \lambda_2, \ldots, \quad \hat{\lambda}_{\hat{p}} = \lambda_{\hat{p}}.$$

A similar effect can be easily shown for the other two deflated pairs $(X^T, \bar{Y}X^T)$ and $(X^T, Y\tilde{X}^T)$. Moreover, all three transformed pairs have the same GSVD, so

$$\left(Y - \frac{\gamma_1}{\alpha_1^2} v_1 q_1^T X\right) X^T = \left(Y - v_1 v_1^T Y\right) X^T$$

$$= Y \left(X^T - \frac{1}{\alpha_1^2} X^T q_1 q_1^T XX^T\right)$$

$$= V\hat{D}_2 Q^{-1}. \tag{6.46}$$

If we also take the limit $N \to \infty$ we obtain

$$R_{yx} - \frac{\gamma_1}{\alpha_1^2} v_1 q_1^T R_x = R_{yx} - v_1 v_1^T R_{yx} \tag{6.47}$$

$$= R_{yx} - \frac{1}{\alpha_1^2} R_{yx} q_1 q_1^T R_x. \tag{6.48}$$

Recursively, p consecutive deflations will result in nullification of the first p generalized eigenvalues so that the $(p + 1)$th component will become dominant.

A straightforward application of deflation to the back-propagation algorithm yields the rest of the components. In particular for neuron p, assuming that the previous $p - 1$ components have already been extracted so that

$$\overline{w}_i = \mu_i v_i, \qquad \underline{w}_i = \mu_i^{-1} \frac{\gamma_i}{\alpha_i^2} q_i.$$

application of the first deflation transform results in the iterative rule

$$\Delta \overline{w}_{p,k} = \beta_k \left[\tilde{y}_k - \overline{w}_{pk} a_{pk}\right] a_{pk}, \tag{6.49}$$

$$\Delta \underline{w}_{p,k} = \beta_k x_k \left[y_k - \overline{w}_{pk} a_{pk}\right]^T \overline{w}_{pk}, \tag{6.50}$$

where $a_p = \underline{w}_p^T x$, and the teacher is deflated:

$$\tilde{y}_k = y_k - \sum_{i=1}^{p-1} \overline{w}_i \underline{w}_i^T x_k. \tag{6.51}$$

Alternatively we may use the teacher

$$\bar{y}_k = y_k - \sum_{i=1}^{p-1} \frac{\overline{w_i}\,\overline{w_i}^T}{\|\overline{w_i}\|^2} y_k \tag{6.52}$$

to obtain the same effect through a deflation of the second type.

6.4   THE LATERAL ORTHOGONALIZATION NET

As in the least-squares problems, orthogonality is a central property in PCA. For example, in standard PCA the eigenvectors (principal components) of the symmetric autocorrelation matrix R_x are orthogonal. In linear approximation APCA the columns of V are orthogonal, and the columns of Q are (XX^T)-orthogonal, namely

$$q_i^T XX^T q_j = 0, \qquad i \neq j \tag{6.23}.$$

It has been also demonstrated in Section 6.3.2 that this orthogonality can be achieved via a generalized deflation transformation.

In some PCA models, such as APEX and Rubner's models, deflation was in effect implemented by a lateral connection network called the anti-Hebbian net. Thus, explicit deflation was replaced by a built-in network deflation which is easily parallelizable [50, 54]. We can extend this idea to the linear approximation APCA problem by introducing the *lateral orthogonalization network (LON)*, which connects the hidden units of a bottleneck linear two-layer network (Fig. 6.1b).

Mathematically, orthogonality is defined with respect to an inner product. If a and b are two random vectors the inner product is usually defined as $a \cdot b = E\{a^T b\}$ and orthogonality is the condition

$$a \cdot b = 0.$$

If a and b are two random signals (e.g., the activation values of two neurons), orthogonality is defined as

$$E\{ab\} = 0.$$

In the case of two deterministic vectors (e.g., a and b are the synaptic weights of two neurons), the orthogonality criterion becomes

$$a^T b = 0.$$

Two kinds of learning rules can be used to train the LON [90].

Local Orthogonalization Rule Let a_1 and a_2 be two random scalars denoting the activation values of two neurons A_1 and A_2. Let c be the value of the synaptic weight connecting A_1 and A_2, and assume that either a_1 or a_2 is a function of c. A local orthogonalization rule for c is characterized by the form

$$\Delta c = \beta \, a_1 \, a_2. \tag{6.53}$$

The rule is considered *local* because the values a_1 and a_2 used for updating c are the activations of the neurons at both ends of the synapse corresponding to c.

Assume that the overall system with which (6.53) is combined is asymptotically stable; then (6.53) approximates the differential equation

$$\Delta c = E\{a_1 a_2\} \tag{6.54}$$

and

$$E\{a_1 a_2\} \to 0,$$

so a_1 and a_2 are asymptotically orthogonal.

As an example consider the case where $a_2 = b_2 - ca_1$ and a_1 is independent of c. The local rule corresponds to the equation

$$\Delta c = E\{a_1 b_2\} - cE\{a_1^2\}.$$

Thus c tracks the value

$$c^* = \frac{a_1 \cdot b_2}{a_1 \cdot a_1},$$

which is the Gram-Schmidt orthogonalization parameter (see Fig. 6.2).

Immediate Orthogonalization Rule Let w_1 and w_2 be the weight vectors of two neurons A_1 and A_2. Assume that w_1 is constant and w_2 is a function of c. It is sometimes possible to construct the overall learning dynamics of the system such that $c = w_1^T w_2$ and $c \to 0$. Consequently, the learning rule for c is

$$\Delta c = \beta \, w_1^T \Delta w_2. \tag{6.55}$$

We call this rule immediate because c is the immediate inner product of the two vectors.

One example is the APEX lateral orthogonalization network described in Section 4.2.6. The lateral weight rule was of the form

$$\Delta c = \beta \left[a_1 a_2 - c a_2^2 \right] \tag{6.56}$$

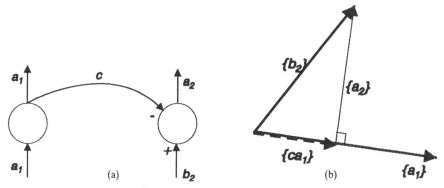

Figure 6.2. (a) The lateral orthogonalization network is based on the principle of removing any duplication of old components from a new component. (b) The part to be removed in order to achieve orthogonality may be depicted as the projection from the new component to the old component. As shown, after the removal, the residue is orthogonal to the old component.

for the synapse between neurons 1 and 2, where $a_1 = w_1^T x$, $a_2 = w_2^T x$. Assume that w_1 is constant, namely the first unit has converged to a fixed value. Since the rule for w_2 is

$$\Delta w_2 = \beta \left[a_2 x - w_2 a_2^2 \right],$$ (6.57)

we clearly have

$$\Delta c = w_1^T \Delta w_2,$$

which is an immediate orthogonalization rule.

6.4.1 Deflation Using LON

The model is depicted in Figure 6.1b. Assume that the first $p-1$ components have already been extracted, namely

$$\overline{w}_i = \mu_i v_i, \qquad \underline{w}_i = \mu_i^{-1} \frac{\gamma_i}{\alpha_i^2} q_i.$$

The proposed rule for the pth neuron is

$$\Delta \overline{w}_p = \beta [y a_p' - \overline{w}_p a_p^2],$$ (6.58)

$$\Delta \underline{w}_p = \beta x \left[b_p' - \|\overline{w}_p\|^2 a_p \right],$$ (6.59)

where

$$a'_p = a_p - \sum_{i<p} c_{pi} a_i, \qquad a_i = \underline{w}_i^T x, \quad i \le p, \tag{6.60}$$

$$b'_p = b_p - \sum_{i<p} \overline{c}_{pi} b_i \qquad b_i = \overline{w}_i^T y, \quad i \le p, \tag{6.61}$$

Orthogonality leads to the optimal conditions

$$\overline{c}_{pi} = \frac{\overline{w}_i^T \overline{w}_p}{\|\overline{w}_i\|^2}, \tag{6.62}$$

$$\underline{c}_{pi} = \frac{E\{a_i a'_p\}}{E\{a_i^2\}}. \tag{6.63}$$

Here the optimal value of $\overline{c}_{pi}$ is readily available at every iteration, while the optimal value of $\underline{c}_{pi}$ must be tracked through a local orthogonalization rule

$$\Delta \underline{c}_{pi} = \beta \, a'_p a_i = \beta \left(a_i a_p - \sum_{j<p} \underline{c}_{pj} a_j a_i \right). \tag{6.64}$$

Since a_i, a_j are assumed already orthogonal, (6.64) simplifies to

$$\Delta \underline{c}_{pi} = \beta (a_i a_p - \underline{c}_{pi} a_i^2). \tag{6.65}$$

Example 6.1 (Simulations). We ran simulation experiments using the back-propagation model with LON on artificially created data. The data set consisted of 100 (x, y) pairs from two colored random sequences, repeated cyclically in sweeps where the input dimension is $n = 4$ and the output dimension is $m = 3$. The y-axis corresponds to the component estimation error, while the x-axis corresponds to the number of iterations (each sweep contains 100 iterations so the plot contains results from 100 sweeps). We experimentally found the value $\beta = 0.01$ to be a good step-size constant.

All the units were allowed to learn concurrently. It is, however, expected that no unit will converge to the final state before all its previous units have done so.

The results of the simulation are depicted in Figure 6.3. As expected, the pth unit does not converge before the first $p-1$ units have done so. This is best demonstrated by the behavior of the third unit in Figure 6.3. Notice that for the first 2000 iterations (or 20 sweeps) this unit is actually moving away from the correct component. This is because it receives the wrong "clue" from one or both the previous units that have not yet converged. After the 2000 iteration mark, however, the unit starts converging because by that time the second unit (and the first one before it) had already converged to its corresponding components.

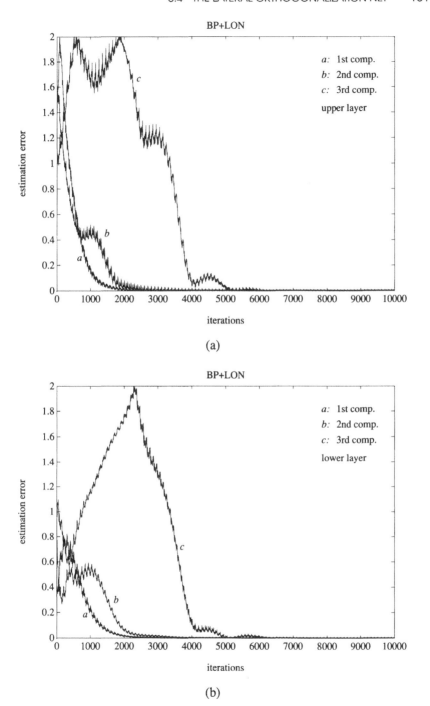

Figure 6.3. The parallel model with three hidden units using LON. (a) The component estimation error $\|v_p - \underline{w}_p/\|\underline{w}_p\|\|^2$ of the upper layer. (b) The component estimation error $\|q_p/\|q_p\| - \underline{w}_p/\|\underline{w}_p\|\|^2$ of the lower layer.

6.4.2   The Cascade Correlation Net

The lateral network idea with the growing number of hidden units is not unique for the APCA networks. For instance, in 1989 Fahlman and Lebiere [95] had proposed a network architecture employing a lateral connection network similar to LON. Their *cascade correlation* model consists of a set of n input units m output units and a variable number of hidden units. The structure of the network is shown in Figure 6.4: there is a set of feedforward connections from input to output, and initially there are no hidden units.

The target is to learn the heteroassociation of N pairs of vectors $\langle x_k, d_k \rangle$, $x_k \in \mathbb{R}^n$, $d_k \in \mathbb{R}^m$, $k = 1, \ldots, N$. First we train the input-output weights using a gradient descent technique on the quadratic error cost

$$ J = \sum_{k=1}^{N} \|d_k - y_k\|^2, \tag{6.66} $$

where y_k is the output vector corresponding to the input pattern x_k. When the error does not decrease any further we freeze the input-output weights and introduce a candidate hidden unit. The activation of the hidden unit may contain a nonlinearity

$$ a = f(w^T x), $$

where f is typically the sigmoid function $1/(1 + e^{-x})$. This hidden unit is not yet connected with the output nodes. It receives input from the input nodes and from any previously introduced hidden units (if it is not the first hidden unit introduced).

The weights of this candidate hidden node can be updated by an iterative algorithm which maximizes the magnitude of the correlation between the unit's response

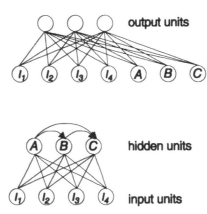

Figure 6.4. The cascade correlation network architecture employs a lateral network similar to LON.

a and the output error $e = d - y$:

$$S = \sum_{i=1}^{m} \left| \sum_{k=1}^{N} (a_k - \bar{a})(e_{k,i} - \bar{e}_i) \right|,$$

where $e_{k,i}$ is the error at the *i*th output unit for the *k*th pattern and $\bar{a}$, $\bar{e}_i$ are the averages of a_k and $e_{k,i}$ over all patterns. The iterative rule that maximizes S can be a gradient ascent procedure

$$\Delta w = \beta \frac{\partial S}{\partial w},$$

$$\Delta w = \beta \sum_{k,i} \sigma_{k,i} (e_{k,i} - \bar{e}_i) f'(w^T x_k) x_k,$$

where f' denotes the derivative of f. Once these weights are trained they freeze and now the hidden unit is connected with the output units. Thus the output units receive their input from all the input units and all the currently available hidden units. We train the output node weights again using a descend procedure on the quadratic cost (6.66) and stop when the error is low enough. Otherwise, we continue by introducing another hidden unit, and so on.

The philosophy behind the correlation maximization is that we should add a unit that is related with the error behavior at the output. The unit is meant for lowering the output error. So, it should be active (i.e., assume an activation away from the mean) when the error is high and nonactive when the error is low. Of course, this is an intuitive argument for adopting the correlation maximization rule, but Fahlman and Lebiere have demonstrated experimental success in various classification problems.

Although there is no immediate relation between APCA and the cascade correlation network, it is interesting to note that the variance maximization is an objective of PCA as well as of the cascade correlation model. Variance maximization is also the main theme of the cross-correlation APCA problem to be discussed next.

6.5 CROSS-CORRELATION APCA

Another PCA generalization path is the maximization of the cross-correlation cost

$$J_{\text{APCA}} = \text{tr}\{\underline{W} R_{xy} \overline{W}\}$$

with a suitable choice of the matrices $\underline{W} \in \mathbb{R}^{n \times p}$, $\overline{W} \in \mathbb{R}^{p \times m}$, $p < \min\{m, n\}$, under the assumption that the rows of $\underline{W}$ and the columns of $\overline{W}$ form two orthonormal sets. If there were no constraints on the size of the matrices, clearly the problem would have been ill-posed. Under the orthogonality constraint, the problem is related to the SVD of the cross-correlation matrix, as shown by the following results.

Lemma 6.1. Let $A \in \mathbb{R}^{m \times n}$ and $W \in \mathbb{R}^{n \times m}$ for some m, n, $m < n$. We have

$$\max_{W^T W = I} \text{tr}(AW) = \text{tr}(AV_m U^T) = \sum_{i=1}^{m} \sigma_m,$$

where $A = U \Sigma V^T$, $\Sigma = \text{diag}[\sigma_1, \ldots, \sigma_m]$ is the SVD of A, and V_m is the matrix composed of the first m columns of V.

Proof. Define $P \equiv V^T W U$. Then

$$\text{tr}(AW) = \text{tr}(U \Sigma V^T W) = \text{tr}(\Sigma P),$$

$$\text{tr}(AW) = \sum_{i=1}^{m} p_{ii} \sigma_i. \tag{6.67}$$

The constraint $W^T W = I$ implies $P^T P = I$, or $\sum_{k=1}^{n} p_{ki}^2 = 1$, so $-1 \leq p_{ii} \leq 1$. Then from (6.67) we get

$$\text{tr}(AW) \leq \sum_{i=1}^{m} \sigma_m,$$

and the maximum is clearly attained for

$$W = V_m U^T. \qquad \blacksquare$$

Theorem 6.5. The solution to the cross-correlation APCA problem is given by

$$\underline{W} = Q U_p^T, \qquad \overline{W} = V_p Q^T,$$

where $Q \in \mathbb{R}^{p \times p}$ is any orthogonal matrix, $R_{xy} = U \Sigma V^T$ is the SVD of R_{xy}, and the matrices $U_p \in \mathbb{R}^{n \times p}$, $V_p \in \mathbb{R}^{m \times p}$ are composed of the first p columns of U and V respectively. The maximum error is

$$\max J_{\text{APCA}} = \sum_{i=1}^{p} \sigma_i,$$

where $\sigma_1, \ldots, \sigma_{\min\{m,n\}}$ are the singular values of R_{xy}.

Proof. Let

$$\underset{n \times p}{U_{1p}} \; \underset{p \times p}{\Sigma_{1p}} \; \underset{p \times p}{V_1^T} \;=\; R_{xy} \overline{W},$$

$$\underset{p \times p}{U_2} \; \underset{p \times p}{\Sigma_{2p}} \; \underset{p \times m}{V_{2p}^T} \;=\; \underline{W} R_{xy}$$

be the SVDs of the corresponding right-hand sides. According to Lemma 6.1, $\text{tr}\{\underline{W}R_{xy}\overline{W}\}$ is maximized for

$$\underline{W} = V_1 U_{1p}^T, \qquad \overline{W} = V_{2p}U_2^T.$$

So

$$U_{1p}\Sigma_{1p}V_1^T = R_{xy}V_{2p}U_2^T,$$

$$U_2\Sigma_{2p}V_{2p}^T = V_1U_{1p}^TR_{xy},$$

$$\Sigma_{1p}V_1^T U_2 = U_{1p}^TR_{xy}V_{2p},$$

$$V_1^T U_2\Sigma_{2p} = U_{1p}^TR_{xy}V_{2p},$$

$$V_1^T U_2 = I \Rightarrow V_1 = U_2 \equiv Q,$$

$$\Sigma_{1p} = \Sigma_{2p} = U_{1p}^TR_{xy}V_{2p}.$$

Therefore, the columns of U_{1p} and V_{2p} are left and right singular vectors of R_{xy}. Then a simple inspection shows that $\text{tr}\{\underline{W}R_{xy}\overline{W}\} = \text{tr}\{U_{1p}^TR_{xy}V_{2p}\}$ is maximized if we choose the singular vectors corresponding to the p largest singular values. ■

The left and right singular vectors $u_1,\ldots,u_p,\ v_1,\ldots,v_p$ of R_{xy} will be called *left* and *right cross-correlation principal vectors* of the pair x, y, while the random variables $u_1^T x,\ldots,u_p^T x,\ v_1^T y,\ldots,v_p^T y$ will be called *left* and *right cross-correlation principal components*.

Example 6.2. Consider the pair of random vectors

$$y = [y_1,\ldots,y_m], \qquad x = [x_1,\ldots,x_n],$$

and assume that both vectors are generated by a set of $p < \min(m, n)$ hidden uncorrelated random variables $\theta = [\theta_1,\ldots,\theta_p]$ through the mappings

$$x = A\theta, \qquad y = B\theta.$$

The variables θ_i can be thought of as hidden factors that explain the joint variance of y and x. The cross-correlation between x and y in this case is

$$R_{xy} = AR_\theta B^T.$$

Since $\theta_1,\ldots,\theta_p$ are assumed uncorrelated,

$$R_\theta = \text{diag}\left[E\{\theta_1^2\},\ldots,E\{\theta_p^2\}\right] \equiv \Sigma \in \mathbb{R}^{p\times p}.$$

If the columns of A and B are orthonormal, namely if $A^T A = B^T B = I$, then the equation $R_{xy} = A\Sigma B^T$ becomes the SVD of R_{xy}. Therefore the columns of A and B are left and right cross-correlation principal vectors. Assuming there are no repeated singular values in R_{xy}, the normal cross-correlation principal vectors are unique up to a sign. Thus, the cross-correlation principal components are equal to each other and to the common hidden factors up to a sign; i.e., if U and V are a pair of left and right singular matrices of R_{xy} we have

$$U^T x = V^T y = [\pm\theta_1 \cdots \pm\theta_p].$$

Clearly, we also have

$$x = UV^T y \quad \text{and} \quad y = VU^T x.$$

Example 6.3. Assume the same situation as in the previous example, except now

$$x = A\theta, \quad y = B\theta + e,$$

where e is an additive noise term. If e is uncorrelated to θ, we still have

$$R_{xy} = A\Sigma B^T,$$

and thus A, B comprise the left and right cross-correlation principal component vectors. Now the left and right principal components are not equal to each other. However,

$$U^T x = [\pm\theta_1 \quad \cdots \quad \pm\theta_p],$$

so the hidden common factors are still uncovered with the use of x. Observe that the transform

$$\hat{y} = VU^T x = y$$

is a filter achieving complete removal of the noise term e from y.

6.5.1 The Cross-Coupled Hebbian Rule

The discussion in this section is based on [91]. Consider the two linear units depicted in Figure 6.5a (ignore the dotted line for the moment) with inputs $x \in \mathbb{R}^n$, $y \in \mathbb{R}^m$, and outputs

$$a = \underline{w}^T x, \tag{6.68}$$

$$b = \overline{w}^T y. \tag{6.69}$$

The following simple cross-coupled rule

$$\Delta\overline{w}_k = \beta_k a_k y_k, \tag{6.70}$$

$$\Delta\underline{w}_k = \beta_k b_k x_k, \tag{6.71}$$

is of Hebbian type, hence the name (and the dotted line in Fig. 6.5a). In order to impose stability on this rule we may normalize (6.70), (6.71), as we did with Oja's

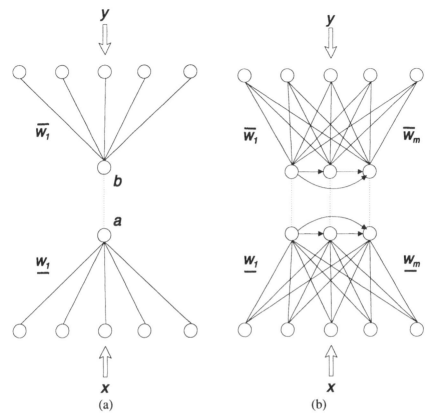

Figure 6.5. (a) A single-hidden-unit cross-correlation network. (b) A multiple-hidden-units cross-correlation network with lateral inhibition parameters.

single-unit PCA rule, to obtain

$$\Delta \overline{w}_k = \beta_k \left[y_k - \overline{w}_k b_k \right] a_k, \tag{6.72}$$

$$\Delta \underline{w}_k = \beta_k \left[x_k - \underline{w}_k a_k \right] b_k. \tag{6.73}$$

Algorithm (6.73), (6.73) is related to the SVD of R_{yx}. Notice that for $y_k = x_k$, (6.73) and (6.73) become Oja's learning rule.

Theorem 6.6. [91] Consider the algorithm described by (6.73) and (6.73) and assume that x_k and y_k are at least wide-sense stationary sequences. Let $\sigma_1 > \sigma_2 \geq \sigma_3 \geq \cdots \geq \sigma_q \geq 0$ be the singular values of R_{xy}. Then with probability 1, $\overline{w}_k \to \pm u_1$ and $\underline{w}_k \to \pm v_1$ as $k \to \infty$.

The proof outline is again based on the associated ODE

$$\frac{d\overline{w}}{dt} = R_{yx}\underline{w} - \overline{w}[\overline{w}^T R_{yx}\underline{w}],$$

$$\frac{d\underline{w}}{dt} = R_{xy}\overline{w} - \underline{w}[\overline{w}^T R_{yx}\underline{w}],$$

which is shown via the Lyapunov function

$$V = \sigma_1 - \overline{w}^T R_{yx}\underline{w}/(\|\overline{w}\|\|\underline{w}\|) \tag{6.74}$$

to have a global attractor $\overline{w} = \pm u_1$, $\underline{w} = \pm v_1$ (all other fixed points can be shown to be unstable).

Assuming that the first $p-1$ components have already been extracted, deflation is accomplished via the transforms

$$\tilde{y} = y - \sum_{i=1}^{p-1} \overline{w}_i \overline{w}_i^T y, \tag{6.75}$$

$$\tilde{x} = x - \sum_{i=1}^{p-1} \underline{w}_i \underline{w}_i^T x. \tag{6.76}$$

We may transform only y, or only x, or both. In all three cases the pth component will become dominant and the $p - 1$ principal components will cancel.

The learning rule for the pth component is

$$\Delta\overline{w}_{p,k} = \beta_k \left[y_k - \overline{w}_{pk} b_{pk} \right] a'_{pk}, \tag{6.77}$$

$$\Delta\underline{w}_{p,k} = \beta_k \left[x_k - \underline{w}_{pk} a_{pk} \right] b'_{pk}, \tag{6.78}$$

where

$$a'_p = a_p - \sum_{i<p} \underline{c}_{pi} a_i, \qquad a_i = \underline{w}_i^T x, \quad i \le p, \tag{6.79}$$

$$b'_p = b_p - \sum_{i<p} \overline{c}_{pi} b_i \qquad b_i = \overline{w}_i^T y, \quad i \le p. \tag{6.80}$$

The units are connected with lateral synaptic weights (see Fig. 6.5b) as with the linear approximation problem. The synaptic strengths $\overline{c}_{pi}$, $\underline{c}_{pi}$, of the LON should be equal to

$$\overline{c}^*_{pi} = \overline{w}_i^T \overline{w}_p \qquad \text{and} \qquad \underline{c}^*_{pi} = \underline{w}_i^T \underline{w}_p. \tag{6.81}$$

These values can be straightforwardly computed as inner products. Alternatively, we may employ a learning rule which also results in computational savings.

Premultiplying (6.77) by $\overline{w}_i^T$ and (6.78) by $\underline{w}_i^T$, we obtain the (immediate) lateral orthogonalization rule

$$\Delta \overline{c}_{pi,k} = \beta_k \left[b_{ik} - \overline{c}_{pi,k} b_{pk} \right] a'_{pk}, \qquad (6.82)$$

$$\Delta \underline{c}_{pi,k} = \beta_k \left[a_{ik} - \underline{c}_{pi,k} a_{pk} \right] b'_{pk}. \qquad (6.83)$$

Equations (6.82), (6.83) contain $O(1)$ floating-point multiplications/additions per iteration as opposed to $O(n)$ operations in (6.81).

Simulations   Figure 6.6 shows the convergence of the network, using 200 random pairs (x_k, y_k) processed in sweeps. The input dimension is 10, the output dimension is 8, and the step-size parameter β is 0.01 derived empirically.

We see that the weights converge to the corresponding normal singular vectors as theoretically predicted. Figure 6.7 depicts the behavior of the Lyapunov function V in (6.74). Since the system only approximates the differential equations (6.74) and (6.74), we don't expect the Lyapunov energy to decrease monotonically; however, we clearly see the monotonic trend *on the average*, which makes the energy eventually vanish.

Relation between the Two Kinds of APCA   The relation between the cross-correlation and linear approximation APCA can be demonstrated rather straightforwardly by studying the corresponding cost functions. If x_k is a white noise sequence then the linear approximation APCA cost

$$J'_{APCA} = E\{\| y_k - \overline{w} \underline{w}^T x_k \|^2\}$$

is equivalent to

$$E\{\| y_k \|^2\} + \| \overline{w} \|^2 \| \underline{w} \|^2 - 2\overline{w}^T R_{yx} \underline{w}.$$

Under the condition that $\| \overline{w} \| = \rho = $ fixed, $\| \underline{w} \| = \mu = $ fixed, then the minimizer of J'_{APCA} is also a minimizer of J_{APCA}; therefore, the linear approximation APCA solution will be the singular vectors of R_{yx}, like the cross-correlation APCA solution. The only difference is in the scaling of the solution vectors: in linear approximation the two vectors are automatically scaled so that $\rho\mu = \sigma_1$, while in the cross-correlation case ρ and μ are fixed, i.e., independent of x_k and y_k. Clearly, one can scale either x_k or y_k so that $\sigma_1 = \rho\mu$ for the cross-correlation case as well; however, the scaling factor is usually not available a priori.

6.6 NONLINEAR PCA

The purpose of principal component analysis is to identify linear correlations between random variables. The target is dimensionality reduction of the data. The distribution of the variables is explained by a few features or principal components.

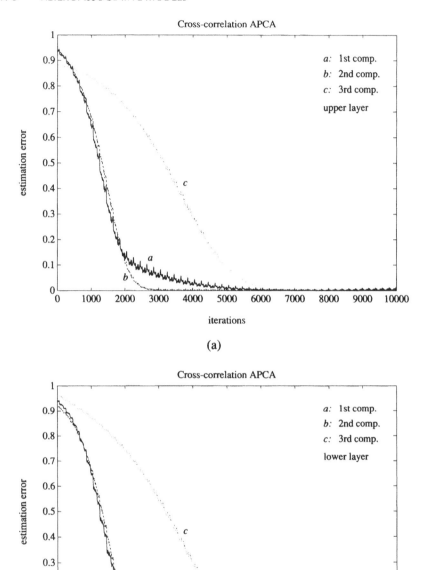

Figure 6.6. Simulation results for the cross-correlation network. (a) The component estimation error $\|u_p - \overline{w}_{pk}\|^2$ for the upper layer. (b) The error $\|v_p - \underline{w}_{pk}\|^2$ for the lower layer.

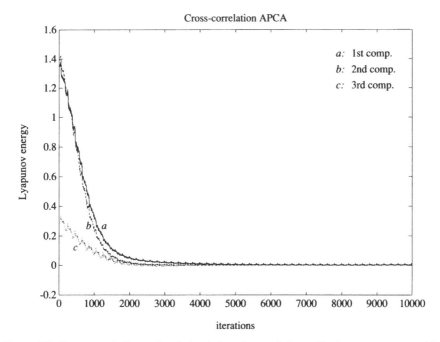

Figure 6.7. Cross-correlation network simulation: the evolution of the Lyapunov energy V.

In PCA, these features are constrained to be linear functions of the variables. Furthermore, the reconstruction of the variables from the hidden factors is also linear. The mapping from the data space to the feature space is referred to as *coding* and the reverse mapping as *decoding*. Thus, PCA assumes that both coding and decoding functions are linear. This may be an appropriate assumption in many situations, as we saw in previous chapters.

In some cases, however, it may be more appropriate to assume that the hidden factors are nonlinear functions of the variables. Furthermore, the reconstruction of the variables from the factors may also be a nonlinear map. Thus in the most general case both the coding function $h : \mathbb{R}^n \mapsto \mathbb{R}^p$ and the decoding function $g : \mathbb{R}^p \mapsto \mathbb{R}^n$, $p < m$, are members of the sets S_c, and S_d of nonlinear functions. Naturally, the problem

$$\text{minimize}_{g,h} \ J = E\|x - g(h(x))\|^2, \qquad x \in \mathbb{R}^n, \ g \in S_c, \ h \in S_d, \quad (6.84)$$

will be called the **Nonlinear PCA** problem. The problem is well defined if we specify the sets S_c and S_d. One possibility is to assume that g and h are continuous and bounded functions on $\mathbb{R}^p$ and $\mathbb{R}^n$ respectively. Ordinary (linear) PCA is now a special case for $S_c = L_{n \mapsto p} = \{h : \exists \underline{W} \in \mathbb{R}^{p \times n} \ h(x) = \underline{W}x\}$ and $S_d = L_{p \mapsto n} = \{g : \exists \overline{W} \mathbb{R}^{n \times p} \ g(y) = \overline{W}y\}$. The elements of the vector

$$[y_1 \quad \cdots \quad y_p] = h(x)$$

will be called *nonlinear principal components*. They are the nonlinear features that underlie the distribution of the data x. As we shall see immediately these nonlinear factors are not unique, and in fact the optimal choice h^*, g^* of coding the decoding functions is not unique.

Example 6.4. Let $x_1, \ldots, x_n$ be a set of random variables forming vector x. Assume that these variables are actually generated by a single underlying variable $\theta \in \mathbb{R}$

$$x_1 = f_1(\theta), \ldots, x_n = f_n(\theta),$$

where $f_1(\cdot), \ldots, f_n(\cdot)$ are nonlinear continuous functions $\mathbb{R} \mapsto \mathbb{R}$. Although the dimensionality of the data vector x is n, this number ignores the relation between the variables. The n variables are so closely related that there is really just one degree of freedom, the hidden variable θ. We may say then that n is the superficial dimensionality of the data while the intrinsic dimensionality is 1.

Assume further that one of the generating functions, say f_i, is invertible. Then the functions

$$h^*(x) = f_i^{-1}(x_i), \qquad g^*(y) = \begin{bmatrix} f_1(y) \\ \vdots \\ f_n(y) \end{bmatrix} \tag{6.85}$$

obtain $x = \hat{x} = g^*(h^*(x))$, and thus achieve the absolute minimum error $E\|x - g(h(x))\|^2 = 0$. Note that $g(\cdot)$ and $h(\cdot)$ are the nonlinear PCA solution for x, but they are not unique: The same error is achieved by any pair of functions of the form $[g^*(q(\cdot)), q^{-1}(h^*(\cdot))]$ for any invertible function $q : \mathbb{R} \mapsto \mathbb{R}$, since $g^*(h^*(x)) = g^*(q(q^{-1}(h^*(x))))$. This also means that the actual variable θ cannot be retrieved unless we know something more about the generating functions $f_1, \ldots, f_n$.

Clearly, the solution to the nonlinear PCA problem depends on both the choice of the sets S_c and S_d and the distribution of x. Even if we don't know the distribution of x we can still obtain some interesting results, starting from the following basic theorem.

Theorem 6.7 [96]. Let the variables $x \in \mathbb{R}^n$ and $y \in \mathbb{R}^p$ be jointly distributed. Then the best estimate of x by a function of y is the conditional expectation of x given y, namely

$$\min_{\hat{x}} E\{\|x - \hat{x}(y)\|^2\} = E\{\|x - g(y)\|^2\},$$

where

$$g(y) = E\{x \mid y\}.$$

Thus, given the function h, the cost (6.84) is minimized for

$$g(y) = E\{x \mid y = h(x)\}. \tag{6.86}$$

If we know the cumulative probability distribution $P(x)$ of x and we define $h^{-1}(y) \equiv \{x : h(x) = y\}$, then (6.86) becomes

$$g(y) = \int_{x \in h^{-1}(y)} x \, dP(x). \tag{6.87}$$

The function h is a many-to-one function since it maps a higher-dimensional space to a lower-dimensional one. The set $h^{-1}(y)$ is the isometric surface or contour of h corresponding to the value y. Moreover, the function, $g(y)$ is a p-parametric surface. For example, if $p = 1$, $g(y)$ is a monoparametric curve, and, by (6.86) $g(y)$ is the center of gravity of the set $h^{-1}(y)$ weighted by the distribution of x. Figure 6.8 shows an example.

As we mentioned in the above example, if a pair of functions $[g(\cdot), h(\cdot)]$ obtains the minimum nonlinear PCA error, then the same is also true for the functions $[g_q = g(q(\cdot)), h_q = q^{-1}(h(\cdot))]$, where $q : \mathbb{R}^p \mapsto \mathbb{R}^p$ is any invertible function. Observe, however, that the set $I(h_q)$ of isometric curves $\{h_q^{-1}(y), \ \forall y \in \mathbb{R}^p\}$ is invariant with respect to q. Indeed, we have $h_q^{-1}(y) = h^{-1}(q(y))$; therefore $I(h_q) = \{h^{-1}(q(y)), \ \forall y \in \mathbb{R}^p\} = \{h^{-1}(y'), \ \forall y' \in \mathbb{R}^p\} = I(h) \equiv I$. Since $g(y) = E_{x \in h^{-1}(y)}\{x\}$ the set $C = \{g(y) : \ y \in \mathbb{R}^p\}$ is also invariant. The important conclusion is that, although h and g are not unique, the following two objects are unique and characterize x:

a. The contour set I of h

b. The p-parametric surface C generated by g

We shall call C the p-parametric *nonlinear principal component surface* of x.

For ordinary PCA the contours of $h(x) = \underline{W}x$ are the $(n - p + 1)$-dimensional hyperplanes: $y = \underline{W}x$, each contour for a different value of y. Similarly, the principal component surface C is a p-dimensional hyperplane span$(\overline{W})$.

The performance of nonlinear PCA cannot be worse than linear PCA if S_c and S_d contain all linear mappings of the corresponding dimensions. However,

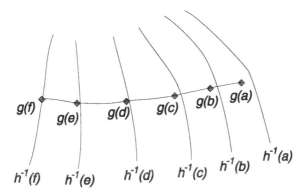

Figure 6.8. The contours of the function h define $g(y)$ as the mean of the contour $h^{-1}(y)$.

computationally the drawback is that the nonlinear optimization problem is much harder to solve, as there is, in general, no closed-form solution. Usually iterative techniques are employed after the problem has been parametrized, namely after it has been assumed that h and g belong to some parametric families of functions.

Example 6.5. We may assume that the h and g are second-order functions of their arguments

$$h(x) = \begin{bmatrix} h_1(x) \\ \vdots \\ h_p(x) \end{bmatrix},$$

$$h_l(x) = h_l(x_1,\ldots,x_n) = \sum_{i=1}^{n}\sum_{j=1}^{n}\eta_{ij}x_ix_j + \sum_{i=1}^{n}\eta_ix_i,$$

$$g(y) = \begin{bmatrix} g_1(y) \\ \vdots \\ g_n(y) \end{bmatrix},$$

$$g_l(y) = g_l(y_1,\ldots,y_p) = \sum_{i=1}^{p}\sum_{j=1}^{p}\gamma_{ij}y_iy_j + \sum_{i=1}^{p}\gamma_iy_i.$$

Under this assumption, the cost J in (6.84) is a function of the parameters η_{ij}, η_i, γ_{ij}, γ_i. The gradient descent rules (for example)

$$\frac{d\eta_{ij}}{dt} = -\frac{\partial J}{\partial \eta_{ij}},$$

$$\frac{d\eta_i}{dt} = -\frac{\partial J}{\partial \eta_i},$$

$$\frac{d\gamma_{ij}}{dt} = -\frac{\partial J}{\partial \gamma_{ij}},$$

$$\frac{d\eta_i}{dt} = -\frac{\partial J}{\partial \eta_i}$$

can be used to minimize J.

6.6.1 Network Models and Examples

A very important parametrization of the nonlinear PCA problem is the use of neural networks. For example, we have already found that linear autoassociative networks with bottleneck hidden layer perform ordinary PCA (see Section 4.5). One may easily (but wrongly) hypothesize that two-layer autoassociative networks with nonlinear units perform nonlinear PCA.

A word of caution is in order here. We recall from Section 4.5 that usage of nonlinear units in the hidden layer does not improve the performance of the network. The linear network achieves the minimum error, which is the best rank-p approximation error of the centered data matrix X', while the nonlinear case performance is not better.

This result can also be generalized in the case of multilayer autoassociative networks with the next-to-last layer having reduced size $p < n$ (Fig. 6.9). This is true because A', the centered activation matrix of the next-to-last layer, can be equal to the optimal $M^{-1}\Sigma_p V_p^T$. If the previous layers are not reduced, this is easy to show using arguments similar to the ones used in Section 4.5.

Does this analysis render nonlinearities in autoassociative networks totally useless? The answer is no. The analysis only implies that in order for the nonlinearities to improve the performance it is necessary that the network have more than two layers, and even in that case the next-to-last layer should not be reduced.

Consider for example, the network shown in Figure 6.10. The subnetwork comprising the layers 1 and 2 is the coding subnetwork which maps the input to the feature space. The feature layer (layer 2) has reduced number of units $p < n$. The subnetwork mapping the features to the output (layers 3 and 4) is the decoding subnetwork. Layers 1 and 3 must be nonlinear for the coding and decoding functions to be nonlinear. We may use the sigmoid nonlinear function $f(x) = 1/(1 + e^{-x})$. The feature layer and the output layer may be linear or nonlinear (layers 2 and 4).

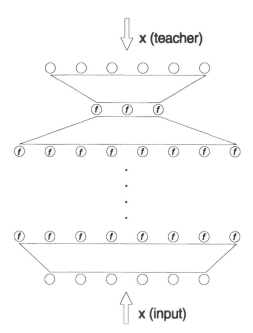

Figure 6.9. A multilayer autoassociative network with reduced next-to-last layer. Using a nonlinear f does not improve the error over a linear f.

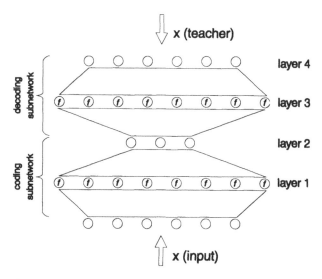

Figure 6.10. An autoassociative nonlinear network performing nonlinear PCA.

It is known [97, 98, 99] that the functions of the form

$$\sigma(x) = \sum_{i=1}^{N} \overline{w}_i f(\underline{w}_i^T x + \underline{\theta}_i) + \overline{\theta} \tag{6.88}$$

are universal approximators; that is, they can approximate any continuous bounded function with arbitrary accuracy provided that N can be arbitrarily large. But $\sigma(x)$ is the function implemented by a two-layer neural network with linear output unit and sigmoid hidden units. Therefore, the coding subnetwork and the decoding subnetwork in Figure 6.10 can implement any continuous bounded function with any degree of accuracy. This is the reason why we do not need to consider the case where layers 2 and 4 are nonlinear. For simplicity we'll assume that they are linear.

Such a network is described in [100]. Let $a_i(l)$ be the activation of unit i in layer l, $w_{ij}(l)$ be the synaptic strength of the connection between unit i in layer l and unit j in layer $l - 1$, and call $\theta_i(l)$ the bias for unit i in layer l. With this notation we have

$$a_i(l) = \begin{cases} f(u_i(l)) & \text{if } l = 1 \text{ or } l = 3, \\ u_i(l) & \text{if } l = 2 \text{ or } l = 4, \end{cases}$$

where

$$u_i(l) = \sum_{j=1}^{N_{l-1}} w_{ij}(l) a_j(l - 1) + \theta_i(l).$$

The number of units in layer l is denoted by N_l. We also define the activation of the zeroth layer to be the input $a_i(0) = x_i$.

The input to the network is the same as the teacher, and we seek to minimize the usual quadratic error

$$J_{\text{NET}} = \frac{1}{2} \sum_{k=1}^{P} \sum_{i=1}^{n} (a_{i,k}(4) - x_{i,k})^2. \tag{6.89}$$

There are n output units and P training data vectors $x_1, \ldots, x_P$. The value $a_{i,k}(4)$ is the activation of the output unit i, in layer 4, for input pattern k.

The back-propagation algorithm [42] can be used to optimize J_{NET}. The iterative equations are

$$\Delta w_{ij}(l) = -\beta \delta_i(l) a_j(l - 1), \tag{6.90}$$

$$\Delta \theta_i(l) = -\beta \delta_i(l), \tag{6.91}$$

where

$$\delta_i(4) = a_i(4) - x_i, \tag{6.92}$$

$$\delta_i(l) = d_i(l) \sum_{j=1}^{N_{l+1}} \delta_j(l + 1) w_{ji}(l + 1), \qquad l = 1, 2, 3, \tag{6.93}$$

$$d_i(l) = \begin{cases} 1 & \text{if } l = 2, \\ f'(u_i(l)) & \text{otherwise.} \end{cases}$$

f' denotes the derivative of the nonlinear activation function f.

Example 6.6. We tried the model of Figure 6.10 for a set of two-dimensional data generated by the equations

$$x_1 = \sin(\phi) + \varepsilon_1,$$

$$x_2 = 2\cos(\phi) + \varepsilon_2.$$

The scalar variable ϕ is uniformly distributed between 0 and 2π, while the variables ε_1, ε_2 are uniformly distributed between -0.05 and 0.05 and are independent of ϕ and of each other. We chose small dimensionality $n = 2$ to aid the visualization of the data and the results.

The feature layer has size $p = 1$, while we experimented with various sizes of the layers 1 and 3. Figure 6.11 shows the results of the experiments for $N_1 = N_3 = 5$, $N_1 = N_3 = 10$, and $N_1 = N_3 = 20$. The network was trained in each case using 1000 sweeps of the back-propagation algorithm with constant step-size parameter $\beta = 0.05$. The figure depicts the nonlinear principal component curve in each case (solid line), which approaches the shape of the ellipse as the number of the

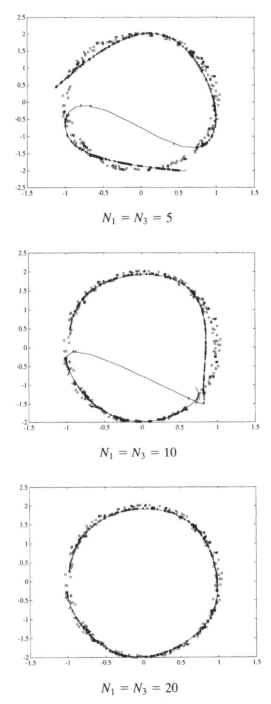

$$N_1 = N_3 = 5$$

$$N_1 = N_3 = 10$$

$$N_1 = N_3 = 20$$

Figure 6.11. The nonlinear principal component of the data approximated by neural networks with size $2 - N_1 - 1 - N_3 - 2$ for different values of N_1 and N_3.

hidden units in layers 1 and 3 increases. This, of course, is expected since more hidden units imply better capability for the coding and decoding subnetworks to approximate the correct nonlinear principal component curve.

In this example the ordinary principal component curve would be a straight line parallel to the main axis of the ellipse (i.e., the horizontal axis). Clearly this line is a very poor approximation of the data, and the ellipsoid principal component curve achieves much better approximation.

Example 6.7. Similar data as in the previous example were used in this experiment as well. In particular,

$$x_1 = 2\sin(\phi) + \varepsilon_1,$$

$$x_2 = 2\cos(\phi) + \varepsilon_2.$$

The difference is that now the data have a semicircular shape and larger noise variance. In this experiment ϕ is uniform between 0 and π, and ε_1, ε_2 are uniform between -0.25 and 0.25.

Figure 6.12 shows three different results for network sizes $N_1 = N_3 = N = 3$, 5, and 10. We are able to see the contours of the functions implemented by the coding subnetwork (layers 1 and 2). These are approximations of the optimal contours of h^*. The principal component curve in all three cases has semicircular shape as we can see and runs like the skeleton of the distribution. We can see that every point in the principal component curve is the center of gravity of the data lying along the corresponding contour.

6.7   APPLICATION EXAMPLES

Nonlinear PCA networks have been applied as nonlinear feature extractors in signal processing applications. Specifically, many chemical processes are described by nonlinear (often chaotic) equations which need to be modeled in order to study, for example, the effects of system parameter changes. Another very intriguing problem is the time-series prediction of the observation data corresponding to these systems since they may exhibit bifurcations, chaotic attractors, etc. Regarding the use of Nonlinear PCA networks (and standard PCA) in tackling these problems, the reader may refer to [101, 102] and the references therein.

Another class of applications for nonlinear PCA networks is pattern recognition as described below.

Example 6.8 (Face and Gender Recognition). Golomb et al. [103] have used nonlinear principal component neural networks for identifying sex from human faces. Their system consisted of two processing stages: (a) a feature extraction stage and (b) a classification stage. Both stages were implemented using neural networks.

The feature extraction network comprised two layers (excluding the input layer). The input and the output layers had 900 nodes equal to the number of pixels in

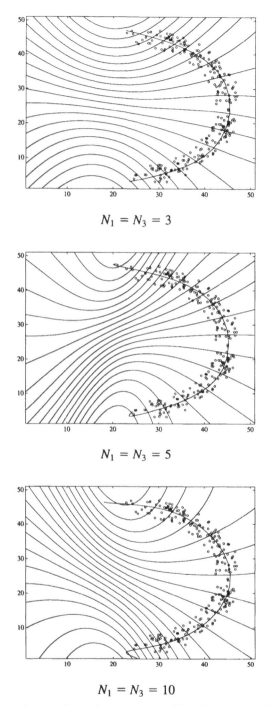

$N_1 = N_3 = 3$

$N_1 = N_3 = 5$

$N_1 = N_3 = 10$

Figure 6.12. The nonlinear principal component of the data approximated by neural networks with different numbers of hidden units. The plots also show the contours of the different mappings implemented by the coding subnetwork.

the 30 × 30 input images. The hidden layer consisted of 40 units with sigmoidal activation function. This is a typical nonlinear PCA network. The authors claim that 50 linear principal components produce reasonable likeness of faces, but nonlinear compression is more efficient since it needs fewer components.

The sex-discriminating network (called SexNet) received input from the activation values of the hidden layer of the compression net. It had 2, 5, 10, 20, and 40 hidden units and one output unit. Training in both networks was done using simple back-propagation.

The 90 test images (45 male and 45 female) were black-and-white photos calibrated so that the distance between the eyes and the distance from the eyes to the mouth was similar in all images. No obvious cues relating to sex (e.g., facial hair, jewelry, clothing, etc.) were present in any picture.

The results of their experiments showed that the network had similar performance, as five human subjects tested on the same images. Humans produced an average misclassification error of 11.6%, while the SexNet with 10 hidden units produced an average error of 8.1%. Both humans and neural network had trouble on the same images and seemed to be affected by similar errors. For example, a certain male image was misclassified by the network when taken as a test image, or took long to train when taken as a train image. The same image was mis-sexed by the human subjects. It is also interesting to note that, according to the same authors, a single network classifier (without a compression subnetwork) with 900 inputs, 40 hidden units, and 1 output unit failed to generalize, although it was able to train well on the same image set.

A similar, but more complicated, classification problem involving human faces was studied by Cottrell and Metcalfe [104]. They also used two networks, one for feature extraction and one for classification. The feature extraction network consisted of 4096 input nodes (64 × 64 images), 40 hidden nodes, and 4096 output nodes. The activation function was the usual sigmoid scaled and shifted in the range from −1 to 1. The activations of the 40 hidden nodes are again given as input to the classification network. The objectives of the classifier are multiple, unlike the previous experiment. The network must decide the gender, the name, and the emotional state of the person in the picture.

The image set consisted of 160 images: 8 pictures for every person in a set of 20 persons (10 male, 10 female). Different pictures of the same person correspond to different feigned emotional states of that person, such as astonishment, delight, sleepiness, relaxation, anger, boredom, etc.

The authors report a perfect recognition rate of the network on the training images in the problem of sex discrimination and near perfect rate (99%) in the problem of identification. In the emotion recognition problem the results were not as good but could be compared with similar results from human subjects.

7

SIGNAL ENHANCEMENT
AGAINST NOISE

This chapter extends ordinary PCA into the constrained PCA (CPCA) and oriented PCA (OPCA) problems. These extensions arise when components from certain subspaces are known to be undesirable. For example, certain subspaces could be known a priori to be contaminated by a certain type of noise or interference. Such a priori knowledge may be exploited for the selection of "best" representative components. In the formulation of CPCA, those unwanted subspaces are completely avoided. In comparison, the OPCA offers a relatively more flexible formulation at the expense of higher computational cost. It searches for an optimal solution oriented toward the directions where the unwanted direction has minimum energy while maximizing the projection energy of input signal. The OPCA is actually closely related to the generalized eigenvalue problem of two random signals.

7.1 CONSTRAINED PCA

The problem of CPCA arises when certain subspaces are less preferred than others, thus affecting the selection of "best" components. In CPC, we assume that there is an undesirable subspace $\mathcal{L}$, spanned by the orthonormal columns of a *constraint matrix* V. $\mathcal{L}$ may stand for the interference subspace in interference-cancellation applications or for a redundant subspace in applications of extracting novel components.

More formally, the CPC problem can be defined as follows: given an n-dimensional stationary stochastic vector process $\{x_k\}$ and an l-dimensional ($l < n$) constraint process $\{v_k\}$, such that

$$v_k = Vx_k, \qquad V^TV = I, \qquad \mathcal{L} = \text{span}(V),$$

find the most representative m-dimensional ($l + m \leq n$) subspace $\mathcal{L}_m$ in the principal component sense constrained to be orthogonal to $\mathcal{L}$. "In the principal component sense" means that we are looking for the optimal linear transformation

$$y_k = Wx_k,$$

where $W \in \mathbb{R}^{m \times n}$, $WW^T = I$, such that the square reconstruction error

$$J_e = E\|x - \hat{x}\|^2, \tag{7.1}$$

$$\hat{x} = W^T y = W^T Wx \tag{7.2}$$

is minimal under the constraint

$$WV = 0. \tag{7.3}$$

The matrix $W^T W$ is the projector operator on the subspace $\mathcal{L}_m = \text{span}(W)$ which is orthogonal to $\mathcal{L}$, and $\hat{x}_k$ is simply the projection of x_k. Like the standard PCA problem, minimization of the reconstruction error under the constraint (7.3) is equivalent to maximization of the variance

$$J_v = \text{tr}\big(E\{yy^T\}\big) = \text{tr}\big(E\{\hat{x}\hat{x}^T\}\big) = \text{tr}(WR_x W^T) \tag{7.4}$$

under the same constraint. The problem was first analyzed in [105] and subsequently in [50, 53]. We present here the main result.

Theorem 7.1. The optimal solution to the CPC problem is

$$W^* = [\pm e_1 \quad \cdots \quad \pm e_m]^T, \tag{7.5}$$

where $e_1, \ldots, e_m$, are the principal eigenvectors of the *projected correlation matrix*:

$$R_p = (I - VV^T)R_x(I - VV^T), \tag{7.6}$$

while the minimum error is

$$\min J_e = \sum_{i=m+1}^{n} \tilde{\lambda}_i, \tag{7.7}$$

$$\max J_v = \sum_{i=1}^{m} \tilde{\lambda}_i, \tag{7.8}$$

where $\tilde{\lambda}_1, \tilde{\lambda}_2, \ldots, \tilde{\lambda}_n$ are the eigenvalues of R_p in decreasing order.

In addition, the nonzero eigenvalues of R_p and their corresponding eigenvectors are also eigenvalue/vector pairs to the *skewed correlation matrix* $R_s = (I - VV^T)R_x$.

Proof. First we shall deal with the last statement in Theorem 7.1. The following facts can be easily shown [50]:

1. All eigenvalues of R_s are real and nonnegative. $I - V^T V$ is a projector matrix, i.e., $(I - V^T V)^2 = (I - V^T V)$. Let e be a right eigenvector of R_s associated with eigenvalue $\tilde{\lambda}$. Assume for the moment that e is complex; then

$$e^* R_x (I - V^T V) R_x e = \tilde{\lambda} e^* R_x e,$$

so

$$\|(I - V^T V) R_x e\|^2 = \tilde{\lambda} \|R_x^{1/2} e\|^2$$

where $*$ denotes conjugate transpose. Therefore, $\tilde{\lambda}$ is not only real but also $\tilde{\lambda} \geq 0$, and e is also real.

2. There are exactly l zero eigenvalues of R_s and the remaining $n - l$ eigenvalues are positive. This is true because the null space of $(I - V^T V)$ has dimension l and R_x is nonsingular.

3. Eigenvectors corresponding to different nonzero eigenvalues are orthogonal. Indeed, let

$$R_s e_i = \tilde{\lambda}_i e_i, \quad R_s e_j = \tilde{\lambda}_j e_j, \qquad \tilde{\lambda}_i, \tilde{\lambda}_j > 0, \ \tilde{\lambda}_i \neq \tilde{\lambda}_j.$$

Then

$$e_i^T R_x (I - V^T V) R_x e_j = \tilde{\lambda}_i e_i^T R_x e_j = \tilde{\lambda}_j e_i^T R_x e_j,$$

$$e_i^T R_x (I - V^T V) R_x e_j = 0.$$

But

$$e_i^T R_x (I - V^T V) R_x e_j = \tilde{\lambda}_i \tilde{\lambda}_j e_i^T e_j = 0,$$

$$e_i^T e_j = 0.$$

4. Eigenvectors of R_s corresponding to nonzero eigenvalues are orthogonal to V. This is obvious since $(I - VV^T) R_x e = \lambda e$ implies $\lambda V^T e = V^T (I - VV^T) R_x e = 0$.

5. If (λ, e) is an eigenvalue/vector pair of R_s, with $\lambda > 0$ then it is also an eigenvalue/vector pair for R_p. From the previous statement $(I - VV^T) e = e$, so $(I - VV^T) R_x e = \lambda e$ implies $(I - VV^T) R_x (I - VV^T) e = \lambda e$.

The proof of the remaining part of the theorem proceeds as follows. Since $W \perp \mathcal{L} = \text{span}(V)$, $W = W(I - VV^T)$ so the problem becomes

$$\text{maximize } \text{tr}(W(I - VV^T) R_x (I - VV^T) W^T)$$

$$\text{subject to } W^T W = I, \text{and } WV = 0.$$

The solution under the first constraint alone is

$$W^* = [\pm e_1 \quad \cdots \quad \pm e_m]^T,$$

but this also satisfies the second constraint $WV = 0$, so it must be the optimal solution under both constraints. ∎

If the columns of V are orthonormal eigenvectors of R_x then $R_p = R_s$ and $(I - VV^T)$ is a deflation operator. Clearly, the problem then reduces to finding the principal eigenvectors orthogonal to the principal l-dimensional eigenspace. This is the PCA problem for the components $l + 1, l + 2, \ldots, n$.

7.1.1 Neural Models for CPC

We'll show now that the APEX model tackles the CPC problem defined above. Consider the APEX network in Figure 7.1a where the first l units correspond to the undesirable components $v_1, \ldots, v_l$. We shall call them *constraint units*. We train the first nonconstraint neuron with the APEX rule

$$\Delta w_k = \beta_k(y_k x_k - y_k^2 w_k), \tag{7.9}$$

$$\Delta c_k = \beta_k(y_k v_k - y_k^2 c_k), \tag{7.10}$$

where

$$y = w^T x - c^T v = (w^T - c^T V)x.$$

We can prove the following

Theorem 7.2 [50]. Consider the algorithm defined above. Then with probability 1, the quantity $q_k = w_k - V^T c_k$ converges to $\pm e_1$ as $k \to \infty$.

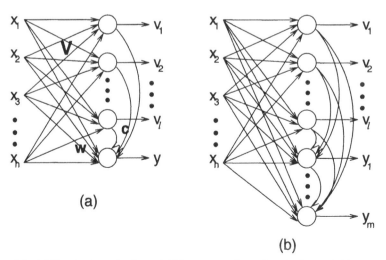

Figure 7.1. (a) The single-output model. The connections denote the weights w_i, c_j which are trained. (b) The multiple-output model.

In the general case for CPC, it is not true that $c_k \to 0$. In the special case where the rows of V are principal eigenvectors of R_x then the problem is reduced to the standard principal component analysis and Theorem 4.3 applies.

The CPC problem can be solved recursively by the APEX model. Since the components are orthogonal, once the first component has been extracted it can be appended to the rows of V to obtain a new orthogonal constraint matrix

$$V' = \left[\begin{array}{c} V \\ e_1^T \end{array} \right],$$

which will be used to obtain the next component.

7.1.2 Simulation Results

Figure 7.2 depicts the convergence of the APEX network for the CPC problem. The data are artificially created and have dimension $n = 64$. There $l = 8$ constraint neurons, while the orthonormal constraint matrix V is randomly picked. The convergence is exponential as in the PCA case.

7.2 ORIENTED PCA

In this section we extend the standard principal component analysis problem by introducing OPCA [50, 106, 107] which corresponds to the generalized eigenvalue problem of two random signals and bears the same relationship to generalized eigenvalue decomposition (GED) as PCA bears to ordinary eigenvalue decomposition (ED). More precisely, the goal is to find the direction vector w that maximizes the signal-to-signal ratio

$$J_{\text{OPC}} = \frac{E\{(w^T x)^2\}}{E\{(w^T v)^2\}} = \frac{w^T R_x w}{w^T R_v w}, \tag{7.11}$$

where $R_x = E\{xx^T\}$ and $R_v = E\{vv^T\}$. We assume that R_v is strictly positive definite, hence nonsingular. Quite often $\{x_k\}$ and $\{v_k\}$ are stationary stochastic processes, whence $R_x = E\{x_k x_k^T\}$ and $R_v = E\{v_k v_k^T\}$ and OPCA is still defined via (7.11). As usual there is little difference between random vectors and stationary random processes, and we'll use the term OPCA for both cases interchangeably.

The optimal solution to (7.11) will be called the *principal oriented component* of the pair (x, v). Referring to Fig. 7.3, the adjective "oriented" is justified by the fact that the principal component of x is now *steered* by the distribution of v: it will be oriented toward the directions where v has minimum energy while trying to maximize the projection energy of x. J_{OPC} is nothing but the generalized Rayleigh quotient for the matrix pencil (R_x, R_v), so the principal oriented component is the principal generalized eigenvector of the symmetric generalized eigenvalue problem [108]

$$R_x w = \lambda R_v w. \tag{7.12}$$

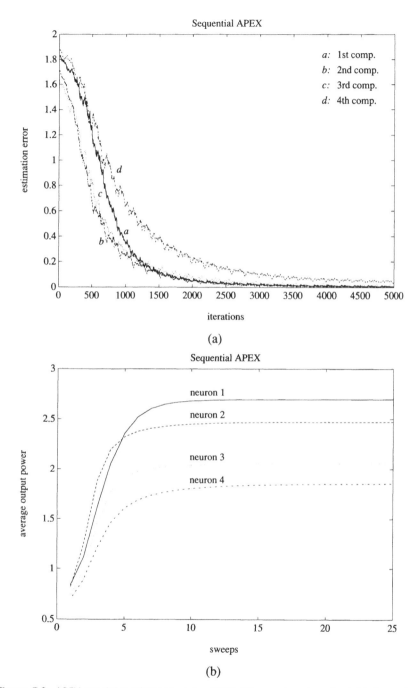

Figure 7.2. APEX model performance for CPC. We use two hundred 64-dimensional data vectors repeated in sweeps. (a) The convergence of the error $\|q_k - e_m\|^2$ for each neuron m. (b) The output variance: $average\{y^2\}$ over each sweep for each neuron. The final variance approximately equals to the corresponding eigenvalue $\tilde{\lambda}_m$.

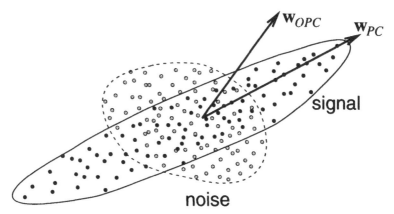

Figure 7.3. A visual interpretation of oriented principal component analysis: although the principal component w_{PC} is along the major axis of the signal, the oriented principal component w_{OPC}, is "steered" by the distribution of the noise.

Since R_x and R_v are symmetric, all the generalized eigenvalues are real and nonnegative and the eigenvectors are also real. The second, third, etc., generalized eigenvectors (ordered by decreasing associated eigenvalue) will also be called oriented principal components. So, if the generalized eigenvalues are $\lambda_1 \geq \lambda_2 \geq \cdots \geq \lambda_n$, then the associated eigenvectors $e_1, e_2, \ldots, e_n$ will be called the first, second, $\ldots$, nth *oriented principal component* respectively.

All the components maximize (7.11) but under different constraints; namely the second component has to be R_v-orthogonal and R_x-orthogonal to the first one, the third component has to be the same to the first two, etc. Formally, for the ith component, $i \geq 2$, we have

$$\frac{E\left\{(e_i^T x)^2\right\}}{E\left\{(e_i^T v)^2\right\}} = \text{a maximum,}$$

$$\text{under} \quad \begin{matrix} R_v\text{-orthogonality: } e_i^T R_v e_j = 0 \\ R_x\text{-orthogonality: } e_i^T R_x e_j = 0 \end{matrix} \quad \forall j < i. \tag{7.13}$$

If $R_v = \sigma I$, then v is isotropically distributed in all directions and provides no "steering" for w. In this case the generalized eigenvalue problem $R_x w = \lambda R_v w$ reduces to the standard eigenvalue problem $R_x w = \lambda \sigma w$ of R_x. The OPCA criterion (7.11) results in a w that will simply maximize the projected energy of x, a solution which is of course equivalent to ordinary PCA.

When $\{v_k\}$ is a stochastic process with $R_v = \sigma I$ we refer to it as *white noise*. Thus OPCA is more general than ordinary PCA and is different from it only when $\{v_k\}$ is a colored random process.

Example 7.1. Consider two random vectors x and v generated as linear combinations of the columns of an invertible $n \times n$ matrix Q:

$$x = Q\theta, \qquad v = Q\phi,$$

where the random vectors θ, ϕ have diagonal correlation matrices

$$R_\theta = \text{diag}[\sigma_{\theta_1} \quad \cdots \quad \sigma_{\theta_n}],$$
$$R_\phi = \text{diag}[\sigma_{\phi_1} \quad \cdots \quad \sigma_{\phi_n}].$$

Assume that $\sigma_{\phi_i} > 0$, for all i. Then the correlation matrices for the vectors x and v are simultaneously diagonalized by Q^{-1}:

$$Q^{-1}R_xQ^{-T} = R_\theta,$$
$$Q^{-1}R_vQ^{-T} = R_\phi.$$

It follows that the columns of Q^{-T} are generalized eigenvectors of the pair (R_x, R_v). Indeed, we have

$$Q^{-1}R_xQ^{-T} = Q^{-1}R_vQ^{-T}R_\phi^{-1}R_\theta,$$

which can be rewritten as

$$R_xQ^{-T} = R_vQ^{-T}\Lambda,$$

with Λ denoting the diagonal matrix of the generalized eigenvalues:

$$\Lambda = \text{diag}[\sigma_{\theta_1}/\sigma_{\phi_1} \quad \cdots \quad \sigma_{\theta_n}/\sigma_{\phi_n}].$$

Clearly any column q_i of Q^{-T} satisfies the generalized eigenvalue equation $R_xq_i = \lambda_i R_vq_i$.

Example 7.2. Let x and v be two-dimensional zero-mean vectors generated by the equations

$$x = \begin{bmatrix} 0.9 & 1 \\ 1 & -1.1 \end{bmatrix} \begin{bmatrix} \theta_1 \\ \theta_2 \end{bmatrix},$$

$$y = \begin{bmatrix} 0.9 & 1 \\ 1 & -1.1 \end{bmatrix} \begin{bmatrix} \phi_1 \\ \phi_2 \end{bmatrix}.$$

Let the random variables θ_1, θ_2, ϕ_1, and ϕ_2 have zero means and variances

$$E\{\theta_1^2\} = 0.1, \qquad E\{\theta_2^2\} = 1,$$
$$E\{\phi_1^2\} = 1, \qquad E\{\phi_2^2\} = 0.3.$$

Also let the pairs θ_1, θ_2, and ϕ_1, ϕ_2 be uncorrelated. In this situation the variances of the elements of x and v are as follows

$$E\{x_1^2\} = 0.9^2 \cdot 0.1 + 1 \cdot 1 = 1.081,$$

$$E\{x_2^2\} = 1 \cdot 0.1 + 1.1^2 \cdot 1 = 1.31,$$

$$E\{y_1^2\} = 0.9^2 \cdot 1 + 1 \cdot 0.3 = 1.11,$$

$$E\{y_2^2\} = 1 \cdot 1 + 1.1^2 \cdot 0.3 = 1.363.$$

Observe that x_1 and y_1 have the same mean (zero) and almost the same variance (1.081 versus 1.11). This is also true for x_2 and y_2 (variances 1.31 versus 1.363). If we were to use the second-order statistics of x_1, x_2, y_1, and y_2 to distinguish between x and y, the resulting test would have been very poor.

According to the previous example, the columns of the matrix

$$U_0 = \begin{bmatrix} 0.9 & 1 \\ 1 & -1.1 \end{bmatrix}^{-T} = \frac{1}{1.99} \begin{bmatrix} 1.1 & 1 \\ 1 & -0.9 \end{bmatrix}$$

are oriented principal eigenvectors of x and v. Thus, performing OPCA on x and v we obtain two scaled eigenvectors of the form

$$e_1 = \alpha\,[1.1 \quad 1]^T, \qquad e_2 = \beta\,[1 \quad -0.9]^T.$$

Since there is no constraint in the size of the eigenvectors the values α and β can be arbitrary. This is unlike ordinary PCA where the eigenvectors are usually assumed to be unit length. Whatever the length of the eigenvectors the oriented component transformation

$$\begin{bmatrix} \hat{\theta}_1 \\ \hat{\theta}_2 \end{bmatrix} = \begin{bmatrix} e_1^T \\ e_2^T \end{bmatrix} x,$$

$$\begin{bmatrix} \hat{\phi}_1 \\ \hat{\phi}_2 \end{bmatrix} = \begin{bmatrix} e_1^T \\ e_2^T \end{bmatrix} v$$

yields the following variances:

$$E\{\hat{\theta}_1^2\} = \alpha^2 E\{\theta_1^2\} = 0.1\alpha^2,$$

$$E\{\hat{\theta}_2^2\} = \beta^2 E\{\theta_2^2\} = \beta^2,$$

$$E\{\hat{\phi}_1^2\} = \alpha^2 E\{\phi_1^2\} = \alpha^2,$$

$$E\{\hat{\phi}_2^2\} = \beta^2 E\{\phi_2^2\} = 0.3\beta^2.$$

Now the variances of the components are distinctly different. The variance of $(e_1^T x)$ is equal to one-tenth of the variance of $(e_1^T v)$, while the variance of $(e_2^T x)$ is

3.3333 times larger than the variance of $(e_2^T v)$. A test for distinguishing x from v based on the second-order statistics of the components $\hat{\theta}_i$, $\hat{\phi}_i$ would be much more successful than the original test.

7.2.1 Gaussian Signal Detection and Matched Filtering

OPCA is related to the detection problem of deciding between two Gaussian assumptions and a certain type of optimal test statistic called *matched filter*. The *binary detection* problem is the problem of choosing between two hypotheses H_0 and H_1 concerning the value of a parameter vector θ involved in the distribution underlying some statistical observation.

A test statistic $f(r)$ is a function of the observation $r = [r_1, r_2, \ldots, r_N]^T$ that is used to form a test

$$f(r) \begin{cases} > \tau, & \text{choose } H_0 : \theta \in \Theta_0, \\ \leq \tau, & \text{choose } H_1 : \theta \in \Theta_1, \end{cases}$$

for choosing between the two alternatives H_0 and H_1. The parameter τ is the detection threshold, while the sets Θ_0, Θ_1 are assumed disjoint sets that cover all the possible values of θ. The observation r is a random vector whose distribution depends on θ. Very often the hypotheses have the simple form $H_0 : \theta = \theta_0$ and $H_1 : \theta \neq \theta_0$ for some fixed value θ_0.

The *size* of the test is the probability of false alarm (probability of choosing H_0 while in fact H_1 is true):

$$(\text{size}) \ \alpha = \text{Prob}(f(r) > \tau \mid H_1),$$

and the *power* of the test is the probability of hit (probability of choosing H_0 when indeed H_0 is true):

$$(\text{power}) \ \beta = \text{Prob}(f(r) > \tau \mid H_0).$$

There is a trade-off between α and $1 - \beta$: the bigger the threshold τ the smaller the probability of false alarm α, but also the smaller the power β. Conversely, smaller τ implies larger probability of hit but also larger probability of false alarm. Typically one wants to minimize α while maximizing β. In many applications (especially of military nature) a false alarm can be a very costly mistake. Therefore, one usually is not interested in tests with $\alpha > \alpha_0$ for some fixed α_0, and under this constraint one wishes to maximize β. A test that does this is called **uniformly most powerful** (UMP). Formally, a test (f, τ_1) is called UMP with size α_0 if

$$\text{Prob}(f(r) > \tau_1 \mid H_0) \geq \text{Prob}(g(r) > \tau_2 \mid H_0)$$

for all tests $(g(r), \tau_2)$ such that

$$\text{Prob}(g(r) > \tau_2 \mid H_1) \leq \text{Prob}(f(r) > \tau_1 \mid H_1) = \alpha_0.$$

Consider now the detection problem

$$H_0 : r = x + v,$$
$$H_1 : r = v, \tag{7.14}$$

where x, v, are zero-mean, independent Gaussian vectors with variance $E\{vv^T\} = R_v$ and $E\{xx^T\} = R_x$. The distribution of r under H_0 is Gaussian with zero mean and variance $E\{rr^T\} = R_x + R_v$:

$$p_{H_0}(r) = \frac{1}{(2\pi)^{n/2} |R_x + R_v|^{1/2}} \exp\left[-\tfrac{1}{2} r^T (R_x + R_v)^{-1} r\right],$$

while under H_1 the distribution is

$$p_{H_1}(r) = \frac{1}{(2\pi)^{n/2} |R_v|^{1/2}} \exp\left[-\tfrac{1}{2} r^T R_v^{-1} r\right].$$

The *log-likelihood ratio* is defined as

$$
\begin{aligned}
l(r) &= \log(p_{H_1}(r)/p_{H_0}(r)) \\
&= C - \tfrac{1}{2} r^T \left[R_v^{-1} - (R_x + R_v)^{-1}\right] r, \tag{7.15}
\end{aligned}
$$

where C is a constant.

According to the Neyman-Pearson theorem [93] the uniformly most powerful test for the alternatives H_0, H_1 is

$$l(r) \begin{cases} > \tau & \text{choose } H_1, \\ \leq \tau & \text{choose } H_0, \end{cases}$$

where τ is selected so that the size of the test be $\alpha = \alpha_0$.

Let the columns of the matrix $E = [e_1, \ldots, e_n]$ be the generalized eigenvectors of (R_x, R_v), so $E^T R_x E = D_x = \text{diag}[d_{x1}, \ldots, d_{xn}]$, $E^T R_v E = D_v = \text{diag}[d_{v1}, \ldots, d_{vn}]$. The quadratic form $q(r) = r^T [R_v^{-1} - (R_x + R_v)^{-1}] r$ in (7.15) becomes

$$
\begin{aligned}
q(r) &= r^T \left[E D_v^{-1} E^T - (E^{-T} D_x E^{-1} + E^{-T} D_v E^{-1})^{-1}\right] r \\
&= r^T E \left[D_v^{-1} - (D_x + D_v)^{-1}\right] E^T r \\
&= \sum_{i=1}^{n} \frac{d_{xi}}{d_{vi}(d_{xi} + d_{vi})} (r^T e_i)^2. \tag{7.16}
\end{aligned}
$$

We can rewrite the test as

$$q(r) \begin{cases} \geq \tau_1 & \text{choose } H_0, \\ < \tau_1 & \text{choose } H_1, \end{cases}$$

where the threshold τ_1 has been properly modified from τ. So the optimal test statistic is the weighted sum of the power of the oriented components of r.

Another interesting relation between OPCA and detection theory comes again from the binary decision problem (7.14) only now under the following setting: $x =$ fixed vector, $v =$ zero-mean Gaussian noise with variance R_v. The log-likelihood ratio results in the following statistic:

$$l(r) = C - \frac{1}{2}\left[r^T R_v^{-1} x - (r - x)^T R_v^{-1}(r - x)\right] \tag{7.17}$$

$$= C_1 - r^T R_v^{-1} x, \tag{7.18}$$

where $C_1 = C + x^T R_v^{-1} x$ is a constant (not a function of the observation r). The principal generalized eigenvector of $(R_x = xx^T, R_v)$ satisfies

$$R_x e_1 = \lambda_1 R_v e_1$$

$$R_v^{-1} x \frac{x^T e_1}{\lambda_1} = e_1.$$

Thus, ignoring the constants C_1 and $(x^T e_1)/\lambda_1$, the optimal statistic can take the form

$$f(r) = r^T e_1,$$

which is nothing but the projection of the observation on the oriented principal component subspace. This function is equivalent to the *matched filter* [109] a classical tool used in detection and communications applications.

Pattern Classification (Fisher's Linear Discriminant)   In the pattern classification context the vectors $\{x_k\}$ and $\{v_k\}$ are random samples drawn from two different classes of data which have different distributions. The task is to classify observed patterns into their corresponding classes as correctly as possible given some knowledge about the distributions or given a set of training samples from which the classifier can learn these distributions. A classical second-order classification technique (i.e., based only on first- and second-order statistics) is Fisher's linear discriminant analysis. It is based on the principal generalized eigenvector of a pair of symmetric matrices S_w and S_b called the *within-cluster* and *between-cluster* scatter matrices. In particular, let m_1, m_2, be the means of the two classes and u_{1k}, u_{2k} the samples drawn from each class. Then the Fisher criterion is

$$\text{maximize } J = \frac{(w^T m_1 - w^T m_2)^2}{E\left\{\left[w^T(u_1 - m_1)\right]^2\right\} + E\left\{\left[w^T(u_2 - m_2)\right]^2\right\}}$$

$$= \frac{w^T S_b w}{w^T S_w w}, \tag{7.19}$$

where $S_b = (m_1 - m_2)(m_1 - m_2)^T$ and $S_w = E\{(u_1 - m_1)(u_1 - m_1)^T\} + E\{(u_2 - m_2)(u_2 - m_2)^T\}$. Fisher's analysis opts to separate the two classes as much as possible using one-dimensional projection by maximizing the distance between the projection means normalized by the spread of the projection (for more details see [110, Chapter 5]). The problem is easily transformed into an OPC formulation by setting $x_k = m_1 - m_2$ and $v_k = u_{2k} - m_2$ or $v_k = u_{1k} - m_1$, in which case $R_x = S_b$ and $R_v = S_w$.

Another popular group of methods for pattern classification based on PCA is *subspace classifiers* [111–113]. In order to battle the curse of dimensionality, subspace classifiers describe each class by a small dimensional principal component subspace. The main criticism against these methods is that the representation of each class is not taking into account the relative difference with the other classes. For example, in the cases where the first few principal components of two classes are very similar to each other subspace classifiers have very poor classification performance. Many attempts have been carried out for improving the PC-based methods by introducing coupling terms from the other classes [114], but these methods are rather heuristic. OPC analysis offers a PC-like alternative for taking the other-class information into consideration and has the advantage that it is based on a specific optimality criterion.

7.2.2 Network Models for OPC Extraction

We initially focus on the extraction of the first component. Next we'll suggest a proper deflation approach for extracting multiple components.

Single-Component Extraction   The maximum value of J_{OPC} in (7.11) is the principal generalized eigenvalue λ_1. Therefore, the function

$$V(w) = \frac{1}{2}\left(\lambda_1 - J_{\text{OPC}}(w)\right)$$

is such that $V(w) \geq 0$, and $V(w) = 0$ only for $w = e_1$, so V may serve as a Lyapunov energy function for a system to be proposed. The proper gradient descent algorithm would be

$$\frac{dw}{dt} = -\nabla V = \frac{1}{w^T R_v w}\left(R_x w - \frac{w^T R_x w}{w^T R_v w}R_v w\right) \tag{7.20}$$

with the globally asymptotically stable fixed point $w = e_1$.

In fact, even the simpler equation

$$\frac{dw}{dt} = \left(R_x w - \frac{w^T R_x w}{w^T R_v w}R_v w\right) \tag{7.21}$$

is stable since

$$\frac{dV}{dt} = \frac{dw^T}{dt}\nabla V = -\frac{1}{w^T R_v w}\left\|R_x w - \frac{w^T R_x w}{w^T R_v w}R_v w\right\|^2 \le 0 \qquad (7.22)$$

and again the point $w = e_1$ is the globally asymptotically stable attractor.

R_x or R_v *Known.* In some situations we may know the covariance matrix R_v of the noise $\{v_k\}$, and we are just interested in adapting our system to the unknown statistical properties of $\{x_k\}$. In the signal detection context, this scenario may happen when attempting to detect the presence of a signal in a stationary background, e.g., the detection of a submarine under water. The ambient noise of the sea has known[1] and stationary statistics; thus there is no point for attempting to adaptively estimate them.

Such knowledge greatly simplifies the algorithm formulation. For example, the single neuron $y = w^T x$, equipped with the adaptive rule

$$\Delta w_k = \beta_k \left(y_k x_k - \frac{y_k^2}{w_k^T R_v w_k}R_v w_k\right) \qquad (7.23)$$

has associated ODE (7.21). So $w_k \to e_1$, as $k \to \infty$.

Similarly simple is the situation where R_x is known. This corresponds to the case where the signal or its statistics is known and the noise environment is unknown. Again for a single neuron $z = w^T v$ we use the rule

$$\Delta w_k = \beta_k \left(z_k^2 R_x w_k - (w_k^T R_x w_k)z_k v_k\right), \qquad (7.24)$$

which also corresponds to the ODE (7.21) and results in $w_k \to e_1$ as $k \to \infty$.

Adaptive Model 1. If neither R_x nor R_v is known then the problem is much more complicated. In [107] the authors suggested a single-unit network with weight vector $w = [w_1, w_2, \ldots, w_n]$ and linear input-output mapping

$$\text{output} = \begin{cases} y = w^T x & \text{if input is } x, \\ z = w^T v & \text{if input is } v. \end{cases} \qquad (7.25)$$

The unit is trained with the following learning rule:

$$\Delta w_k = \beta_k \left[(z_k^2/\|w\|^2)q_k - v_k\right],$$
$$\Delta q_k = \beta_k [y_k x_k - y_k^2 q_k],$$

---

[1] Of course, in reality we never "know" any statistics. This is a working assumption which translates into "we have a very good approximate model for all practical purposes."

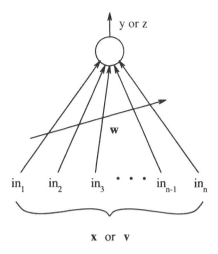

Figure 7.4. The proposed OPC linear neuron unit.

where $q \in \mathbb{R}^n$ is an auxiliary vector. The rule has been found to converge to the principal oriented component solution very slowly. In addition, it is nonlocal and rather artificial for biological justification.

Adaptive Model 2. Two improvements have been proposed in [50, 106]. The model proposed in [106] is a simplified linear neuron with adaptable weights (Fig. 7.4) similar to the model proposed for ordinary PCA by Oja.

The learning rule is also similar to the normalized Hebbian rule except that it is duplicated for both signal and noise, and an additional adaptable parameter, ξ, is introduced which plays a crucial role in the correct functioning of the algorithm. The system has n inputs $\{in_1, in_2, \ldots, in_n\}$, driven interchangeably by the two n-dimensional random processes $\{x_k\}$ and $\{v_k\}$, and one output defined by (7.25) where $w \in \mathbb{R}^n$ is the weight vector.

Although there is no *teacher* process involved in the training, there is an implicit teacher in the sense that the system knows whether each incoming pattern belongs to the process $\{x_k\}$ or $\{v_k\}$.

In the proposed algorithm, the input data are grouped in blocks of size B, where B is some large positive integer. It is assumed that $\{x_k\}$ and $\{v_k\}$ are at least wide-sense stationary, and R_v is strictly positive definite in order to avoid the complications of infinite eigenvalues.

Algorithm 7.1.

1. Initialization: Set θ larger than the largest eigenvalue of R_v. For example, $\theta = \alpha E\{\|v\|^2\}$, $\alpha > 1$. Also set $w_0 = $ any value $\neq 0$, $\sigma_0^{(x)} = \sigma_0^{(v)} = $ any value, $\xi_0 = 0$.

II. *Within Block τ:*
  if input is $\{x_k\}$,

$$\Delta w_k = \beta_k(y_k x_k - y_k^2 w_k), \tag{7.26}$$
$$\Delta \sigma_k^{(x)} = c\beta_k(y_k^2 - \sigma_k^{(x)}) \tag{7.27}$$

else if input is $\{v_k\}$,

$$\Delta w_k = -\xi_\tau \beta_k(z_k v_k - z_k^2 w_k) + \theta\beta(1 - \|w_k\|^2)w_k, \tag{7.28}$$
$$\Delta \sigma_k^{(v)} = c\beta_k(z_k^2 - \sigma_k^{(v)}), \tag{7.29}$$

  where c is any positive constant.
III. *End of Block τ:*

$$\xi_{\tau+1} = \xi_\tau + \gamma\left(\frac{\sigma_{\tau B}^{(x)}}{\sigma_{\tau B}^{(v)}} - \xi_\tau\right), \qquad 0 < \gamma \le 1. \tag{7.30}$$

Clearly, (7.26) and the first term on the right-hand side of (7.28) are Oja's rules corresponding to x_k and v_k. However, the term in (7.28) is negatively weighted by $-\xi$. The intuitive interpretation is that the network must keep away from the principal component of v_k and close to the principal component of x_k with the value ξ representing the compromise between the two extremes. The total rule corresponds to Oja's single-unit algorithm for the matrix $R_x - \xi R_v + \theta I$. Here comes the necessity of the last term in (7.28): it offers a bias that is needed to keep the matrix $R_x - \xi R_v + \theta I$ positive definite (otherwise the weights may converge to 0). The whole philosophy of the algorithm is based on the following simple result.

Lemma 7.1. Let ρ_1 be the largest eigenvalue of the matrix $R_x - \xi R_v$, and let (λ_1, e_1) be the principal generalized eigenvalue/vector pair of the pencil (R_x, R_v). Then

(a) $\rho_1 > 0$ if $\lambda_1 > \xi$,
(b) $\rho_1 < 0$ if $\lambda_1 < \xi$,
(c) $\rho_1 = 0$ if $\lambda_1 = \xi$, and the eigenvector corresponding to ρ_1 is e_1.

Proof. (a) It is sufficient to show that at least one eigenvalue of $R_x - \xi R_v$ is positive. Notice that

$$e_1^T(R_x - \xi R_v)e_1 > e_1^T(R_x - \lambda_1 R_v)e_1 = 0,$$

so indeed the matrix in question can be neither negative definite nor negative semidefinite.

(b) For all generalized eigenvectors e_i,

$$q_i = e_i^T(R_x - \xi R_v)e_i < e_i^T(R_x - \lambda_1 R_v)e_i \le 0.$$

Since the generalized eigenvectors are linearly independent, any vector z can be expanded in e_i: $z = \sum_{i=1}^{n} \alpha_i e_i$, so

$$z^T (R_x - \xi R_v)z = \sum_{i=1}^{n} \alpha_i^2 q_i < 0.$$

It follows that the matrix in question is negative definite.

(c) We have

$$(R_x - \xi R_v)e_1 = (R_x - \lambda_1 R_v)e_1 = 0,$$

while for all i,

$$e_i^T (R_x - \xi R_v)e_i \leq e_i^T (R_x - \lambda_1 R_v)e_i = 0,$$

so the matrix in question is seminegative definite and e_1 is an eigenvector with an associated eigenvalue equal to 0. ∎

Under the condition $B \to \infty$, $\lim_{\tau \to \infty} \xi_\tau \to \lambda_1$ and $w_{\tau B}$ converges to the normalized principal eigenvector of $R_x - \lambda_1 R_v$, which is equal to e_1 as shown in Lemma 7.1.

Adaptive Model 3. Motivated by reducing the complexity of the previous model for OPC extraction, an alternative model is proposed in [50].

The critical issue in totally adaptive OPC approaches is the estimation of the ratio $w^T R_x w / w^T R_v w$ since the matrices R_x and R_v are not readily available. Our model will have to track this ratio as the data are processed. This can be achieved by the following simple adaptive rule:

$$\Delta w_k = \beta_k(y_k x_k - \|w_k\|^2 z_k v_k), \tag{7.31}$$

which is basically formed by two counterbalanced Hebbian rules (the terms $y_k x_k$ and $z_k v_k$). The differential equation associated with (7.31) is

$$\frac{dw}{dt} = R_x w - \|w\|^2 R_v w. \tag{7.32}$$

The dynamics of $\|w\|^2$ are determined by premultiplying (7.32) by $2w^T$ to obtain

$$\frac{d\|w\|^2}{dt} = 2(w^T R_x w - \|w\|^2 w^T R_v w). \tag{7.33}$$

Observe that $w = 0$ is an unstable fixed point of (7.32). Indeed, a small perturbation $\|w\|^2 = \delta^2 > 0$ results in

$$\frac{d\delta^2}{dt} = w^T R_x w - \delta^2(w^T R_v w) > \rho_n^x \delta^2 - \rho_1^v \delta^4,$$

where ρ_n^x, ρ_1^v are the largest and smallest eigenvalues of R_x and R_v respectively. Therefore, if $\delta^2 < \rho_n^x / \rho_1^v$ then $d\delta^2/dt > 0$, yielding an increase of δ^2. If $\|w(0)\|^2 \neq 0$ then $\|w(t)\|^2 \neq 0$ for all t and the ratio $J = w^T R_x w / w^T R_v w$ is well defined.

Unfortunately, it is not very easy to analyze the stability properties of the remaining fixed points $w = \sqrt{\lambda_i}e_i$, $i = 2, \ldots, n$. Equation (7.33) indicates that $\|w\|^2$ tracks J_{OPC}, since $\|w\|^2$ increases if it is less than J_{OPC}, and decreases if greater. If we substitute J_{OPC} for $\|w\|^2$ in (7.32), we obtain the gradient descent rule (7.20).

Simulation experiments show that the rule (7.31) indeed extracts the principal oriented component for the two random sequences. However, we found that the performance can be significantly improved in terms of the variance of the estimation if the norm $\|w_k\|^2$ in (7.31) is replaced by another parameter ξ_k which tracks it and has smoother evolution in time. So in the following we will propose a slight modification of rule (7.31) defined below:

$$\Delta w_k = \beta_k(y_k x_k - \xi_k z_k v_k), \qquad (7.34)$$

$$\Delta \xi_k = \beta_k(\|w_k\|^2 - \xi_k). \qquad (7.35)$$

Again we find it very difficult to rigorously prove that model (7.34)–(7.35) indeed extracts the required components, and we'll content ourselves with the demonstration of the convergence via simulation experiments.

Simulation Results. We tested Algorithm 7.1 using various artificially created random sequences for various input dimensions and block sizes B. Figure 7.5 shows a typical run for an input dimension $n = 10$ and block size $B = 200$. In order to demonstrate the convergence ability of the algorithm, we repeat the same set of 200 data points in sweeps. The input data were constructed by time-windowing two signals using a window of size $n = 10$. The signals were colored by passing two white noise sequences through different AR filters. The value of γ was set at 0.95 while the value of β was determined according to our discussion in Section 4.2.6 since within each block the algorithm is equivalent to the Oja rule, which in turn is a special case of APEX. So our discussion regarding the value of the step-size constant for APEX applies here, too. The parameter θ was estimated by averaging $\|v_k\|^2$ for 100 iterations before starting the algorithm (notice that in the plots of Fig. 7.5 the adaptation really starts at $k = 200$ or $\tau = 1$). In Eqs. (7.27) and (7.29) we used a constant learning rate $1/5B$ instead of $c\beta_k$. Any other small constant value in the range $1/B$ to $1/10B$ would do a reasonable job; however, outside this range the convergence of ξ could be very slow.

We compare the performance of model 3 with model 2, running the algorithm on the same data used in the simulation experiments of the previous section. Figure 7.6 shows the performance of model 3. The value of the step-size constant was set, after experimentation, at $\beta = 0.01$. Part (a) of the plot shows the estimation error between w_k and the actual component e_1, while part (b) shows the evolution of the estimator ξ_k, of the eigenvalue λ_1. Although ξ converges slower than for model 2 and it follows a characteristic damped oscillation, we observe that the convergence of w_k is both exponential and significantly faster than the convergence of model 2 (notice that in Fig. 7.5a the x-axis extends from 0 to 20,000 while here it only extends to 10,000). Furthermore, model 3 is simpler, contains fewer parameters and appears more aesthetically appealing. The disadvantage of this model is that

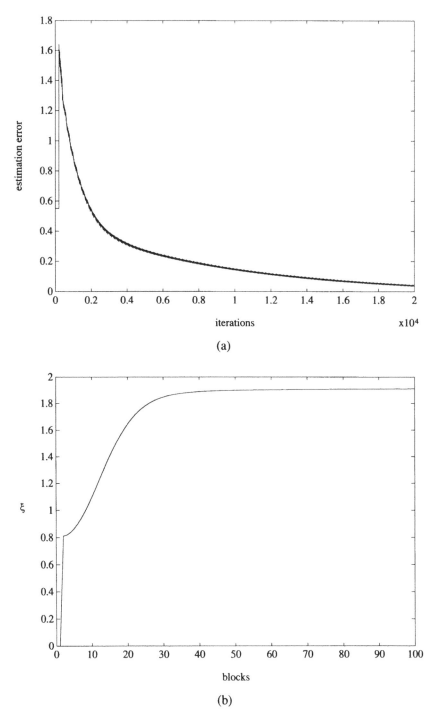

(a)

(b)

Figure 7.5. OPC Model 2: (a) plot of the estimation error $\|e_1 - w_k\|^2$, (b) evolution of ξ_τ.

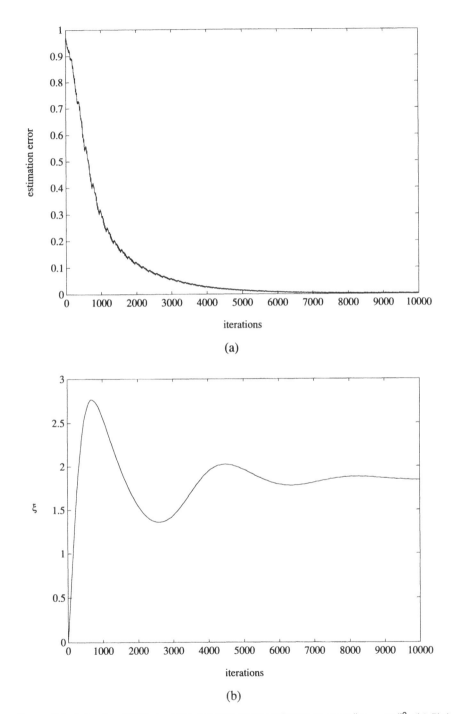

Figure 7.6. Adaptive OPC model 3. (a) Plot of the estimation error $\|e_1 - w_k\|^2$. (b) Plot of ξ_k.

the final convergence vector is not normalized and in fact its norm is equal to λ_1, which can be significantly large if R_v is near-singular. Luckily, when v_k is noise, the condition number of R_v (i.e., the ratio between its largest and smallest eigenvalue) is not very high, and assuming x and v are reasonably scaled, λ_1 is a reasonably sized scalar.

7.2.3 Extracting Multiple OPCs

Once the first generalized eigenvector e_1 is extracted a deflation procedure is followed similar to the classical PC case in order to extract the rest of the components.

Definition 7.1. Any of the mappings

$$(R_x, R_v) \rightarrow \left(\left\{ I - \frac{R_x e_1 e_1^T}{e_1^T R_x e_1} \right\} R_x \left\{ I - \frac{e_1 e_1^T R_x}{e_1^T R_x e_1} \right\}, R_v \right), \qquad (7.36)$$

$$(R_x, R_v) \rightarrow \left(\left\{ I - \frac{R_v e_1 e_1^T}{e_1^T R_v e_1} \right\} R_x \left\{ I - \frac{e_1 e_1^T R_v}{e_1^T R_v e_1} \right\}, R_v \right), \qquad (7.37)$$

$$(R_x, R_v) \rightarrow \left(R_x \left\{ I - \frac{e_1 e_1^T R_x}{e_1^T R_x e_1} \right\}, R_v \right), \qquad (7.38)$$

$$(R_x, R_v) \rightarrow \left(R_x \left\{ I - \frac{e_1 e_1^T R_v}{e_1^T R_v e_1} \right\}, R_v \right) \qquad (7.39)$$

is called a *deflation transformation* of the matrix pair (R_x, R_v) with respect to the generalized eigenvalue problem.

As with the standard PCA case, the matrix resulting after deflation has the same eigenvalue/vector pairs except that the eigenvalue associated with e_1 becomes 0. So, after deflation, the original second component becomes dominant. One can easily verify the above claims by showing that if $(\tilde{R}_x, R_v)$ is any of the four pairs resulting after deflation, then

$$\tilde{R}_x e_1 = 0,$$

while

$$\tilde{R}_x e_i = R_x e_i, \quad i > 1,$$

based on the fact that the generalized eigenvectors are R_x- and R_v-orthogonal. Therefore, the relationship

$$\tilde{R}_x e_i = \tilde{\lambda}_i R_v e_i$$

holds for all i, where now $\tilde{\lambda}_1 = 0$ and $\tilde{\lambda}_i = \lambda_i$ for all $i > 1$.

We can achieve deflation directly on the data, for example, through the transformation

$$\tilde{v}_k = v_k,$$ (7.40)

$$\tilde{x}_k = x_k - y_k \frac{E\{y_k x_k\}}{E\{y_k^2\}} = x_k - \frac{R_x w}{w^T R_x w} y_k,$$ (7.41)

assuming that the weight vector w is proportional to the principal eigenvector e_1. Then the autocorrelation matrices $\tilde{R}_x = E\{\tilde{x}_k \tilde{x}_k^T\}$, $\tilde{R}_v = E\{\tilde{v}_k \tilde{v}_k^T\} = R_v$ form a deflated pair of the first type in Definition 7.1.

(a)   (b)

(c)   (d)

Figure 7.7. CPC analysis is applied to remove interference (rain) from a picture. The constraint matrix V is set equal to the "rain" component. Shown here are images of (a) picture with rain (i.e. $\alpha = 0.$); (b) using a "hard" factor $\alpha = 1$, note that the "white rain" is converted to the "dark rain"; (c) using a softer $\alpha = 0.5$, the "white rain" becomes lighter but is still on the "white" side, hinting a harder factor needed; (d) using a "harder" factor $\alpha = 0.6$, the rain almost disappears.

7.3 APPLICATION EXAMPLES

Example 7.3 (Interference Cancellation). The CPC problem formulation can be used for removing unwanted interference in signal restoration applications [107]. For example, in the case of null-steering beam-forming applications the task is to locate the desired target signals while suppressing the interference from jamming signals. The jamming signals lie in a subspace $\mathcal{L}_i$. In order to remove such interference the basic CPC approach is to set the constraint matrix V such that $\text{span}(V) = \mathcal{L}_i$ and search for the principal components of the signal orthogonal to V.

Using this brute-force approach all the signal energy in the subspace $\mathcal{L}_i$ will be canceled, including the energy of the desired signal that lies on this subspace. A soft-constraint principal components approach can be adopted to incorporate a certain degree of flexibility in the interference-removing process, ranging from a hard (total) blocking to a moderate interference suppression. In order to provide such flexibility, Kung et al. [107] introduce a scaling factor $0 < \alpha < 1$, for the constraint matrix; thus V is replaced by αV. The APEX model still converges to the principal eigenvectors of the new skewed autocorrelation matrix $[I - \alpha^2 V^T V]R_x$. The larger the value of α the harder are the constraint and the more forceful the reorientation of the PCs. In the two extremes lie the pure CPC analysis ($\alpha = 1$) and the pure PCA ($\alpha = 0$).

Figure 7.7 depicts the results of soft-constraint PC analysis applied to remove interference (rain) from a picture. The interference was created from a known orthogonal matrix V. Different scaling factors $\alpha = 0.0, 0.5, 0.6, 1.0$ were experimented. With proper choice of α ($= 0.6$) the rain almost totally disappears and the picture becomes clear again.

8

VLSI IMPLEMENTATION

The practical application of PCA neural models relies heavily on their successful computer implementation. A software solution on a conventional single processor hardware has speed limitations, but it may be sufficient for applications such as acoustics or speech, where the throughput requirement is low. Still, many real-time applications in signal processing, pattern recognition, etc., deal with fast sampling frequencies or large data volumes and are very demanding in computation and/or storage requirements. Neural processing architectures for such applications may require enormous amounts of computation for the training phase as well as high throughputs for the recognition or retrieving phase. Under such circumstances, the single-processor software solution is often inadequate, and parallel VLSI solutions (analog or digital) may become necessary.

Research on PCA neural hardware architectures remains largely virgin territory. Nevertheless, it holds a great deal of potential. Neural PCA models, for instance, offer an alternative approach for PCA computation over classical eigenvector techniques. The latter are not easily parallelizable due to their essentially sequential recursive deflation methodology (see Chapter 3).

A thorough theoretical understanding of explicit and inherent parallelism in neural models can help design cost-effective real-time processing hardware. Most artificial neural network models involve primarily repetitive and regular operations, which may be efficiently mapped to parallel architectures. Principal component neural models are no exception. In fact, they may have an advantage over other neural models because, in the absence of nonlinear functions, they involve linear matrix-vector operations, which are known to have a high degree of parallelizability. For these classes of algorithms, a special-purpose systolic array-type architecture built on local interconnects is an attractive approach.

We demonstrate that all the PCA neural models are quite parallelizable, just like back-propagation networks, whose parallel processing architectures have been studied in great detail in [53]. This paves the way for massively parallel processing, which represents the most promising future solution to digital real-time neural information processing.

Unlike digital implementation, the analog approach for neural PCA models has been the focus of some previous research effort [67, 115]. This chapter studies both digital and analog implementations of PCA models. It would be too early to make a final judgment on which approach is more viable, since both are good for different reasons. The analog approach has the advantage of speed but lacks programmability and scalability, which are the major advantages of the digital approach.

8.1 DIGITAL IMPLEMENTATION[1]

The engineer who wants to design a parallel implementation of neural PCA algorithms faces the basic choice between (a) mapping the algorithms on a general-purpose parallel machine and (b) designing a special-purpose architecture. The general-purpose approach utilizes existing machines, such as the Cray Y-MP C-90 [116], the Intel Paragon [117], MasPar [118], KSR [119], etc. There is also a class of programmable but special-purpose neurocomputers, such as the Siemens Synapse [120, 121], Adaptive Solutions CNAPS [122], the Hitachi neurocomputer [123], etc.

Siemens' Synapse Neurocomputer has a 2-D systolic array architecture, which is designed to support neural algorithms. The interface hardware with real world (namely image acquisition) is included to support an input image data rate up to 80 MByte/sec. The array consists of 4×2 MA16 ASIC chips, each representing a specific VLSI neural signal processor chip, containing a systolic array of 16 fixed-point multipliers. For the retrieving phase, each chip can perform up to 640 megaconnections per second.

In the design of a special-purpose machine, an important decision is whether to use commercially available components or custom-made processors. Popular off-the-shelf components include microprocessors, DSPs (digital signal processors), and FPGAs (field-programmable gate arrays). The drawback against the adoption of such components is mainly that they are designed for general purposes and may not efficiently address the requirements of the application specifications on communication bandwidth, support for special operations, physical size, etc. However, they do offer some important advantages:

- *Fast Turnaround Time from Concept to Implementation:* since the components are readily available and tested, the design effort will be spent only on the development of the architecture;

---

[1]This section is based on "Systolic Array Implementation for Adaptive Principal Component EXtraction (APEX) Algorithm," Technical Report by Yun-ting Lin, Princeton University, 1994.

- *Low Cost Compared to a Custom-Processor Solution:* there will be no cost for developing, fabricating and testing the components;
- *Software Tools* (e.g., compilers): these aid the development of a complete system along with its associated software.

In contrast, from the custom design perspective the above assessments on the pros and cons are reversed. In the custom-design approach there is a development time and cost for fabrication and testing of the designed component. Furthermore, since custom components are usually not demanded in large quantities (unlike the commercial components) the amortized expense becomes higher. Finally, on the software side, difficult low-level code has to be developed that will control the signals of the custom component. However, the custom processor is designed to meet exactly the needs of the application and yields optimal performance. The custom approach is preferred when performance is at a premium. The key in this approach is to find the best mapping of the algorithm on the existing architecture so as to best utilize the inherent parallelism of the algorithm.

Most neural PCA models described in Chapter 4 allow the concurrent extraction of multiple principal components. These models are also computationally iterative and intensive and demand very high throughput. They mostly use matrix-multiplication-type operations, which are very suitable for systolic massively parallel implementation. The structure of these algorithms matches very well the design principle of a VLSI system, which exploits modular, pipelined, and parallel architectures and reduces the communication hardware to mostly local interconnections.

We discuss a special-purpose systolic design for the APEX model. This is only an example demonstrating the design methodology for the mapping of any PCA model into systolic arrays. The same methodology can be applied to derive a special-purpose architecture exploiting the parallelism, e.g., in Rubner's model (which is in network structure identical to APEX), the GHA model, the subspace method, etc. This example helps the theoretical study of the amenability of the above models to parallel architecture implementation.

8.1.1 Design Example: The APEX Model

For the systolic array design of the APEX algorithm, we adopt the design methodology proposed in [124]. First assume that the network has n input units $x_1,...,x_n$ and m output units $y_1,...,y_m$.

Systolic Array for the Retrieving Phase   The mapping of the input to the output in APEX—the *retrieving phase*—is described by the equation (see Chapter 4)

$$y_i = \sum_{j=1}^{n} w_{ij}x_j - \sum_{j=1}^{i-1} c_{ij}y_j. \tag{8.1}$$

The first step of the design is the construction of the dependence graph (DG) for the retrieving phase, as in Figure 8.1a. The DG is a directed graph with nodes that

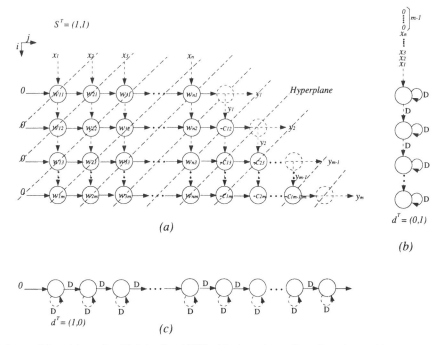

Figure 8.1. (a) Localized DG for the APEX retrieving phase. Functional operation at each node of the DG. (b) Type-I systolic design obtained by selecting $\vec{d} = (0, 1)$ and $\vec{s} = (1, 1)$. (c) Type-II systolic array obtained by selecting $\vec{d} = (1, 0)$ and $\vec{s} = (1, 1)$.

correspond to computations and arcs that correspond to the logical dependencies among the computations. For example, if an operation A needs data produced as the results of operation B there is a directed arc emanating from B and pointing to A. The matrix-vector multiplication algorithm used in the retrieving phase of APEX has a 2-D regular DG structure as shown in the figure. The 2-D array is indexed by the integers i and j, which roughly correspond to the dimension of the output (m) and input (n) respectively.

Each node in the DG corresponds to a multiply-accumulate operation (MAC): the east-going arc is the result of multiplying the data coming from north by the value stored in the node (e.g., the weight w_{ij}) and adding to the product the value coming from west; the south-going arc simply passes on the value coming from north. The dashed nodes on the right end correspond to dummy operations which simply pass the data on from left to right.

From DG to Systolic Array. The next step in the design is the projection of the DG onto an array of processing elements. For this we need to define a projection direction $\vec{d}$ and a linear schedule $\vec{s}$. The projection direction dictates which operations (DG nodes) are executed by each processor in the array. For example, the vector $\vec{d} = [i = 0, \ j = 1]$ dictates that each processor executes a row of the DG

(Fig. 8.1b), while the direction $\vec{d} = [1\ 0]$ associates each processor with a column of the DG (Fig. 8.1c).

The schedule vector $\vec{s}$ defines a family of *equitemporal hyperplanes*, namely those orthogonal to $\vec{s}$. All DG nodes on the same hyperplane are executed at the same time, each node executed on the processor selected by $\vec{d}$. Figure 8.1a shows the hyperplanes corresponding to the schedule $\vec{s} = [1\ 1]$.

A DG arc $\vec{e}$ connecting nodes A and B is mapped into an array arc $\vec{e}_1$ connecting the processors P_A, P_B, which will execute A, B, respectively, according to the projection $\vec{d}$. The arc $\vec{e}_1$ has an associated delay (D) which is the difference between the execution times of A and B, according to the schedule $\vec{s}$.

For the mapping to be implementable (i.e., computationally feasible) the *causality* and *positive pipeline period* conditions must be satisfied [124]. They require that

$$\vec{s}^T \vec{e} \geq 0 \qquad \text{and} \qquad \vec{s}^T \vec{d} > 0,$$

where $\vec{e}$ is any dependence arc in the DG.

As already discussed, through different projection directions we can derive two different linear arrays with size m (Type-I design) and size $n + m - 1$ (Type-II design), respectively (see Fig. 8.1). Next we'll focus on the Type-I systolic array, shown in Figure 8.1b.

PE Requirements for Type-I Design. The processor elements (PE) comprise the following components:

- *Memory:* The ith PE stores a row of synaptic weights $[w_{1i}, w_{2i}, \ldots, w_{ni}, -c_{1i}, \ldots, -c_{(i-1)i}]$.
- *Communication:* Data are transmitted in one direction between two neighboring PEs.
- *Arithmetic Processing:* It mainly supports the MAC operation.
- *Control Unit:* The local control unit consists of counters and multiplexer (MUX) for redirecting the data.

Data Movements in Type-I Design. Assume that the data $\{w_{ij}^{(k)}, -c_{ij}^{(k)}\}$ are prestored (row by row) in the PEs.

1. The data $x_j^{(k)}$ are input sequentially into the first PE in the original natural order. (As will be explained momentarily, the input port must impose $m - 1$ idle cycles before it can accept the next vector pattern.) They will be subsequently propagated downward (in the transmittent mode) to all other PEs.

2. When $x_j^{(k)}$ arrives at the ith PE (from the top), it is multiplied with the stored data $\{w_{ij}^{(k)}\}$. The result is added to the partial sum being accumulated in the same PE.

3. After $n + 2i - 2$ active clocks, $y_i^{(k)}$ is generated. It will then be propagated downward to the other (lower) PEs in the transmittent mode just like $x_j^{(k)}$.

The *pipeline period* (denoted by α) is the number of basic time unit periods between two successive inputs into any PE. The time unit T must be large enough for the processing of the slowest PE in the array to take place. For example, if all the PEs execute one MAC operation, then T must be greater or equal to the time it takes one PE to execute one MAC. If the pipeline rate of the array is α, then it takes αT time between two successive inputs into any PE. For a given projection $\vec{d}$ and schedule $\vec{s}$ it is known that the pipeline rate can be computed as

$$\alpha = \vec{d}^T \vec{s}.$$

The smallest value of α is obviously 1 since the next input should not be received before the processing of the current one has finished.

For either of the two projection choices (Type I or Type II in Fig. 8.1) the pipeline rate is minimal; i.e., $\alpha = 1$. This means that the data are consecutively processed without any cycle gap in the pipeline. The block pipeline period (denoted by α_{BP}) is defined as the time units separating the execution of two input vectors (a block of n inputs $x_1, \ldots, x_n$). The block pipelining period $\alpha_{BP} = n + m - 1$. Therefore, the input port must impose m idle cycles before it can accept the next vector pattern.

Systolic Array for Training Phase   The *training phase* is more computationally demanding than the retrieving phase. It can be partitioned in two subphases: (a) the *preupdating phase*, which computes the synaptic weight changes Δw_{ij} and Δc_{ij}, and (b) the *updating phase*, where the new weights are computed:

$$w_{ij}^{new} = w_{ij}^{old} + \beta \Delta w_{ij}$$

$$c_{ij}^{new} = c_{ij}^{old} + \beta \Delta c_{ij}. \tag{8.2}$$

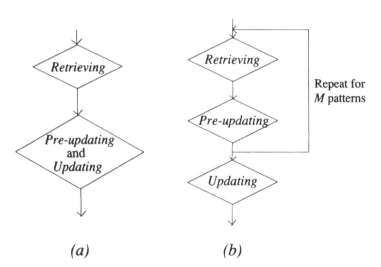

(a)   *(b)*

Figure 8.2. Computation flow diagram of the APEX algorithm for (a) ihe data adaptive (DA) training scheme and (b) the block adaptive (BA) training scheme.

As in all adaptive algorithms, in general, there are two training schemes: data adaptive (DA) and block adaptive (BA). In the DA scheme, the weights must be updated before the next input pattern is processed. So the preupdating equations (8.3) should be computed for each pattern k and be immediately followed by the updating phase (see Fig. 8.2a):

$$\Delta w_{ij} = (y_i^{(k)} x_j^{(k)} - y_i^{(k)2} w_{ij}^{(k)}), \qquad i, j = 1, \ldots, n,$$

$$\Delta c_{ij} = (y_i^{(k)} y_j^{(k)} - y_i^{(k)2} c_{ij}^{(k)}), \qquad i = 1, \ldots, n, \ j < i. \tag{8.3}$$

In contrast, in the BA scheme, the weight updating is deferred until the end of each training data block (see Fig. 8.2b). The preupdating equations become

$$\Delta w_{ij} = \sum_{k=1}^{M} \left(y_i^{(k)} x_j^{(k)} - y_i^{(k)2} w_{ij}^{(k)} \right), \qquad i, j = 1, \cdots, n,$$

$$\Delta c_{ij} = \sum_{k=1}^{M} \left(y_i^{(k)} y_j^{(k)} - y_i^{(k)2} c_{ij}^{(k)} \right), \qquad i = 1, \cdots, n, \ j < i. \tag{8.4}$$

Note that the BA scheme requires less computation that the DA scheme since the weight updating is done less frequently. Yet it is our contention that the speed of convergence is affected very little by the time lapse in the updating process.

We shall first consider the systolic array design for the BA training scheme. The design can be easily extended to the DA scheme.

As shown in Table 8.1, the preupdating equations can be rewritten in two different forms, whose choice could affect the implementation efficiency. The second representation in the table is more appealing, thanks to the less data storage needed.

In processing each of the input vectors in the BA scheme, the overall DG is one combining one DG for *retrieving mode* and another for *preupdate mode* (see Fig. 8.3). (The missing DG for *update mode* may be embedded in the DG for *preupdating mode*.) Structurewise, we have exactly the same DGs for the *retrieving mode* and the *preupdating mode*. They differ in the functionalities and controls within the computational nodes. More specifically, in the preupdating DG, the computation in each node has two MAC operations, instead of just one MAC operation in the retrieving DG. Also, the output values y_i are now transmittent in the j direction.

Table 8.1. Comparison of Different Representations of the Preupdating Equation

Representation	Op's per Row	Storage
$\Delta w_{ij}^{(k+1)} = \Delta w_{ij}^{(k)} + y_i^{(k)} x_j^{(k)} - y_i^{(k)2} w_{ij}^{(k)}$	$2n + 1$ MULs	$y_i^{(k)}$
$\Delta w_{ij}^{(0)} = 0$	n ADDs	$y_i^{(k)2}$
$\Delta w_{ij}^{(k+1)} = \Delta w_{ij}^{(k)} + y_i^{(k)}(x_j^{(k)} - y_i^{(k)} w_{ij}^{(k)})$	$2n$ MULs	$y_i^{(k)}$
$\Delta w_{ij}^{(0)} = 0$	n ADDs	

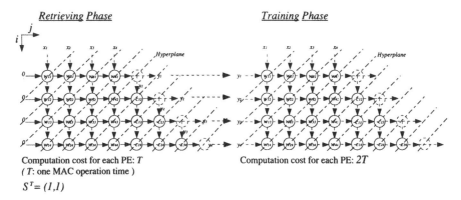

Figure 8.3. Combined DG for the retrieving and training phases ($n = m = 4$).

From DG to Systolic Array. Since the DGs for the retrieving and updating phases are topologically the same, the corresponding arrays for the same projection and scheduling vectors $\vec{d}$ and $\vec{s}$ will also be topologically identical. Specifically, for $\vec{d} = [0 \quad 1]$ we obtain the two arrays shown in Figure 8.4, while for $\vec{d} = [1 \quad 0]$ the two arrays are shown in Figure 8.5. The overall array topology will be called bilinear.

Although the training phase array has the same topology as the retrieving phase array, the processing elements in the two arrays differ. The training phase PEs need to perform a somewhat more complex operation than their retrieving phase counterparts. Next we shall discuss in detail the PE requirements for the training phase.

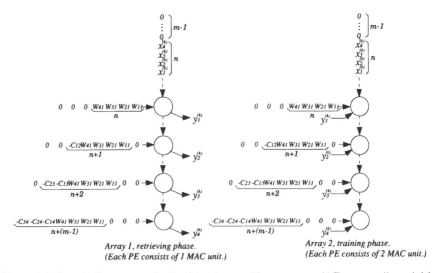

Figure 8.4. Type-I bilinear array for the BA scheme. (Here $n = m = 4$.) The synaptic weights are stored in memory shared by both linear arrays.

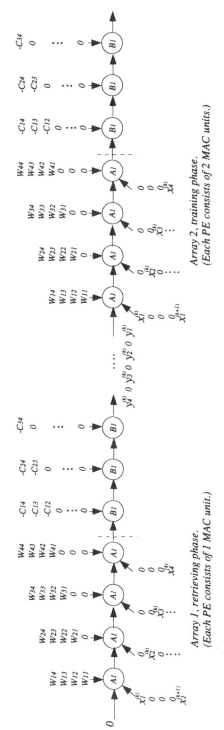

Figure 8.5. Type-II bilinear array for the BA scheme. (Here $n = m = 4$.) The synaptic weights are stored in memory shared by both linear arrays.

PE Design Requirements. The processor element comprises the following components:

- *Memory:* The weights $[w_{1i}, w_{2i}, \ldots, w_{ni}, -c_{1i}, \ldots, -c_{(i-1)i}]$ are again stored in the ith PE. (Note that the synaptic weights are actually stored in the memory space shared by both the retrieving and training arrays.) In addition, y_i from the retrieving phase, β^k, and partial sums Δw_{ij} and Δc_{ij} need to be stored in the training array.
- *Communication:* Data are transmitted in one direction (top-down) between two neighboring PEs.
- *Arithmetic Processing:* To fully support the arithmetic functional capabilities, each PE should contain two MAC units.
- *Control Unit:* The local control unit generates control signals for *preupdate* mode and *update* mode (cf. Fig. 8.2).

Data Movements in (Type-I) Linear Systolic Design. The data movement for preupdate mode is very similar to that in the retrieving phase. The data $\{w_{ij}^{(k)}, -c_{ij}^{(k)}\}$ (row by row), $\{y_i^{(k)}\}$, and the stepsize $\beta^{(k)}$ are stored in the PEs. In addition, the initial partial sums Δw_{ij} and Δc_{ij} will be set to be zero.

1. The data $x_j^{(k)}$ are input sequentially into the first PE in the original natural order. (They will be subsequently propagated downward to all other PEs.)

2. When the data $x_j^{(k)}$ (resp. $y_j^{(k)}$) arrives (from the top) at the ith PE, the first MAC unit computes the product of $y_i^{(k)}$ and $\{w_{ij}^{(k)}\}$ (resp. $\{-c_{ij}^{(k)}\}$) and then subtracts the product from $\{x_j^{(k)}\}$ (resp. $\{y_j^{(k)}\}$). The result is passed to the second MAC unit in the same PE. In the next cycle, the second MAC will multiply the result from the first MAC unit with $y_i^{(k)}$ and this product will be added to the partial sum Δw_{ij} (resp. Δc_{ij}).

3. For the ith PE, after $n + 2i - 1$ active clocks, the computation of the weight adjustment for one input pattern is completed in each PE.

It will take a total of $n + 2m - 1$ time units to complete the computation involving one input pattern.

Actual Updating Step

BA scheme. After one sweep of input patterns (M patterns if M is the block size), the ith PE starts the real updating phase and multiplies β^k by Δw_{ij} (or Δc_{ij}). The product is then added to the original weights $w_{ij}^{(k)}$ (or $-c_{ij}^{(k)}$) in the real-update mode.

DA scheme. The above design proposed for the BA scheme can be extended to the DA mode. In DA scheme, w's and c's are updated after sending each input pattern. Notice that for DA scheme, three MAC cycles will be needed for updating.

8.1.2 Performance Comparison of Bilinear Arrays

For simplicity in our execution time estimate we shall only count the arithmetic processing time and deliberately ignore the time spent on memory access and communication. (In practice, they should count as a significant fraction of processing time.) We also ignore the time spent for the computation of β. Thus, each time unit period T is the time needed to execute one MAC operation.

Referring to Figure 8.4, we note that if only one MAC hardware unit is adopted for the second array, the preupdate training mode would require $\alpha = 2$. This means we need two units of time ($2T$) to perform two MACs by a single MAC hardware unit. Recall that the optimal pipeline period for the first array (for retrieving mode) is $\alpha = 1$. The imbalance between the two processing speeds would incur approximately 50% idle time on the retrieving array. Obviously, this problem may be solved by using two MAC hardware units in each PE of the training array. With two MACs arranged in two pipeline stages, the pipeline period for the second array becomes $\alpha = 1$. Thus, the pipeline speeds of the two arrays are now in perfect synchronization and the processing power may be optimized. This will be explained shortly.

The architectural choice hinges upon several key performance measures, including cost effectiveness of the number of processors, utilization rate, and speedup factor, defined as follows:

$$\text{Utilization rate} = \frac{\text{speed-up factor}}{\text{number of processors}},$$

$$\text{Speedup factor} = \frac{\text{sequential time}}{\text{array time}}.$$

(The array time is equal to the block pipeline period α_{BP}.)

According to the DG displayed in Figure 8.3, the total sequential time for processing each training pattern in the BA scheme is

$$\frac{1}{2}\left(2nm + 2\sum_{i=1}^{m-1} i\right) = m\left(n + \frac{m-1}{2}\right).$$

Bilinear Array (with 1&2 MACs per PE). In this bilinear array, we use one MAC hardware unit for the retrieving linear array and two MAC hardware units per PE for the training linear array. This yields an array time $\alpha_{BP} = n + m - 1$, and we have

$$\text{Speedup factor} = \frac{3(mn + (m-1)/2)}{n + m - 1}, \tag{8.5}$$

$$\text{Utilization rate} = \frac{3m(n + (m-1)/2)}{3m(n + m - 1)}. \tag{8.6}$$

Bilinear Array (with 1&1 MAC per PE). If we use only one MAC hardware unit per PE for the training array, then the array time becomes $\alpha_{BP} = 2(n + m - 1)$, and we have

$$\text{Speedup factor} = \frac{3m(n + (m - 1)/2)}{2(n + m - 1)}, \tag{8.7}$$

$$\text{Utilization rate} = \frac{3m(n + (m - 1)/2)}{2 \times 2m(n + m - 1)}. \tag{8.8}$$

The 1&1 bilinear array delivers only 75% of that of the 1&2 bilinear array in terms of utilization rate. In terms of speedup factor, it has only 50%. Clearly, the 1&2 bilinear array is a preferred design, since it is favored by both criteria.

Bilinear Array for DA Scheme. For the DA scheme, in contrast to the BA scheme, w's and c's need to be updated for each input pattern and an extra (i.e., the third) MAC cycle is needed for the actual updating step (cf. Fig. 8.2). Therefore 3 MAC cycles will be needed for preupdating/updating step in the DA scheme. In designing the bilinear array for the DA scheme, we will again use one MAC hardware unit for the retrieving linear array. However, we will need a total of three MAC hardware units for the training linear array in order to synchronize the speed of the retrieving array. For the 1&3 bilinear array, we have

$$\text{Speedup factor} = \frac{4m(n + (m - 1)/2)}{n + m - 1}, \tag{8.9}$$

$$\text{Utilization rate} = \frac{4m(n + (m - 1)/2)}{4m(n + m - 1)}. \tag{8.10}$$

8.1.3 Other Systolic Design Alternatives

Type-II Bilinear Design   Figure 8.5 depicts a different bilinear systolic design, which consists of $(n + m - 1)$ PEs in each linear array. Note that the PEs are not purely homogeneous (in terms of their control functions). In Figure 8.5, they are distinguished by two different labels: *type A nodes* for the first n PEs and *type B nodes* for the remaining $m - 1$ PEs. The data movements for the Type-II design are very similar to Type I, so the detailed description can be omitted here.

Two-Dimensional Systolic Array for Block Processing   Very often, a block of input patterns (instead of a single pattern) is presented in a continuous manner. The corresponding DG for such principal-component extraction may be visualized as if the same 2-D DG (for single pattern) was being repeated by M folds, where M is the block size. This results in a 3-D DG, with the third dimension of size M. Projecting the 3-D DG back into the ij-plane will result in a 2-D array structure resembling the 2-D DG in Figure 8.1a.

Both the *memory* and *communication* requirements for each PE need some modification. It will need less storage: one weight, either w_{ij} or $-c_{ij}$, needs to be stored in each PE. It will demand more *communication links*: each PE will require four (one-way) channels to communicate with its four neighbors. As to the *data movement*, the data $x_j^{(k)}$ are input from the top of the array in the time-skewed order.

They are will propagate downward to the other PEs along the same column. The partial sums for $y_i^{(k)}$ and the final $y_i^{(k)}$ need to propagate from left to right to the other PEs along the same row.

During the start-up phase the utilization rate is inevitably low, because it takes time to fill up the 2-D array. After this initial period, the processor utilization reaches nearly 100%. With a much larger number of PEs, the 2-D array offers a much higher speedup. In fact, the array achieves the (optimal) block-pipelining period $\alpha_{BP} = 1$; i.e., it can receive one vector input pattern per cycle time.

Table 8.2 shows the comparison of different arrays in terms of array size, latency, block-pipelining period, and utilization rate. Both Type-I and Type-II designs give same latency and processor utilization. Type-I design, however, has an advantage over the other designs in the sense that the array size is independent of n, which is usually larger and has a greater variation for different applications. For real-time processing, the block pipelining period is the most critical criterion. In this regard, the 2-D array offers a (optimal) block-pipelining period $\alpha_{BP} = 1$.

8.1.4 Scalability

If m is fixed and only n is varying, then the Type-I array is still suitable, while the Type-II design needs to be modified. On the other hand, if n is fixed and m will be varying, then the Type-I array will need modification. As an example, for image compression, the subimage blocks are often of a fixed size (say 8×8). Then n can be fixed to $n = 64$, but the number of PCs (m) may vary depending on the application needs. In this case, the Type-II array is more appealing since the variation on m only changes processing time and the fundamental architecture remains intact.

Very often there are situations when both the input dimension n and the output dimension m may increase beyond the physical array sizes. For this, two approaches may be considered:

1. Enlargement of the Physical Array Size: Fortunately, the PEs in a systolic array are quite homogeneous; therefore, scaling the array up in proportion to the new input/output dimension is quite straightforward. For example, if we want to extract more principal components, and, say, m is increased from 4 to 8, the design is easily

Table 8.2. Cost and Performance Analysis of Different Designs[a]

Size	Latency	α_{BP}	Utilization
1-D, m	$n + 2m + 1$	$n + m - 1$	$\dfrac{n + (m - 1)/2}{n + m - 1}$
1-D, $n + m - 1$	$n + 2m + 1$	m	$\dfrac{n + (m - 1)/2}{n + m - 1}$
2-D, $m(n + (m - 1)/2)$	$n + 2m + 1$	1	$\approx 100\%$

[a]According to the table, when n increases, so does the utilization rate.

expandable by concatenating two size-4 Type-I arrays. The only modification will be an expansion of the memory size due to increased number of lateral weights.

2. *Enlargement of the Virtual Array Size*: Another approach is to keep the physical array size the same but enhance the hardware/software/memory to support the processing of a larger problem size (at the expense of processing time, of course). This effectively enlarges the *virtual array size*. This is an important design issue because very often the physical array sizes cannot keep up with the growth of the application problems. Especially, the input dimension n could easily overwhelm the given physical array size.

One prominent approach for enlarging virtual array size is to adopt an algorithm *partitioning* scheme. Let us rewrite the formulas for the retrieving and training phases of the APEX algorithm in matrix form and transform the algorithm partitioning problem into a matrix partitioning problem. Since the DG topology for the training phase is identical to that of the retrieving phase, the training phase partitioning problem should be treated similarly and it will not be separately analyzed. Thus, for the retrieving phase we have

$$Wx - Cy = y, \qquad (8.11)$$

where W is the $m \times n$ feedforward weights matrix and C is a lower triangular matrix (with 0 diagonal) consisting of the lateral weights. $x = [x_1, \ldots, x_n]^T$ is the input pattern and $y = [y_1, \ldots, y_m]^T$ is the output vector.

Locally Parallel Globally Sequential Partitioning for Type-I Arrays   When m is fixed and n has a large variation, then Type-I array design is very appealing. However, if m increases beyond the size of the original array, then the Type-I design needs to be modified. Let us first consider partitioning along the m direction. We divide the original matrix into submatrices; therefore (8.11) can be written as

$$\left[\frac{W_{\{1\}}}{W_{\{2\}}}\right] [x] - \left[\frac{C_{\{1\}}}{C_{\{2\}}}\right] [y] = \left[\frac{y_{\{1\}}}{y_{\{2\}}}\right]. \qquad (8.12)$$

Note that the computation is now divided into two parts. Both W and C are partitioned into upper half and lower half, and each part of the computation will be mapped to the same processors while being executed in different times. The complete DG shown in Figure 8.6a is modified to show the scheduling if the tasks are partitioned in the vertical direction (cf. (8.12)). When $n = 4$ and $m = 4$, the mapping to $m/2$ PEs and the data movements are shown in Figure 8.6b. Note that the vector $y_{\{1\}}$ must be stored in order to be propagated downward later to other PEs, just like the unpartitioned array. The block-pipelining period now becomes $2n + \frac{3}{2}m - 2$.

Locally Sequential Globally Parallel Partitioning for Type-II Array   In practice, we often encounter the situation where $n \gg m$. If m is fixed, then the

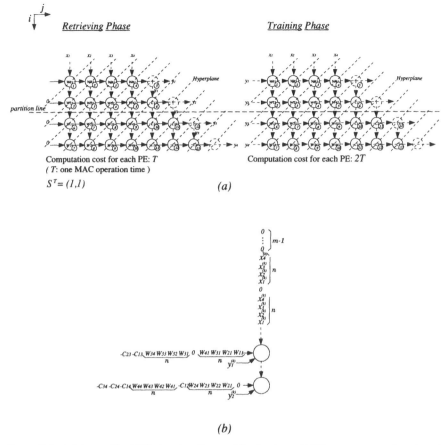

Figure 8.6. (a) A modified DG showing the partitioning in m. (b) The corresponding signal flow graph and data movements.

Type-I array is still suitable. However, the parallel processing power with $O(m)$ PEs will be somewhat limited, especially when n is extremely large. This makes the scalability of Type-II design very critical since n can easily grow beyond any fixed range in many applications. Just as discussed previously, the same LPGS partitioning may be applied to the Type-II design to enlarge the virtual array size. Here we will explore a different LSGP design procedure.

Assume that we are now facing $n' = \kappa n$ but m remains unchanged, where κ is an integer scaling factor. For simplicity, let us assume $\kappa = 2$; i.e., $n' = 8$, doubling the original size $n = 4$. Given a systolic array in Figure 8.5 originally designed for the case $n = 4$ and $m = 4$, we would like the original four-processor Type-II array be modified to support an eight-processor virtual array. Using a special labeling, the eight-dimensional row vector of input data can be expressed as

$$x = [x_{1\alpha}\ x_{1\beta}\quad x_{2\alpha}\ x_{2\beta}\quad x_{3\alpha}\ x_{3\beta}\quad x_{4\alpha}\ x_{4\beta}].$$

Furthermore, let us denote

$$x_{\{i\}} \equiv [x_{i\alpha} \ x_{i\beta}], \qquad i = 1, \ldots, n.$$

Then, the eight-dimensional data vector can be equivalently expressed as

$$x = [x_{\{1\}} \quad x_{\{2\}} \quad x_{\{3\}} \quad x_{\{4\}}].$$

Applying a similar notation to the eight-dimensional weight vector, we have

$$w = [w_{\{1\}} \quad w_{\{2\}} \quad w_{\{3\}} \quad w_{\{4\}}].$$

Note that the product

$$\langle w_{\{i\}} \ x_{\{i\}} \rangle = x_{i\alpha} w_{i\alpha} + x_{i\beta} w_{i\beta} \tag{8.13}$$

will be implemented as an *inner product* instead of an ordinary product. This leads to a notion of a vectorized MAC. This new notion allows us to regard the problem with $n' = 8$ just like the case with $n = 4$. We can use the original DG in Figure 8.1a to treat the scaled-up problem, except now the internal MAC functions in the DG nodes are replaced by a vectorized MAC described in (8.13). Consequently, the same systolic structure in Figure 8.5 will remain intact after the same projection, except now that vectorized MAC hardware units must be adopted in the PE. In order for a vectorized MAC hardware unit to perform an inner product operation, we need to enhance an ordinary MAC with a special counter. The counter can ensure that exactly κ products will be counted and accumulated for the vectorized MAC. (The basic cycle time will also be lengthened to κT.) Another hardware component change is that the memory space need to be increased proportionally to κ.

8.2 ANALOG IMPLEMENTATION

In the analog approach the major processing element is the MOS transistor, and the major building block is the operational amplifier (op amp). The signals processed in an analog implementation have continuous amplitude in contrast to the discrete (binary) quality of the signals processed in the digital approach. The output voltage of an operational amplifier is proportional to the input voltage difference (see Fig. 8.7a):

$$V_{\text{out}} = A(V_1 - V_2).$$

The value A is called the *voltage gain* of the amplifier. Ideally the amplifier has the following properties:

- Infinite input resistance, $R_{\text{in}} = \infty$, thus 0 input current.
- Zero output resistance, $R_{\text{out}} = 0$.

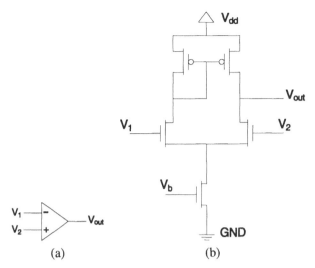

Figure 8.7. (a) Symbolic diagram of an operational amplifier. (b) A simple MOS implementation of an op amp.

- Infinite voltage gain, $A = \infty$.
- Infinite bandwidth.
- $V_{out} = 0$ if $V_1 = V_2$.
- Operational characteristics independent of temperature.

Of course, in practice these ideal characteristics are never met. However, the gain A can be several hundred and the operating voltage range can be quite large. The circuit implementation of a simple op amp is shown in Figure 8.7b.

The major advantage of the op amp is the fact that its input is seen from the rest of the circuit as an open circuit. Since the op amp draws no current it does not affect the operation of the circuit that is connected to its input.

Various important functions, static or dynamic, can be implemented with the help of the op amp. Sampling the most important of them, with respect to PCA neural models, we mention the input follower (Fig. 8.8a), the inverter (Fig. 8.8b), the voltage adder (Fig. 8.8c), and the multiplier-integrator (Fig. 8.8d) functions. The multiplication function, not shown here, can also be implemented in the analog paradigm with the use of special circuits [125].

The follower circuit (Fig. 8.8a) implements the identity function:

$$V_{out} = A(V_{in} - V_{out}),$$
$$V_{out} = (1 + 1/A)^{-1}V_{in}.$$

Under the ideal assumption $A = \infty$ we have $V_{out} = V_{in}$. In most practical situations the 1% error (or so) due to the imperfect A is tolerable. The op amp implementation of the identity function has the following very desirable property: the output and

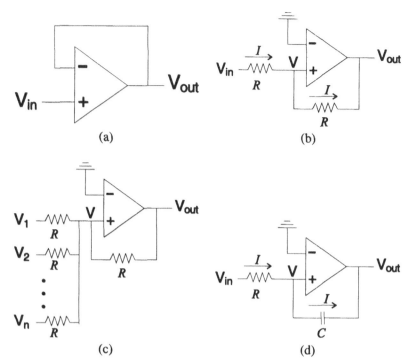

(a)   (b)

(c)   (d)

Figure 8.8. (a) The follower circuit copies the input voltage to the output. The difference between this implementation of the identity function and a simple short between input and output is that the op amp insulates the input from the output. In other words, any load hung on the output of the amplifier does not affect the operation of the circuit that produces the input voltage. (b) The inverter produces the inverse of the input voltage at the output. (c) An analog voltage adder. (d) A simple multiplier-integrator. The output voltage approximates the integral of the input multiplied with the constant $1/RC$.

the input are insulated from each other. This means that any load hooked on the output does not affect the circuit connected to the input of the op amp. Thus, we can safely copy a voltage signal from one point of the circuit to another without worrying about unwanted interactions between the two points.

The inverter circuit (Fig. 8.8b) is a special case of the n-input adder in Fig. 8.8c. We'll analyze the general case (the adder circuit) and derive the inverter function. Using Kirchhoff's current law in the adder circuit we obtain

$$I = I_1 + I_2 + \cdots + I_n,$$

$$\frac{V - V_{\text{out}}}{R} = \sum_i \frac{V_i - V}{R},$$

$$V_{\text{out}} - (n + 1)V = -\sum_i V_i.$$

Since $V_{out} = AV$ we have

$$V_{out} = -\frac{1}{1 - (n+1)/A} \sum_i V_i.$$

Thus, for A very large the output is the sum (with a minus sign) of the input voltages: $V_{out} \approx -\sum_i V_i$. The inverter is a special case for $n = 1$, yielding $V_{out} \approx -V_{in}$. Clearly if we attach an inverter following the adder in Figure 8.8c we obtain a true adder of n voltages without the minus sign.

Finally let us take a look at a dynamic circuit: the multiplier-integrator in Figure 8.8, in which the output approximates the time integral of the input. From Kirchhoff's current law again and from the amplification rule $V_{out} = AV$ we obtain

$$\frac{V_{in} - V}{R} = C\frac{d}{dt}(V - V_{out}),$$

$$\frac{V_{out}}{A} - V_{in} = RC\left(1 - \frac{1}{A}\right)\frac{d}{dt}V_{out}.$$

The solution of this differential equation is

$$V_{out}(t) = -\frac{1}{\tau}\int_{-\infty}^{t} V_{in}(t')e^{(t'-t)/A}\,dt',$$

where

$$\tau = RC(1 - 1/A).$$

As A is a large number we can write

$$V_{out} \approx -\frac{1}{RC}\int_{-\infty}^{t} V(t')\,dt'.$$

For an excellent treatment of analog circuits, especially in relation to the implementation of various neural algorithms, the reader may refer to the work by C. Mead [125]. Mead also describes in detail the design of analog multipliers which are essential in all neural network algorithms.

Equipped with all the above functional blocks the design of analog circuits for the execution of neural PCA algorithms is now possible. The analog implementation of PCA algorithms is appealing for applications where the data arrive in continuous fashion.

The advantages of analog implementation are

- Extremely high speed.
- Low power consumption.

- Certain critical operations such as multiplication or integration require much less silicon area or execution time in the analog paradigm than in the digital implementation.

The disadvantages of analog implementation are

- Low precision; in most cases only 8 to 10 bits of accuracy can be attained.
- Susceptibility to noise and temperature variations.
- Lack of programmability and expandability.

Still, for specific applications with fixed parameters a dedicated analog implementation becomes very attractive. Consider, for example, any neural PCA algorithm among the ones described in Chapter 4 and assume that the input dimension n and the desired number of components m are fixed. Since n and m are not programmable the number of components required in an analog implementation (the number of integrators, adders, multipliers, etc.) is well defined.

Observe that all the neural PCA methods employ simple mathematical operations; in fact, they use only the operations of addition, subtraction, and multiplication. Therefore they can be easily implemented with the basic analog building blocks discussed above. Furthermore, assuming that a good analog design can minimize the effects of noise and of the parameter fluctuation due to temperature, the only real question about the attractiveness of the analog approach is the consequences of low precision.

Such questions were studied by Cichocki and Unbehauen [67, 115], who presented various analog models for eigenvalue decomposition and principal component analysis. These models were analog implementations of gradient descent algorithms based on appropriate energy functions.

For example, consider the case where the observed vector $x(t)$ is a continuous-time stochastic process. The continuous-time Karhunen-Loève theorem applies here, and the subject of the eigenvalue decomposition is the correlation matrix $R_x = E\{x(t)x(t)\}$. Oja's algorithm in the continuous case becomes a differential equation

$$\frac{dw}{dt} = \mu\left(x(t)y(t) - y(t)^2 w(t)\right), \qquad (8.14)$$

where

$$y(t) = w(t)^T x(t) = \sum_{i=1}^{n} w_i(t)x_i(t). \qquad (8.15)$$

Figure 8.9 shows an analog implementation of the continuous PCA model (8.14). The value $y(t)$ is the output of the linear neuron with weights $w_i(t)$. The APEX model can be also implemented using a simple extension of the hardware for Oja's model (see Fig. 8.10).

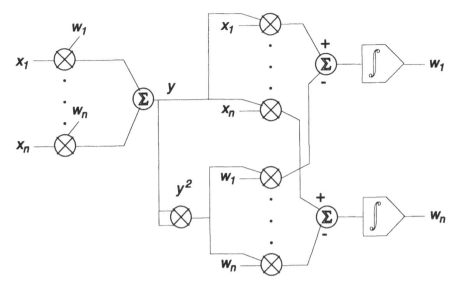

Figure 8.9. The analog implementation of the continuous Oja algorithm.

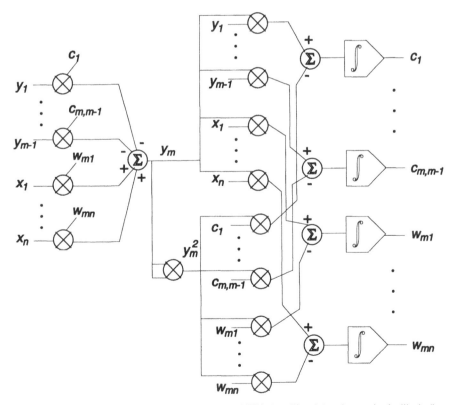

Figure 8.10. The mth neuron in the continuous APEX algorithm is implemented with similar analog hardware as Oja's model.

8.3   CONCLUDING REMARKS

Most neural processing algorithms are computationally iterative and intensive, and they demand very high throughput. From an architectural perspective, the main concern is to systematically derive parallel processing architectures that optimize performance. In particular, PCA-type neural algorithms can be expressed as basic matrix operations (such as inner product, outer product, and matrix multiplications). These operations, in turn, can be mapped to basic processor arrays. Detailed procedures mapping some prominent PCA networks to array architectures are described in this chapter. While the final performance analyses have to depend on a balanced design of *computation, memory,* and *communication* modules, such array architectures can very well harness the pipelined/parallel processing potential offered by VLSI/ULSI technologies.

Dedicated neural implementation is aimed at high-performance for special applications. The implementation efficiency depends very much on the application domain. It is also heavily influenced by the technological choices between analog and digital VLSI implementation. Both analog and digital techniques have demonstrated convincing success in their own application domains. The selection between digital and analog circuits depends on many factors (speed, precision, adaptiveness, programmability, and transfer/storage of signals, e.g.).

8.3.1   Pros and Cons of Analog Circuits

Features of analog designs are fast speed, low precision, and small-scale systems. Although analog designs are always continuous-valued, they can be implemented in continuous-time circuits (e.g., *RC* circuits) or in discrete-time circuits (e.g., analog switch-capacitor circuits and CCD). In dedicated analog devices, a neuron is basically a differential amplifier with synaptic weights implemented by resistors. Thus, many neurons can fit on a single chip. Analog circuits can process more than 1 bit per transistor with a very high speed. The asynchronous updating property of analog devices offers qualitatively different computations from those offered by digital devices [126]. For real-time early vision processing, dedicated analog processing chips offer arguably the most appealing alternative. For example, analog circuits offer inherent advantages on (1) the computation of the sum of weighted inputs by currents or charge packets, and (2) the nonlinear effects of the devices facilitating realization of sigmoid-type functions. Because of the vital integration between analog sensors and information preprocessing/postprocessing, analog circuits will continue to have a major impact on dedicated neuron processing designs.

Although analog circuits are more attractive for biological-type neural networks, their suitability for connectionist-type networks remains questionable. For example, compared with digital circuits, analog circuits are more susceptible to noise, crosstalk, temperature effects, and power supply variations. Although nonvolatile storage of analog weights provides high synaptic density, they are not easily programmable. In fact, the higher the precision, the more chip area is required. Thus, analog precision is usually limited to no more than 8 bits. In resistor-capacitor circuitry, low current consumption calls for high-resistance resistors. In switch-capacitor and resistor-capacitor circuitry, the low-noise constraint limits the minimal transistor surfaces and capacitors. In short, the combined factors of precision, noise, and current consumption lead to a larger chip area.

8.3.2 Pros and Cons of Digital Circuits

For connectionist networks, digital technology offers very desirable features such as design flexibility, learning, expandable size, and accuracy. Digital designs have an overall advantage in terms of system-level performance. Dynamic range and precision are critical for many complex connectionist models. Digital implementation offers much greater flexibility of precision than its analog counterpart. Design of digital VLSI circuits is supported by mature and powerful CAD technology, as well as convenient building-block modular design. Digital circuits also have an advantage in access to commercial design software and fast-turnaround silicon fabrication. The disadvantages of digital circuits are, for example, bulky chip areas and (sometimes) relatively slow speeds.

The design issues confronting digital neural implementation include the relatively larger silicon area, slower speed, and greater interconnection hardware cost. These difficulties, however, are not insurmountable. This chapter has proposed several plausible approaches to getting around them. Digital technique neural networks, when fully developed, can offer many unique and appealing advantages.

In conclusion, this book systematically explores the relationship between PCA and neural networks and studies fundamental issues pertaining to both subjects. In doing so, it covers both structural (neural network) and mathematical (PCA) treatments. The ultimate objective is to provide a synergistic exploration on the *algorithmic*, *applicational*, and *architectural* aspects of principal component neural networks.

APPENDIX A

STOCHASTIC APPROXIMATION

Consider the general formulation of a stochastic recursive algorithm

$$\theta_{k+1} = \theta_k + \beta_k f(x_k, \theta_k), \qquad k = 0, 1, 2, \ldots \qquad (A.1)$$

where $\{x_k \in \mathbb{R}^n\}$ is a sequence of random vectors, $\{\beta_k\}$ is a sequence of step-size parameters, f is a continuous and bounded function characteristic of the algorithm, and $\{\theta_k \in \mathbb{R}^m\}$ is a sequence of approximations of some desired parameter vector θ^*. Most of the neural network techniques that we dealt with in this monograph can be described by an equation in the form of (A.1). In most cases θ^* is an eigenvector of some correlation or covariance matrix or a collection of eigenvectors forming a matrix (remember that matrices form vector spaces, so they are vectors in the formal sense).

Clearly θ_k is a random vector since its value depends on the partial random sequence $x_0, \ldots, x_{k-1}$. Therefore, any statements regarding θ_k may be true only with some probability $p \in [0, 1]$ ("w.p.p" usually stands for "with probability p"). If the algorithm is well designed it is hoped that the larger the index k the larger the probability p with which statements about θ_k can be made. Ultimately it is hoped that asymptotically $\theta_k \to \theta^*$ as $k \to \infty$ w.p.1.

The study of algorithms of the form (A.1) is the topic of stochastic approximation theory. Early publications in this area include the classical papers by Robbins and Monro (1951) [127] and by Kiefer and Wolfowitz (1952) [128]. In the last two decades Ljung (1977) [39], Kushner and Clark (1978) [40], and Ljung and Söderström (1983) [55] made significant progress in understanding the dynamical behavior of such systems. In particular, these authors showed that, under certain conditions, the sequence $\{\theta_k\}$ of (A.1) converges w.p.1 to the solution of an associated deterministic ODE. Therefore, the asymptotic study of (A.1) is reduced to the study of the dynamics of the associated ODE.

229

We describe Kushner's approach, which is, we believe, conceptually the simplest one.

The following assumptions are used:

P-1. The step-size sequence satisfies

$$\beta_k \to 0 \quad \text{and} \quad \sum_{k=0}^{\infty} \beta_k = \infty. \tag{A.2}$$

P-2. $f(\cdot, \cdot)$ is a bounded and measurable $\mathbb{R}^m$-valued function.

P-3. For any fixed x, the function $f(\cdot, x)$ is continuous and bounded (uniformly in x).

P-4. There is a function

$$\overline{f}(\theta) = \lim_{k \to \infty} \frac{\sum_{i=k}^{\infty} \beta_i f(\theta, x_i)}{\sum_{i=k}^{\infty} \beta_i} = \lim_{k \to \infty} E\{f(\theta, x_k)\} \tag{A.3}$$

for all fixed θ. Notice that $\{x_k\}$ is not necessarily a stationary sequence. All that it is required is that it be "stationary in the limit," namely as $k \to \infty$, so taking the expectation results in a function independent of k.

We define the time indices t_k by the formula

$$t_k = \sum_{i=0}^{k} \beta_i, \tag{A.4}$$

and we define the linear interpolation process

$$\theta^0(t) = \frac{1}{\beta_{k+1}} \left[(t_{k+1} - t)\theta_{k+1} + (t - t_k)\theta_k \right], \quad \text{for } t_k \le t \le t_{k+1} \tag{A.5}$$

(see Fig. A.1).

The key role in this method is played by the left-shifted interpolation processes

$$\theta^k(t) = \theta^0(t_k + t), \quad k = 1, 2, \ldots \tag{A.6}$$

Theorem A.1 (Kushner and Clark). Assume P-1 through P-4 and let $\{\theta_k\}$ be bounded w.p.1. The sequence $\{\theta^k(\cdot)\}$ has a convergent subsequence whose limit $\theta(\cdot)$ satisfies the ODE

$$\frac{d\theta}{dt} = \overline{f}(\theta). \tag{A.7}$$

If Θ^* is an asymptotically stable set for (A.7) with domain of attraction $\mathcal{D}(\Theta^*)$, and θ_k enters a compact set $A \subset \mathcal{D}(\Theta^*)$ infinitely often w.p.1, then

$$\theta_k \to \Theta^* \quad \text{as } k \to \infty.$$

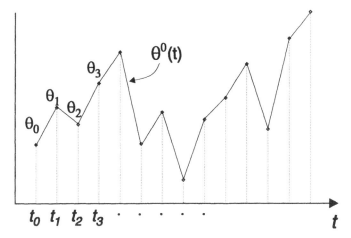

Figure A.1. The time index t is associated with the cumulative sum of β_i. We define the continuous-time process $\theta^0(t)$ via a linear interpolation through the points $t_0, t_1, \ldots$.

A sketch of the proof is outlined below. The cornerstone of the proof is the Arzelà-Ascoli theorem, which helps to show that the sequence $\theta^k(\cdot)$ (or rather a subsequence of it) converges uniformly to a limit $\theta(\cdot)$. This theorem makes use of the concepts of uniform boundedness and equicontinuity.

Definition A.1. A family Φ of continuous functions $\phi_\alpha(\cdot)$ defined on a closed interval $[0, T]$ is said to be **uniformly bounded** if there is a number $M > 0$ such that $|\phi_\alpha(x)| \leq M$ for all $x \in [0, T]$ and all $\phi_\alpha \in \Phi$.

Definition A.2. A family Φ of continuous functions $\phi_\alpha(\cdot)$ defined on a closed interval $[0, T]$ is said to be **equicontinuous** if for any $\varepsilon > 0$ there exists a $\delta > 0$ such that $|x_1 - x_2| < \delta$ implies $|\phi_\alpha(x_1) - \phi_\alpha(x_2)| < \varepsilon$, for all $x_1, x_2 \in [0, T]$ and all $\phi_\alpha \in \Phi$.

Theorem A.2 (Arzelà) [129]. A family Φ of continuous functions $\phi_\alpha(\cdot)$ defined on a closed interval $[0, T]$ is relatively compact if and only if Φ is uniformly bounded and equicontinous.

The important result of relative compactness is that for each infinite sequence $\{k_i\}$ we can find a subsequence $\{k_i'\}$ such that $\phi_{k_i'}(\cdot)$ converges uniformly on bounded intervals. The strategy is then to show that the sequence $\{\theta^k(\cdot)\}$ is bounded and equicontinuous. Then appealing to Arzelà's theorem there is a convergent subsequence $\theta^{k_i'}(\cdot) \rightarrow \theta(\cdot)$ as $i \rightarrow \infty$.

From (A.1) and (A.6) we obtain

$$\theta^k(t) = \theta^k(0) + \int_0^t f\big(\bar\theta(t_k + s), \bar x(t_k + s)\big)\, ds, \tag{A.8}$$

where $\bar{\theta}(\cdot)$ and $\bar{x}(\cdot)$ are the piecewise constant interpolations of θ_k and x_k respectively:

$$\bar{\theta}(t) = \theta_k, \qquad \text{for } t_k \le t \le t_{k+1},$$

$$\bar{x}(t) = x_k, \qquad \text{for } t_k \le t \le t_{k+1}.$$

Uniform boundedness and equicontinuity follows from (A.8), and thus the limit $\theta(\cdot)$ mentioned before does exist. Then (A.8) can be rewritten as

$$\theta^k(t) = \theta^k(0) + f_1^k(t) + \int_0^t f\left(\theta(s), \bar{x}(t_k + s)\right) ds,$$

$$f_1^k(t) = \int_0^t \left[f\left(\bar{\theta}(t_k + s), \bar{x}(t_k + s)\right) - f\left(\theta(s), \bar{x}(t_k + s)\right) \right] ds,$$

and it can be shown that $f_1^k(\cdot) \to 0$ on finite intervals as $k \to \infty$. So in the limit

$$\theta(t) = \theta(0) + \lim_k \int_0^t f\left(\theta(s), \bar{x}(t_k, s)\right) ds.$$

Now, Assumption P-4 implies

$$\int_0^t \left[f\left(\theta, \bar{x}(t_k + s)\right) - \bar{f}(\theta) \right] ds \to 0,$$

so

$$\theta(t) = \theta(0) + \int_0^t \bar{f}\left(\theta(s)\right) ds.$$

As far as the stability assertion is concerned, if $\theta_k \in A$ infinitely often then we can extract a convergent subsequence $\theta_i^k(\cdot) \to \hat{\theta}(\cdot)$. Since the set Θ^* is asymptotically stable, $\hat{\theta}(t) \to \Theta^*$ as $t \to \infty$. It is then rather tedious but not difficult to show that $\theta_k \to \Theta^*$ as well.

Although Theorem A.1 assumes that $\beta_k \to 0$ as $k \to \infty$, in many cases and for practical purposes this is not true. In fact, the well-known trade-off between tracking capability and convergence [55] is present in any adaptive algorithm. One wants to keep the step size small but nonzero in order to be able to follow (track) slow changes in the statistics of the input signal. After all, this is the meaning of the word "adaptive": one "throws" such a system into an unfriendly or unpredictable environment, expecting that the system will follow any changes on its own.

It is known [130, 131] that even if β_k does not go to zero but remains equal to a small constant then the mean value $\langle \theta \rangle$ of θ_k still approximates the ODE (A.7); therefore, in that sense, the algorithm still converges to the solution. However, now in the steady state, the adapted parameters oscillate around the fixed point without ever actually converging to it. This phenomenon is due to the variance of the stochastic input that drives the system. Naturally the amplitude of the oscillation is proportional to this variance as well as to the size of β. However, in many practical applications, a small uncertainty in the final value is tolerable, traded-off for the valuable property of the algorithm to be able to track the changing parameters of the input process and adapt its internal parameters to these changes.

APPENDIX B

DERIVATIVES WITH VECTORS AND MATRICES

The derivative of a matrix

$$A(t) = \begin{bmatrix} a_{11}(t) & \cdots & a_{1n}(t) \\ \vdots & & \vdots \\ a_{m1}(t) & \cdots & a_{mn}(t) \end{bmatrix}$$

with respect to the scalar parameter t is defined as the matrix resulting from the elementwise differentiation of A with respect to t:

$$\frac{dA}{dt} = \begin{bmatrix} \dfrac{da_{11}}{dt} & \cdots & \dfrac{da_{1n}}{dt} \\ \vdots & & \vdots \\ \dfrac{da_{m1}}{dt} & \cdots & \dfrac{da_{mn}}{dt} \end{bmatrix}$$

It is easy to verify that the following properties of matrix differentiation can be generalized from scalar differentiation:

$$\frac{d}{dt}(AB(t)C) = A\frac{dB}{dt}(t)C,$$

$$\frac{d}{dt}(A + B) = \frac{dA}{dt} + \frac{dB}{dt},$$

$$\frac{d}{dt}(AB) = \frac{dA}{dt}B + A\frac{dB}{dt}.$$

As an application we compute the derivative of $A^{-1}(t)$ with respect to t. We have

$$\frac{d}{dt}(A(t)A^{-1}(t)) = \frac{dI}{dt} = 0,$$

$$\frac{dA}{dt}A^{-1} + A\frac{d(A^{-1})}{dt} = 0,$$

$$\frac{d(A^{-1})}{dt} = -A^{-1}\frac{dA}{dt}A^{-1}.$$

Consider now a scalar function $f(X)$ of a matrix argument $X \in \mathbb{R}^{m \times n}$. We define the derivative of f with respect to X, and we denote it by $D_X f$ as follows:

$$D_X f = \begin{bmatrix} \dfrac{\partial f}{\partial x_{11}} & \cdots & \dfrac{\partial f}{\partial x_{1n}} \\ \vdots & & \vdots \\ \dfrac{\partial f}{\partial x_{m1}} & \cdots & \dfrac{\partial f}{\partial x_{mn}} \end{bmatrix}.$$

An important example is the trace function with the following properties:

- $D_X \operatorname{tr}(X) = I$
- $D_X \operatorname{tr}(AX) = A^T$.
  Indeed, $\operatorname{tr}(AX) = \sum_{ij} x_{ij} a_{ji}$, so $\partial \operatorname{tr}(AX)/\partial x_{ij} = a_{ji}$.
- $D_X \operatorname{tr}(AXB) = (BA)^T$ since $\operatorname{tr}(AXB) = \operatorname{tr}(BAX)$.

Similarly, we define the derivative of a vector function $f(x) \in \mathbb{R}^m$ with respect to its vector argument $x \in \mathbb{R}^n$:

$$\frac{df}{dx} = \begin{bmatrix} \dfrac{\partial f_1}{\partial x_1} & \dfrac{\partial f_1}{\partial x_n} \\ \vdots & \vdots \\ \dfrac{\partial f_m}{\partial x_1} & \dfrac{\partial f_m}{\partial x_n} \end{bmatrix}.$$

APPENDIX C

COMPACTNESS AND CONVEXITY

A set X is called a *metric space* if we have defined a function $d : x \times X \mapsto \mathbb{R}$ called the *distance* or *metric* such that

- $\forall x, y \in X, x \neq y \Rightarrow d(x, y) > 0; d(x, x) = 0$.
- $\forall x, y \in X, d(x, y) = d(y, x)$.
- $\forall x, y, z \in X, d(x, y) \leq d(x, z) + d(z, y)$.

For example, if $\| \cdot \|$ is a norm in the Euclidian space $\mathbb{R}^n$ then $d(x, y) = \|x - y\|$ is a metric. The following concepts are defined for a metric space X:

(a) A neighborhood $N(x)$ of a point $x \in X$ is the set of all points y with distance $d(x, y) < r$, for some $r \geq 0$.
(b) A set $F \subseteq X$ is called open if every point $x \in F$ has a neighborhood $N(x) \subset F$.
(c) A set $K \subseteq X$ is called closed if its complement $K^c = X - K$ is open.
(d) A set $F \subseteq X$ is bounded if there is a number $M \in R$ and a point $x_0 \in F$ such that $d(x_0, x) < M$ for all $x \in F$.
(e) A set $F \subseteq X$ is called **compact** if every infinite collection $\{S_a\}$ of open sets such that $\cup_a S_a \supseteq S$ has a finite subcollection whose union also contains S.

The following important result helps to identify compact subsets of Euclidian spaces.

Theorem C.1 (Heine-Borel). A set $F \subseteq \mathbb{R}^n$ is compact if and only if it is closed and bounded.

A subset S of a vector space V is a **convex set** if for all $x, y \in S$ and $0 \leq \alpha \leq 1$, we have $z = \alpha x + (1 - \alpha)y \in S$. For fixed x and y, the locus of points z is the straight line connecting x and y. In other words, a set is convex if the straight line connecting any pair of points in the set also lies in the set. Figure C.1 shows examples and counterexamples of convex sets.

A **convex combination** of the vectors $x_1, \ldots, x_n$ is a linear combination $\alpha_1 x_1 + \alpha_2 x_2 + \cdots + \alpha_n x_n$, where $\alpha_i \geq 0$, $i = 1, \ldots, n$, and $\alpha_1 + \alpha_2 + \cdots + \alpha_n = 1$. A member v of a convex set S is an **extreme point** of S if it cannot be written as a convex combination of any other points in the set except v itself:

$$v = \alpha x + (1 - \alpha)y, 0 \leq \alpha \leq 1 \Rightarrow v = x = y.$$

Not all convex sets have extreme points (e.g., the open right-half plane). However, all compact convex sets have extreme points, either finitely many (e.g., a closed polygon) or infinitely many (e.g., a closed disk). If a convex set has a finite number of extreme points they are also called **vertices**.

Theorem C.2 (Krein-Milman). Every compact convex set is *generated* by its extreme points, namely, every point in the set can be written as a convex combination of the extreme points.

Let S be a subset of a vector space V. A function $f : S \to \mathbb{R}$ is a **convex function** if

$$f(\alpha x + (1 - \alpha)y) \leq \alpha f(x) + (1 - \alpha)f(y)$$

for all $x, y \in S$, $0 \leq \alpha \leq 1$. If the above inequality is reversed, namely if

$$f(\alpha x + (1 - \alpha)y) \geq \alpha f(x) + (1 - \alpha)f(y)$$

for all $x, y \in S$, $0 \leq \alpha \leq 1$, then the function f is called **concave**. In the special case where $S \subseteq \mathbb{R}$ the convexity of a function can be easily tested by the second-order

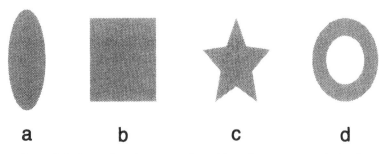

a   **b**   **c**   **d**

Figure C.1. Examples of convex sets (a, b) and nonconvex sets (c, d).

derivative:

$$\text{if } \forall x \in S \quad \frac{d^2 f}{dx^2} \begin{cases} \leq 0, & \text{then } f \text{ is convex,} \\ \geq 0, & \text{then } f \text{ is concave.} \end{cases}$$

Of course, a function may be neither convex nor concave. Some convex functions are x^2, e^x, $-\log(x)$, etc., while $-x^2$, $-e^x$, $\log(x)$ are concave. It is clear that if a function $f(x)$ is convex then the function $-f(x)$ is concave, and vice versa. If f is linear or affine it is both convex and concave.

The optimization of convex or concave functions on compact convex sets is an important problem with several very interesting and useful properties.

Theorem C.3. Let $f : S \rightarrow \mathbb{R}$ be a convex function and let S be a compact convex subset of a subspace V. Then the maximum of $f(x)$, $x \in S$, is attained at an extreme point of S. Similarly, if f is concave, the minimum is attained at an extreme point of S.

Corollary C.1. If f is a linear function defined on a convex set S, then the minimum and maximum are attained at extreme points of S.

BIBLIOGRAPHY

1. G. J. Tomko and D. R. Crapper. "Neural Variability: Nonstationary Response to Identical Visual Stimuli". *Brain Res.*, 79:405–418, 1974.

2. S. J. Hanson. "A Stochastic Version of the Delta Rule". *Physica D*, 42:265–272, 1990.

3. W. S. McCulloch and W. Pitts. "A Logical Calculus of the Ideas Immanent in the Nervous Activity." *Bull. Math. Biophys.*, 5(115), 1943.

4. D. H. Hubel. *Eye, Brain, and Vision.* Scientific American Library, 1988.

5. D. H. Hubel and T. N. Wiesel. "Brain Mechanisms of Vision". *Sci. Am.*, 241:130–144, 1979.

6. F. W. Campbell and J. G. Robson. "Application of Fourier Analysis to the Visibility of Gratings". *J. Physiol. (London)*, 197:551–566, 1968.

7. D. A. Pollen, J. R. Lee, and J. H. Taylor. "How Does the Striate Cortex Begin the Reconstruction of the Visual World?". *Science*, 173:74–77, 1971.

8. C. R. Michael. "Color Vision Mechanisms in Monkey Striate Cortex: Dual-Opponent Cells with Concentric Receptive Fields". *J. Neurophysiol.*, 41:572–588, 1978.

9. D. H. Hubel and T. N. Wiesel. "Cells Sensitive to Binocular Depth in Area 18 of the Macaque Monkey Cortex". *Nature*, 225:41–42, 1970.

10. F. Crick and C. Asanuma. "Certain Aspects of the Anatomy and Physiology of the Cerebral Cortex". In D. E. Rumelhart, J. L. McClelland, and the PDP Research Group, editors, *Parallel Distributed Processing (PDP): Explorations in the Microstructure of Cognition (Vol. 2)*, chapter 20, pages 333–371, MIT Press, Cambridge, MA, 1986.

11. W. M. Cowan. "The Development of the Brain". *Scientific American*, 241:107–117, 1979.

12. R. Linsker. "Self-Organization in a Perceptual Network". *IEEE Comput. Mag.*, 21:105–117, March 1988.

13. J. Rubner and K. Schulten. "Development of Feature Detectors by Self-Organization". *Biol. Cybernet.*, 62:193–199, 1990.

14. T. D. Sanger. "Optimal Unsupervised Learning in a Single-Layer Linear Feedforward Neural Network". *Neural Networks*, 2(6):459–473, 1989.

15. D. O. Hebb. *The Organization of Behavior.* Wiley, New York, 1949.

16. E. Oja. "A Simplified Neuron Model as a Principal Component Analyzer". *J. Math. Biol.*, 15:267–273, 1982.

17. P. Földiák. "Adaptive Network for Optimal Linear Feature Extraction". In *Int. Joint Conf. Neural Networks*, pages 401–406, Washington DC, 1989.

18. S. Y. Kung and K. I. Diamantaras. "A Neural Network Learning Algorithm for Adaptive Principal Component EXtraction (APEX)". In *Proc. IEEE Int. Conf. Acoustics, Speech and Signal Processing*, pages 861–864, Albuquerque, April 1990.

19. J. Rubner and P. Tavan. "A Self-Organizing Network for Principal-Components Analysis". *Europhys. Lett.*, 10(7):693–698, 1989.

20. J. Karhunen and E. Oja. "New Methods for Stochastic Approximation of Truncated Karhunen-Loeve Expansions". In *Proc. 6th Int. Conf. on Pattern Recognition*, pages 550–553, Springer-Verlag, New York, 1982.

21. R. A. Horn and C. R. Johnson. *Matrix Analysis*. Cambridge University Press, 1985.

22. R. A. Horn and C. R. Johnson. *Topics in Matrix Analysis*. Cambridge University Press, 1991.

23. J. S. Lim and A. V. Oppenheim, editors. *Advanced Topics in Signal Processing*. Prentice Hall, Englewood Cliffs, NJ, 1988.

24. H. Hotelling. "Analysis of a Complex of Statistical Variables into Principal Components". *J. Educ. Psychol.*, 24:498–520, 1933.

25. K. Pearson. "On Lines and Planes of Closest Fit to Systems of Points in Space". *Philos. Mag., Ser. 6*, 2:559–572, 1901.

26. D. F. Morrison. *Multivariate Statistical Methods*. 3rd edition, McGraw-Hill,New York, 1990.

27. P. Jolicoeur and J. E. Mosimann. "Size and Shape Variation in the Painted Turtle: A Principal Component Analysis". *Growth*, 24:339–354, 1960.

28. K. S. Fu. *Sequential Methods in Pattern Recognition and Machine Learning*. Academic Press, New York, 1968.

29. K. Karhunen. "Zur Spektraltheorie stochastischer Prozesse". *Ann. Acad. Sci. Fenn.*, 34, 1946.

30. M. Loève. "Fonctions alèatoires du second ordre". In P. Lèvy, editor, Suppl. to *Processus Stochastique et mouvement Brownien*, Gauthier-Villars, Paris, 1948.

31. S. Watanabe. "Karhunen-Loève Expansion and Factor Analysis". In *Trans. 4th Prague Conf. Inf. Theory, Stat. Decision Functions, and Random Proc.*, pages 635–660, Prague, 1965.

32. C. Eckart and G. Young. "The Approximation of One Matrix by Another of Lower Rank". *Psychometrika*, 1:211–218, 1936.

33. R. B. Ash. *Information Theory*. Interscience Publishers, New York, 1965.

34. R. G. Gallager. *Information Theory and Reliable Communication*. Wiley, New York, 1968.

35. P. Baldi and K. Hornik. "Learning in Linear Networks". Preprint, 1992.

36. G. H. Golub and C. F. Van Loan. *Matrix Computations*, 2nd edition, Johns Hopkins University Press, Baltimore, 1989.

37. B. N. Parlett. *The Symmetric Eigenvalue Problem*. Prentice-Hall, Englewood Cliffs, NJ, 1980.

38. J. L. McClelland, D. E. Rumelhart, and G. E. Hinton. "The Appeal of Parallel Distributed Processing". In J. L. McClelland D. E. Rumelhart and the PDP Research Group, editors, *Parallel Distributed Processing*, MIT Press, Cambridge, MA, 1986.

39. L. Ljung. "Analysis of Recursive Stochastic Algorithms". *IEEE Trans. Automat. Control*, AC-22(4):551–575, August 1977.

40. H. J. Kushner and D. S. Clark. *Stochastic Approximation Methods for Constrained and Unconstrained Systems*. Springer-Verlag, New York, 1978.

41. G. Widrow and M. E. Hoff. "Adaptive Switching Circuits". *IRE Western Electronic Show and Convention: Convention Record, Part 4*, 96–104, August 1960.

42. D. E. Rumelhart, G. E. Hinton, and R. J. Williams. "Learning Internal Representations by Error Propagation". In D. E. Rumelhart, J. L. McClelland, and the PDP Research Group, editors, *Parallel Distributed Processing (PDP): Exploration in the Microstructure of Cognition (Vol. 1)*, Chapter 8, pages 318–362, MIT Press, Cambridge, MA, 1986.

43. G. E. Hinton and T. J. Sejnowski. "Learning and Relearning in Boltzmann Machines". In D. E. Rumelhart, J. L. McClelland, and the PDP Research Group, editors, *Parallel Distributed Processing (PDP): Exploration in the Microstructure of Cognition (Vol. 1)*, Chapter 7, pages 282–317, MIT Press, Cambridge, MA, 1986.

44. D. E. Rumelhart and D. Zipser. "Feature Discovery by Competitive Learning". *Cognitive Sci.*, 9:75–112, 1985.

45. E. Oja. "Neural Networks, Principal Components, and Subspaces". *Int. J. Neural Systems*, 1(1):61–68, 1989.

46. T. D. Sanger. "An Optimality Principle for Unsupervised Learning". In D. S. Touretzky, editor, *Advances in Neural Information Processing Systems*, pages 11–19, Morgan Kaufmann, San Mateo, CA, 1989.

47. E. Oja and J. Karhunen. "On Stochastic Approximation of the Eigenvectors and Eigenvalues of the Expectation of a Random Matrix". *J. Math. Anal. Appl.*, 106:69–84, 1985.

48. A. L. Yuille, D. M. Kammen, and D. S. Cohen. "Quadrature and the Development of Orientation Selective Cortical Cells by Hebb Rules". *Biol. Cybernet.*, 61:183–194, 1989.

49. K. Hornik and C.-M. Kuan. "Convergence Analysis of Local Feature Extraction Algorithms". *Neural Networks*, 5:229–240, 1992.

50. K. I. Diamantaras. *Principal Component Learning Networks and Applications*. Ph.D. thesis, Princeton University, 1992.

51. P. Baldi. "Linear Learning: Landscapes and Algorithms". In D. S. Touretzky, editor, *Advances in Neural Information Processing Systems I* (Denver, 1988), Morgan Kaufmann, San Mateo, CA, 1989.

52. W.-Y. Yan, U. Helmke, and J. B. Moore. "Global Analysis of Oja's Flow for Neural Networks". *IEEE Trans. Neural Networks*, 5(5):674–683, September 1994.

53. S. Y. Kung. *Digital Neural Networks*. Prentice Hall, Englewood Cliffs, NJ, 1993.

54. H. Chen and R. Liu. "An Alternative Proof of Convergence for Kung-Diamantaras APEX Algorithm". In B. H. Juang, S. Y. Kung, and C. A. Kamm, editors, *Neural Networks for Signal Processing*, pages 40–49, IEEE, New York, 1991.

55. L. Ljung and T. Söderström. *Theory and Practice of Recursive Identification*. MIT Press, 1983.

56. H. M. Abbas and M. M. Fahmy. "A Neural Model for Adaptive Karhunen Loève Transformation (KLT)". In *Proc. IJCNN-92*, pages 975–980, Baltimore, MD, June 1992.

57. T. P. Krasulina. "Method of Stochastic Approximation in the Determination of the Largest Eigenvalue of the Mathematical Expectation of Random Matrices". *Automat. Remote Control*, 215–221, February 1970.

58. N. L. Owsley. "Adaptive Data Orthogonalization". In *Proc. IEEE Int. Conf. Acoustics, Speech and Signal Processing*, pages 109–112, Tulsa, OK, April 1978.

59. T. Leen. "Dynamics of Learning in Linear Feature-Discovery Networks". *Network*, 2:85–105, 1991.

60. Y. Chauvin. "Principal Component Analysis by Gradient Descent on a Constrained Linear Hebbian Cell". In *Proc. Int. Joint Conf. Neural Networks (IJCNN)*, pages 373–380, Washington, DC, 1989.

61. L. E. Russo. "An Outer Product Neural Net for Extracting Principal Components from a Time Series". In B. H. Juang, S. Y. Kung, and C. A. Kamm, editors, *Neural Networks for Signal Processing*, pages 161–170, IEEE, New York, 1991.

62. R. Lenz and M. Österberg. "A Parallel Learning Filter System That Learns the KL-Expansion from Examples". In B. H. Juang, S. Y. Kung, and C. A. Kamm, editors, *Neural Networks for Signal Processing*, pages 121–130, IEEE, New York, 1991.

63. S. T. Smith. "Dynamical Systems That Perform the Singular Value Decomposition". *Systems Control Lett.*, 16:319–327, 1991.

64. F. Palmieri. "A Self-Organizing Neural Network for Multidimensional Approximation". In *Proc. Int. Joint Conf. Neural Networks (IJCNN)*, pages 802–807, IEEE, Baltimore, June 1992.

65. E. Oja. "Principal Components, Minor Components, and Linear Networks". *Neural Networks*, 5(6):927–935, 1992.

66. R. H. White. "Competitive Hebbian Learning: Algorithm and Demonstrations". *Neural Networks*, 5(2):261–275, 1992.

67. A. Cichocki and R. Unbehauen. "Neural Networks for Computing Eigenvalues and Eigenvectors". *Biol. Cybern.*, 68:155–164, 1992.

68. S. M. Kay. *Modern Spectral Estimation: Theory and Application*. Prentice Hall, Englewood Cliffs, NJ, 1988.

69. C. W. Therrien. *Discrete Random Signals and Statistical Signal Processing*. Prentice Hall, Englewood Cliffs, NJ, 1992.

70. L. Xu, E. Oja, and C. Y. Suen. "Modified Hebbian Learning for Curve and Surface Fitting". *Neural Networks*, 5(3):441–457, 1992.

71. H. Bourlard and Y. Kamp. "Auto-Association by Multilayer Perceptrons and Singular Value Decomposition". *Biol. Cybernet.*, 59:291–294, 1988.

72. P. Baldi and K. Hornik. "Neural Networks for Principal Component Analysis: Learning from Examples without Local Minima". *Neural Networks*, 2:53–58, 1989.

73. J. Hertz, A. Krogh, and R. G. Palmer. *Introduction to the Theory of Neural Computation*. Addison Wesley, Reading, MA, 1991.

74. D. J. C. MacKay and K. D. Miller. "Analysis of Linsker's Simulation of Hebbian Rules". *Neural Computat.*, 2:173–187, 1990.

75. T. Leen, M. Rudnick, and D. Hammerstrom. "Hebbian Feature Discovery Improves Classifier Efficiency". In *Proc. Int. Joint Conf. Neural Networks (IJCNN)*, pages 51–56, San Diego, CA, 1990.

76. V. V. Veeravali and H. V. Poor. "Quadratic Detection of Signals with Drifting Phase". *J. Acoust. Soc. Am.*, 89(2):811–819, February 1991.

77. G. J. Foschini, L. J. Greenstein, and G. Vannucci. "Noncoherent Detection of Coherent Lightwave Signals Corrupted by Phase Noise". *IEEE Trans. Commun.*, COM-36(3):306–314, March 1988.

78. A. D. Whalen. *Detection of Signals in Noise*. Academic Press, New York, 1971.

79. S. Y. Kung, K. I. Diamantaras, and J. S. Taur. "Adaptive Principal Component Extraction (APEX) and Application". *IEEE Trans. Signal Process.*, 42(5):1202–1217, May 1994.

80. B. Picinbono and P. Duvaut. "Optimal Linear-Quadratic Systems for Detection and Estimation". *IEEE Trans. Inform. Theory*, 34(2):304–311, March 1988.

81. C. Georghiades and D. L. Snyder. "A Proposed Receiver Structure for Optimal Communication Systems that Employ Heterodyne Detection and a Semiconductor Laser as a Local Oscillator". *IEEE Trans. Commun.*, COM-33(4), April 1985.

82. D. Le Gall. "MPEG: A Video Compression Standard for Multimedia Applications". *Trans. ACM*, April 1991.

83. A. N. Netravali and B. G. Haskell. *Digital Pictures, Representation and Compression.* Plenum Press, New York, 1988.

84. K. I. Diamantaras and S. Y. Kung. "Compressing Moving Pictures using the APEX Neural Principal Component Extractor". In *Neural Networks for Signal Processing, Proceedings of the third IEEE Workshop*, IEEE, Baltimore, September 1993.

85. K. I. Diamantaras, N. Grammalidis, and M. G. Strintzis. "KLT-Based Coding of Stereo Image Sequences". In *Proc. Int. Conf. on Image Processing*, Budapest, June 1994.

86. D. E. Rumelhart, J. L. McClelland, and the PDP Research Group. *Parallel Distributed Processing (PDP): Psychological and Biological Models (Vol. 2).* MIT Press, Cambridge, MA, 1986.

87. K. Hornik. "Noisy Linear Networks". In R. Mammone, editor, Artificial Neural Networks with Applications in Speech and Vision, Chapman and Hall, London, 1993.

88. K. I. Diamantaras and K. Hornik. "Noisy Principal Component Analysis". In J. Volaufova and V. Witkowsky, editors, *Measurement '93*, pages 25–33, Institute of Measurement Science, Slovak Academy of Sciences, Bratislava, Slovakia, May 1993.

89. R. Linsker. "An Application of the Principle of Maximum Information Preservation to Linear Systems". In D. S. Touretzky, editor, *Advances in Neural Information Processing Systems*, pages 186–194, Morgan Kaufman, San Mateo, CA, 1989.

90. K. I. Diamantaras and S. Y. Kung. "Multi-layer Neural Networks for Reduced-Rank Approximation". *IEEE Trans. Neural Networks*, 5(5):684–697, September 1994.

91. K. I. Diamantaras and S. Y. Kung. "Cross-Correlation Neural Network Models". *IEEE Trans. Signal Process.*, 42(11):3218–3223, November 1994.

92. S. Y. Kung and K. I. Diamantaras. "Neural Networks for Extracting Unsymmetric Principal Components". In B. H. Juang, S. Y. Kung, and C. A. Kamm, editors, *Neural Networks for Signal Processing*, pages 50–59, IEEE, New York, 1991.

93. L. L. Scharf. "The SVD and Reduced-Rank Signal Processing". In R. J. Vaccaro, editor, *SVD and Signal Processing II: Algorithms Analysis and Applications*, pages 3–31, Elsevier, Amsterdam, Netherlands, 1991.

94. C. F. Van Loan. "Generalizing the Singular Value Decomposition". *SIAM J. Numer. Anal.*, 13(1):76–83, March 1976.

95. S. E. Fahlman and C. Lebiere. "The Cascade Correlation Learning Architecture". In D. S. Touretzky, editor, *Advances in Neural Information Processing Systems II* (Denver, 1989), pages 524–532, Morgan Kaufmann, San Mateo, CA, 1990.

96. B. D. O. Anderson and J. B. Moore, editors. *Optimal Filtering.* Prentice Hall, Englewood Cliffs, NJ, 1979.

97. G. Cybenko. "Approximation by Superpositions of a Sigmoidal Function". *Math. Control, Signals Systems*, 2:303–314, 1989.

98. A. R. Barron. *"Approximation and Estimation Bounds for Artificial Neural Networks".* Technical Report #59, Department of Statistics, University of Illinois at Urbana-Champaign, Champaign, IL, February 1991.

99. K. Hornik, M. Strinchcombe, and H. White. "Multilayer Feedforward Networks are Universal Approximators". *Neural Networks*, 2(5):359–366, 1989.

100. M. A. Kramer. "Nonlinear Principal Component Analysis Using Autoassociative Neural Networks". *J. Am. Inst. Chem. Eng. (AIChE)*, 37(2):233–243, February 1991.

101. R. Rico-Martinez, K. Krischer, and I. G. Kevrekidis. "Discrete vs. Continuous-Time Nonlinear Signal Processing of Cu Electrodissolution Data". *Chem. Eng. Comm.*, 118:25–48, 1992.

102. I. G. Kevrekidis, R. Rico-Martinez, R. E. Eske, R. M. Farber, and A. S. Lapedes. "Global Bifurcations in Rayleigh-Bénard Convection. Experiments, Empirical Maps and Numerical Bifurcation Analysis". *Physica D*, 71:342–362, 1994.

103. B. A. Golomb, D. T. Lawrence, and T. J. Sejnowski. "SEXNET: a Neural Network Identifies Sex from Human Faces". In R. P. Lippmann et al., editor, *Advances in Neural Information Processing Systems III* (Denver, 1990), pages 572–577, Morgan Kaufmann, San Mateo, CA, 1991.

104. G. W. Cottrell and J. Metcalfe. "EMPATH: Face, Emotion, and Gender Recognition Using Holons". In R. P. Lippmann et al., editors, *Advances in Neural Information Processing Systems III* (Denver, 1990), pages 564–571, Morgan Kaufmann, San Mateo, CA, 1991.

105. S. Y. Kung. "Adaptive Principal Component Analysis via an Orthogonal Learning Network". In *Proc. Int. Symp. on Circuits and Systems*, pages 719–722, New Orleans, May 1990.

106. K. I. Diamantaras and S. Y. Kung. "An Unsupervised Neural Model for Oriented Principal Component Extraction". In *Proc. Int. Conf. Acoustics, Speech, Signal Processing*, pages 1049–1052, Toronto, Canada, 1991.

107. S. Y. Kung, K. I. Diamantaras, and J. S. Taur. "Neural Networks for Extracting Pure / Constrained / Oriented Principal Components". In R. J. Vaccaro, editor, *SVD and Signal Processing II: Algorithms, Analysis and Applications*, Elsevier Science Publishers, New York, 1991.

108. B. De Moor, J. Staar, and J. Vandewalle. "Oriented Energy and Oriented Signal to Signal Ratio Concepts in the Analysis of Vector Sequences and Time Series". In E. F. Deprettere, editor, *SVD and Signal Processing*, pages 209–232, Elsevier Science Publishers, New York, 1988.

109. J. B. Thomas. *An Introduction to Communication Theory and Systems*. Springer-Verlag, 1988.

110. R. O. Duda and P. E. Hart. *Pattern Classification and Scene Analysis*. Wiley, New York, 1973.

111. K. Fukunaga and W. C. G. Koontz. "Applications of the Karhunen Loeve Expansion to Feature Extraction and Ordering". *IEEE Trans. Comput.*, C-19:311–318, 1970.

112. J. Kittler. "The subspace Approach to Pattern Recognition". In R. Trappl, G. J. Klir, and L. Ricciardi, editors, *Progress in Cybernetics and Systems Research*, Hemisphere, Washington, 1978.

113. E. Oja. *Subspace Methods for Pattern Recognition*. Research Studies Press, Letchworth, Hertfordshire, England, 1983.

114. E. Oja and J. Parkkinen. "Texture Subspaces". In P. A. Devijver and J. Kittler, editors, *NATO ASI Series*, pages 21–33, Springer-Verlag, Berlin, Heidelberg, 1987.

115. A. Cichocki and R. Unbehauen. "Robust Estimation of Principal Components by Using Neural Network Learning Algorithms". *IEE Electron. Lett.*, 29(21):1869–1870, October 1993.

116. Cray. *The Cray Y/MP C-90 Supercomputer System*. Cray Research Inc., Eagan, MN, 1991.

117. Intel. *Paragon XP/S Product Overview*. Supercomputers System Division, Intel Co., Beaverton, OR, 1991.

118. MasPar. *The MasPar Family Data-Parallel Computer*. MasPar Computer Co., Sunnyvale, CA, 1991.

119. H. Burkhardt. *Technical Summary of KSR-1*. Kendall Square Research Co., Waltham, MA, 1992.

120. U. Ramacher. "SYNAPSE-A Neurocomputer that Synthesizes Neural Algorithms on a Parallel Systolic Engine". *J. Parallel Distrib. Comput.*, 14:306–318, 1992.

121. U. Ramacher, J. Beichter, and N. Bruls. "Architecture of a General-Purpose Neural Signal Processor". In *Int. Joint Conf. on Neural Networks*, pages 443–446, Seattle, WA, 1991.

122. D. Hammerstrom. "A VLSI Architecture for High-Performance, Low-Cost, On-Chip Learning". In *Proc. Int. Joint Conf. Neural Networks (IJCNN)*, pages 537–544, San Diego, CA, 1990.

123. M. Yasunaga et al. "Design, Fabrication and Evaluation of a 5-inch Wafer-Scale Neural Network LSI composed of 576 digital neurons". In *Proc. Int. Joint Conf. Neural Networks (IJCNN)*, page 527, San Diego, CA, 1990.

124. S. Y. Kung. *VLSI Array Processors*. Prentice-Hall, Englewood Cliffs, NJ, 1988.

125. C. Mead. *Analog VLSI and Neural Systems*. Addison-Wesley, Reading, MA, 1989.

126. J. J. Hopfield and D. W. Tank. Neural computation of decision in optimization problems. *Biol. Cybernet.*, 52:141–152, 1985.

127. H. Robbins and S. Monro. "A Stochastic Approximation Method". *Ann. Math. Statist.*, 22:400–407, 1951.

128. J. Kiefer and J. Wolfowitz. "Stochastic Estimation of the Maximum of a Regression Function". *Ann. Math. Statist.*, 23:462–466, 1952.

129. A. N. Kolmogorov and S. V. Fomin. *Introductory Real Analysis*. Prentice Hall, Englewood Cliffs, NJ, 1970.

130. H. J. Kushner and H. Huang. "Asymptotic Properties of Stochastic Approximations with Constant Coefficients". *SIAM J. Control Optim.*, 19:87–105, 1981.

131. A. Benveniste and G. Ruget. "A Measure of the Tracking Capability of Recursive Stochastic Algorithms with Constant Gains". *IEEE Trans. Automatic Control*, AC-27(3):639–649, 1982.

INDEX

Printed and bound by CPI Group (UK) Ltd, Croydon, CR0 4YY

27/10/2024

14580332-0001